FOOD AND BEVERAGE SERVICE

Wiley Professional Restaurateur Guides

FOOD AND BEVERAGE
S·E·R·V·I·C·E

BRUCE H. AXLER   ❖   CAROL A. LITRIDES

WILEY

John Wiley & Sons

New York   Chichester   Brisbane   Toronto   Singapore

Library of Congress Cataloging-in-Publication Data

Axler, Bruce H.
    Food and beverage service / Bruce Axler, Carol Litrides.
      p. cm. — (Wiley professional restaurateur guides)
    ISBN 0-471-62176-5
    1. Table service. 2. Waiters. 3. Waitresses. I. Litrides,
Carol. II. Title. III. Series.
TX925.A89 1990
642'.6--dc20   89-28391
                                       CIP

Printed in the United States of America
90 91   10 9 8 7 6 5 4 3 2 1

PREFACE

Anyone who goes to a restaurant encounters service staff with three distinct types of skills. Although any given staff member may excel in one or more of these areas, few excel in all three. These fundamental skills are:

♦ *Guest courtesy skills,* or "people skills": making each guest feel comfortable and satisfied, with a desire to return
♦ *Basic food and beverage service skills:* getting food and beverages to the table in an attractive, timely manner
♦ *Wine and liquor beverage service skills:* enhancing the meal with rituals governing the service of wine or other alcoholic drinks

Each of these skills is made up of many abilities, involving a myriad of details. So instead of trying to cover them all in one massive book, we decided to split them into three separate guides. *Food and Beverage Service* is the first guide in the series because so many people are engaged in the service of food and beverages, and because these professional skills are so much in demand. The forthcoming second guide, *Wine and Liquor Beverage Service,* covers wine, wine service, cocktails, cocktail service, and liquor service—everything a server needs to know about alcoholic beverage service. The forthcoming third guide, *Guest Courtesy,* details how to meet, greet, and seat guests, as well as how to organize a restaurant, a front desk, and coat-check station.

Each guide provides step-by-step instructions for the many procedures vital to a successful restaurant. Special how-to sections include recipes; a glossary is also included for reference. (All three guides are a part of the series Wiley Professional Restaurateur Guides.)

These guides are designed to help restaurant service personnel enhance skills in areas they are already proficient in, and to learn more about areas they want to improve. The guides are also intended for managers—to offer guidance on structuring the jobs in their restaurants, to suggest alternate methods of accomplishing various tasks, to train employees, and to provide job descriptions and sample forms.

We hope you will enjoy all three guides.

ACKNOWLEDGMENTS

Our utmost thanks to Mr. Warner LeRoy, owner of the *Tavern on the Green* restaurant in New York City, for allowing us to use his spectacular restaurant as a setting for the photographs you'll soon see, and for providing the restaurant as a place for us to test various procedures and techniques. By the process of elimination only the best "tried-and-true" techniques are described herein. All of the basic techniques (Chapters One and Two) are standard procedure for the service staff at *Tavern on the Green,* who have proven to themselves that good service does, in fact, result in better tips!

We'd also like to thank the *NCR Corporation* for permission to use the NCR 2760 and NCR 2160 computer foodservice systems for illustrative purposes and examples in ordering, cost control, menu and sales tracking, and other restaurant controls, as well as for providing templates.

Thanks also to *The Culinary Institute of America* and its President, Ferdinand E. Metz, for permission to reference *The Escoffier Restaurant* and the *American Bounty Restaurant* at *The Institute.* We'd like to thank members of the Institute's staff for all of their help and support. Special thanks to the wonderful tableservice instructors for their assistance, especially Mr. Ivan Salgovic, who received many a morning phone call, asking for resolution of a fine point of service, before teaching a class of would-be-servers.

Other staff members at *The Culinary Institute of America* who have been very helpful are Mr. Manny Ketterer, Mr. Tom Schmitter, Mr. Ken Carlson, and Mr. Heinz Holtmann, Tableservice Department Chairman.

And most of all, for her continuing support, Mrs. Dell Hargis Minacapilli.

Other restaurateurs (in alphabetical order) whom we'd like to thank for giving us permission to feature them or their restaurants as examples include the following:

♦ Chef Siegfried Werner Eisenberger, *Chef Sigi's,* Nashville, Tenn.
♦ Rafael J. Garcia, *Tavern on the Green,* New York City
♦ Mr. Michael Kelly, *Jimmy Kelly's,* Nashville, Tenn.

CONTENTS

❖ One: BUSSER   1

❖   Two: **SERVER**   59

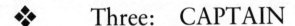

Three: CAPTAIN   129

INTRODUCTION

Taking an order and serving food and beverages to a table involves many tasks. Each customer must be met, greeted, seated; the order must be taken, the specials described, the water glasses filled, the bread brought to the table, the food and beverages served and cleared, and the check paid. This book shows how these basic operations, and many more, can be accomplished while a professional level of service and courtesy to guests is provided.

For ease of description, the tasks to be performed in a dining room have been categorized into job titles based on a four-person "team": captain, front server, back server, and busser. Often the duties of a front server and back server are combined or overlap, so people performing those tasks are generally referred to as servers in this book.

The positions and the tasks and techniques associated with them are introduced in the following order, according to the level of skill they require:

♦ Bussers
♦ Servers
♦ Captains

The titles captain, server, and busser are used for illustrative purposes, to help show the "flow" of a meal and to clarify the tasks often associated with each title in restaurants utilizing team organization. Whether the tasks of the captain, server, and busser are performed by individuals doing everything, or by captains, servers, and bussers, each with their own subtasks, depends on the establishment. Some operations use teams, others don't. Ultimately, it does not matter whether the tasks are accomplished by one person with several responsibilities or by several people, each with a particular responsibility. The important thing is to provide a professional level of service and not to worry about the position or title of the person performing a particular task.

On the other hand, isn't it nice to know what's expected for each position? Well, that's what job descriptions are for. Typical job descriptions—based on a team approach and given in a generalized format—are in the front of each chapter. Bear in mind that these are general descriptions, and that the tasks outlined in one job description may be performed by someone else in any given restaurant. Also, one person may be performing many of the jobs, so several job descriptions may pertain to one person at any given restaurant.

We provided these job descriptions to outline briefly the jobs or tasks that are commonly performed in a restaurant, using the job titles often associated with those tasks. Our goal was to present an organized method for serving guests in a timely manner but it's up to you to review the specifics of each job and to change these descriptions to suit your individual restaurant. In addition, each specific skill required for effective service is outlined in a how-to format, making it easy to practice that skill until it is mastered, and then to teach others.

 ## BASIC SELLING

Basic foodservice involves sales skills—not only for selling food and beverage items but also for selling the whole experience to the guests, the ambience, the foods, the wines, the specials, so that they will want to come back. If a guest leaves a restaurant as a satisfied customer, eager to return, the service staff has been successful.

Selling is at the heart of the jobs of the captains, servers, and bussers, since these are the people who have primary responsibility for interacting with the guests. In any operation, those who interact with the customers are responsible for the sales, the return guests, the repeat customers, and the good word-of-mouth advertising.

Regardless of whether you master the other skills described in these three guides, if you do not master salesmanship, the others are for naught. While specific sales techniques are not the focus of this guide, certain "selling behavior" techniques are necessary for all of those in the foodservice industry:

◆ *Create a positive experience for your guests*
From the moment a guest walks into the restaurant, an impression is being created. The service staff members must ensure that it is a good impression, and sell themselves as representatives of the restaurant by being polite and well-groomed and by having a good attitude, especially since the service staff gives the first and last impression of a restaurant.

♦ *Make the guests feel welcome*
Welcome them with a "Hello" or bid farewell with a "Have a good day, we hope to see you again soon." Guests like to be acknowledged, so acknowledge them. If a guest's name is known, use it. Make guests feel special, because they are the heart of the restaurant. If you make them feel special, they'll act special—buying what you suggest!

♦ *Smile, smile, smile*
A smile is the fastest way to make a guest feel welcome. Smile—a lot.

♦ *Sell, sell, sell*
Guests are out to have a good time—sell by suggesting something every chance you get. Suggest drinks, suggest the specials, suggest wines that complement their food choices. If you suggest, the majority of the time the guests will order whatever it is that you suggested. Guests don't want to have to make decisions—they want to enjoy themselves!

In addition to selling skills and making the guests feel welcome, it is equally important to have good service skills if the foods and drinks ordered are to be delivered in a timely and professional manner. That's what the rest of this guide is about—the how-tos of professional service.

❖ BASIC SKILLS

Whether you are a captain, server, busser, or an all-in-one person, you must master certain skills to be effective and professional in a restaurant. Of all the important skills, four are basic; utilized day after day, they must become automatic:

♦ Loading and carrying a tray with food and/or beverages
♦ Loading and carrying a bus box or tray with soiled wares
♦ Handling serviceware
♦ Clearing a table during service

Two additional skills are necessary for restaurants that use a more elegant service. Summarized here because of their universality, these skills are reviewed in detail in the server and busser chapters, respectively:

♦ Russian and/or French service: that is, service using a serving spoon and fork from a platter (Russian) or plating using a serving spoon and fork (French) often from a gueridon
♦ Resetting a table during service, including the changing of linens in the dining room with a minimum of disruption and baring of the table

These skills, with the basics of selling, will give you a start in providing professional tableservice to your guests.

❖ SERVICE TEAM OVERVIEW

While each member of the restaurant organization has a particular job to do, it is the responsibility of all to

- Ensure that customers have a wonderful meal, with impeccable service, and wish to return.
- Set all tables perfectly, to specifications, and check them before service.
- Ensure that table linens are not faded, that they are free of wrinkles, stains, and holes, and that they are centered on the table.
- Ensure that chairs and banquettes are clean, and free from crumbs, foods, and other debris after changing table linens.
- Make sure that flowers are nicely arranged on tables, and fresh.
- Check that salt and pepper shakers are filled and clean every day. Keep condiment bottles clean; keep the inside of caps and the tops of jars clean.
- At banquettes, pull out the tables when customers are arriving and leaving.
- Approach guests with a smile and greet them with "Good morning," "Good afternoon," or "Good evening," as appropriate. Hand each person a menu and wine list; obtain a beverage order, and if possible, a food order.
- Serve cocktails as soon as possible. The back server (if there is one) must help with cocktail service at the start of the meal period and when not busy.
- After water has been requested and served, keep water glasses filled automatically until the dessert course.
- Assist guests with descriptions of menu items and wines. Sell specials, desserts, coffees, espresso, cappuccino, liquors. Ensure that wine, if ordered, is presented and opened prior to, or at approximately the same time as, the course it is to be served with arrives and is served. Red wines need to "breathe" so they should be presented and opened, but not necessarily poured, before the arrival of the course.
- Refill wine glasses one-third to one-half full if a standard wine glass (not oversized goblets). Offer another bottle when the first one is almost finished. (A 750-ml bottle should provide six to eight 3- to 4-ounce servings [six 4-ounce servings or eight 3-ounce servings].)
- Watch tables carefully, keeping them clean and well tended .
- Wipe the rims of dishes before you serve them if there is any food or sauce on the rim.
- Offer fresh pepper when appropriate. Provide ketchup, mustard, and

other condiments, when appropriate, prior to or with the placing of the food on the table. A guest should never have to ask for the condiments typically served with particular foods, for example, ketchup with hamburgers.

♦ Crumb the table (if necessary) and set proper silverware before each course is served.

♦ Keep ashtrays clean. They should be emptied several times during the course of a meal if there are smokers present.

♦ Provide fingerbowls or steamed towels with a lemon wedge on a bread-and-butter (B&B) or other small plate after messy items.

♦ Remove glasses, plates, and silverware as soon as all the guests at the table have finished (or follow house policy if different).

♦ After the entree course, offer coffee and dessert. Offer second cups of coffee automatically. Offer after-dinner drinks or cigars. If serving coffee, decaffeinated coffee, and/or tea, make sure it's *hot*. There's nothing worse than ending a meal with a cold cup of coffee.

♦ Never leave a table uncovered during service in a restaurant that uses tablecloths. When changing the table linen, remove the soiled linen only if another linen is ready to cover the table. Learn how to change linens properly, with a minimum baring of the table and without removing the flowers, ashtrays, and so on from the tabletop (described in detail in the section on bussers).

♦ Continue to followup service even after the check has been paid. If the customers are still sitting there and talking, offer liqueurs, cognac, armagnac, or the like. Don't assume that they're finished. You can always start another check.

♦ Communicate, cooperate, and coordinate with team members to ensure the smooth working of the station and to find out if a guest has requested something special. Work together at all times.

♦ Be professional and have pride in what you are doing. Be courteous, be polite, and smile.

If there are teams at the restaurant, each member of the service team will have specific responsibilities. If not, then each server must perform all of the tasks mentioned above and detailed in the following chapters.

A specific breakdown of the steps in service, including general time frames for each step of service, can be found in Table 2.4 in the chapter on servers.

It's basically simple: In order to serve guests in a restaurant, someone's got to do the jobs and tasks described throughout this book! By knowing all of the tasks and skills that are needed, you're ready for any position in any restaurant, and will probably earn increased tips from serving the guests in a professional, courteous manner. That's what this book is about—helping you to make yourself a better professional!

One

B·U·S·S·E·R

When you think of a busser, you probably imagine a person removing soiled dishes and glassware from a table. But this is only a small part of a busser's job, and in many operations not large enough for a busser, these tasks are performed by others in the organization.

In some operations there are specific individuals doing various tasks while in other operations one person does everything in a station. The tasks described here may or not be performed in each operation. They are meant to provide an overview of tasks typically performed or at least considered in an operation—for example: Is water served automatically or upon request? Are rolls served to everyone or only to those ordering complete dinners? Is a relish tray offered to every table? Only during certain meal periods? If so, when, and to which tables if not all?

The descriptions and how-tos provided are meant to be modified by each operation. Examples give an idea of one method of providing that service, but service is meant to be just that—service to the guest. And the best way to accomplish it is to adjust what is described below to a specific operation, to what your guests desire and expect.

❖ JOB DESCRIPTION: BUSSER

Job Summary

The busser is responsible for the following:

- The set-up of the station
- Water, coffee, and tea service
- Bread and butter service
- Clearing of soiled dishes, glassware, and flatware from tables
- Resetting of tables

Duties and Responsibilities

◆ Clean, wipe and stock the sidestand before service with all supplies needed by the team during service, including napery, china, glassware, and flatware.

◆ Steam, clean, and wipe silverware for the team, stocking the sidestand, before service.

◆ Arrange tables in proper position in station; arrange chairs in proper position and 24 inches from the edge of the table.

◆ Ensure the prompt, courteous service of all guests.

◆ Serve ice water to guests on request. Serve water glasses from a bar tray held in the *left* hand, and serve with the *right* hand, to the *right* side of the guest, keeping your hand on the lower portion of the glass.

◆ Refill low or empty water glasses automatically, without being requested to do so by either the guest or the captain. Once dessert has been served, stop refilling water glasses automatically; refill only on request.

◆ Obtain bread and butter for guests at each table as soon as they are seated.

◆ Ensure that adequate ice water, hot coffee, and hot tea are available on the station during service; refill coffeepots and customers' cups as necessary, and without being motioned to do so.

◆ Bus dirty dishes from tables, using the right hand and stacking dishes on the left hand, wrist, and arm; move dishes to oval trays and/or bus boxes.

◆ Ensure the sidestand is kept clean and clear of dirty dishes and trays throughout service, bussing trays as needed, so there is always a landing area on the sidestand.

◆ Use a napkin to cover trays of dirty dishes, flatware, and glassware being carried into the kitchen, so that customers do not see soiled china and glassware.

◆ Clear and reset tables as guests leave.

◆ Change table linens during service without baring the table; without removing flowers, lanterns, ashtrays, or other accessories from the table; and keeping the linen close to the table, so as not to "hang out the laundry" for the whole dining room to see.

◆ Crumb tables as required: between courses (always between the entree and dessert courses), and whenever else the table is exceptionally "crummy."

◆ Provide any and all other services to guests, as directed by the captain of the team or management, including:

 · Cleaning duties: dusting, washing mirrors, vacuuming
 · Transporting equipment and supplies, especially linen
 · Cleaning after accidents
 · Filling dispensers—for example, those for milk and ice

In short, bussers have two major areas of work—preopening duties, to be done before service begins, and duties directly related to customer service, to be done with customers present.

The busser duties are presented in the order that a busser would perform them, from the time he or she arrives for the shift to the opening for service ("Getting Ready to Serve"), and then the duties during service ("Once the Customers Arrive").

❖ GETTING READY TO SERVE

Serving the guests and clearing and resetting tables quickly and professionally are possible only if another part of the busser's job has been performed properly—the sidework, or getting ready for service. Sidework takes time; it can occupy as much time as the actual service. The work required of each staff member depends on the establishment and, in most cases, on the organization of the dining room. Sidework usually consists of three major areas of activity.

1. Preparing the dining room for service. This starts at the close of business and continues in the morning before the first meal period.
2. Cleaning and polishing serviceware, which includes china, glassware, silverware or flatware, and service pieces such as platters, bowls, and so on.
3. Preparing sidestands, sideboards, or booster stations.

People may be hired specifically to do certain tasks (vacuuming, rug shampooing, cleaning mirrors, polishing the silver platters and copper pans, and so on), or the service staff might be responsible. Check with management to determine which, if any, of the above are service staff responsibilities.

In classical organization specific jobs are assigned to individuals on the basis of their roles during service. Bussers and assistant servers have the most "outside of service" work, with captains having the least. An operation that uses pool organization attempts to apportion the work in the same way tips are divided, equally among all individuals on the staff; chores are rotated. Station organization places the responsibility for a number of tables and all they require with a single individual or with the team that shares the tips from that group of tables. If several individuals are involved, they may divide the work.

In all cases, the overall responsibility is given to someone—the captain, maitre d', or some representative of management. In operations where there are union contracts, the nature and the extent of sidework are usually defined further.

Preparing the Dining Room for Service

Preparation of the dining room starts the evening before, at the close of business. Both high-volume and gourmet dining rooms require the same kind of attention, although specific activities may differ. The dining room must be immaculate for the start of service.

Some sidework to be performed at the close of business is listed here.

- Electrical appliances are disconnected; gas equipment is shut off.
- Plastic and leatherette surfaces are washed; cloth surfaces are vacuumed.
- Stainless steel is washed with a stainless steel detergent, then polished with a stainless steel cleaning compound.
- Tables are cleared of dishes, flatware, and table coverings. Chairs are removed from the floor (they are often placed atop the tables) to allow cleaning of the floor.
- Clean utensils are placed in appropriate place.
- Perishables in the dining room are returned to the kitchen or placed in appropriate storage facilities.
- Dispensers for cream or milk are emptied and washed.
- Water pitchers are emptied and washed.
- Ice buckets are emptied and placed in appropriate overnight storage area.
- Condiment containers (sugar, salt, mustard, relish) are emptied and sent to warewashing. Salt and pepper shakers are filled and wiped clean. If the containers need washing, they need to be emptied and sent to warewashing.
- Coffeepots and coffee urns are washed completely or are sent to warewashing.
- Ashtrays are emptied and washed.
- Side stations and booster stations are completely emptied, cleaned, and restocked (or restocked before the start of business the next day).
- All consumables are restocked: matches, toothpicks, single-service napkins, dishes, cups, flatware, and so on.
- The first menu of the next business day is brought into the dining room.

Many of these sidework tasks will be discussed in detail below.

Cleaning Before Opening

Heavy cleaning of the dining area is most often the responsibility of a specialized cleaning crew, either an operation's own porters or contract cleaners. Cleaning as sidework consists mainly of dusting walls and furniture and polishing mirrors and glass. Chemically treated cloths and dust mops are often used to dust so that the procedure actually removes dust rather than spreading it through the air. Neither the dustcloth nor the mop should ever be wet, as a residue of dirt will be left on the "clean" surfaces. Dust furniture before floors. Clean mirrors and glass last.

Technique: Dusting Furniture

1. Fold a square yard of cloth end to end four times to make a flat 9-inch square dustcloth with 32 usable surfaces. Do not bunch the cloth into a ball. As it becomes soiled, refold it to a clean side.
2. Dust high surfaces first, and work downward.
3. Move objects to dust under them.
4. Hold light objects over their original positions and replace them immediately.
5. Dust the undersides and backs of furniture.

Technique: Dusting Floors

1. Place a clean dustcloth in the corners of the room and pull it out so that soil from the corners is drawn into the room.
2. Dust the main part of the room by walking forward in a straight line swinging the dust mop in a side-to-side motion. Or, push the dust mop directly ahead while walking forward.
3. Once the dusting of an area has been started, don't lift, jar, or shake the dust mop, or stroke it like a pushbroom, or take it from the floor, as this will release the dust.
4. Proceed to the back of the house area and dispose of the debris.

Technique: Cleaning Coffee Urns

Coffee urns should be cleaned as part of the closing routine every day, or the coffee will taste bitter. At least twice a week they should be cleaned using an urn cleaner, which is generally supplied by the coffee purveyor. The basic procedure is to add the cleaning solution and allow the solution to remain in the urn 35 to 40 minutes before scrubbing it (step 4).

1. Remove filter or bag holder.
2. Drain any coffee that remains in urn.

3. Rinse urn and then partially fill with hot water from the urn reservoir to about the coffee stain line.
4. Using a "gong" brush, vigorously scrub the sides of the urn and the inside of the cover.
5. Meanwhile place all used bags (if it is a bag machine) in cold water to soak.
6. Drain urn. Flush at least once with hot water, several times if a cleaner has been used.
7. Remove glass gauge by removing fastening nut at top of tube. Using a gauge brush, clean glass tube. Rinse.
8. Remove faucet from shank. Scrub inside of faucet and rinse. Scrub shank.
9. Reassemble faucet and urn gauge.
10. Partially fill urn with water.
11. Clean outside of urn.

Manufacturers of coffee urns and of other types of coffee-making equipment will generally furnish complete instructions about how to clean their machines, as well as how to make coffee with them.

Cleaning Serviceware

Clean dishes, glassware, and flatware are the responsibility of the warewashers (who wash the wares—silverware, chinaware, and glassware), or "dishwashers," in a foodservice operation. Although the service staff does not wash the servicewares, they are often asked to polish silverware or servicewares.

China

Even though warewashing machines are effective, if food has been allowed to dry onto plates before washing, there may be some residue. Therefore it is essential that bussers examine every glass, plate, cup, and other piece of china for dirt, cracks, and chips. Return any chinaware that is dirty to the warewashing station for soaking and rewashing. Before the meal starts remove from service any chinaware that is chipped or cracked. (This procedure is often called "reading the plates.")

Although this is the sanitary procedure that all restaurants should follow, it is an expensive proposition to discard automatically any chipped or cracked pottery or china. You should ask for an explanation of the "chip policy" of your restaurant. Some operations continue to use dishes which have chips removed from the underside (underchips) but reject dishes with chips on the top (overchips). Sometimes "star cracks" are acceptable to the management. Rejected pieces should be saved for the manager to discard.

Soap film, bits of food particles on surfaces, and stain build-up indicate an improper warewashing procedure. If these are evident, the manufacturers of the warewashing equipment are usually prepared to perform troubleshooting services to determine if it is the water temperature, type of chemicals used, hardness or softness of the water, or another problem. In any case, management needs to address the problem.

Glassware

If the glasswashing equipment is adequate and dedicated only to glasswashing, service personnel may never have to polish glassware by hand. Warewashing systems that do china, silverware, and glassware often recycle the same dirty soapy dishwater. If the rinse cycle is not hot enough, or the chemicals not sufficiently strong to effect a "sheeting" action on the glass, streaking or cloudiness may result.

If the glassware is streaked or cloudy the service staff should steam the glassware and hand-dry each glass with a lint-free cloth prior to service. How to steam glassware is described here:

❖ *Technique:* Steaming Glassware

1. Place a full-size hotel pan chafing dish assembly on the worktable. Fill the hotel pan half full with hot water (from the coffee urn, carried over in coffeepots). Ignite the Sternos (solid fuel).
2. Place a wire mesh over the top of the hotel pan. Place the glasses to be steamed atop the wire mesh, upside down, allowing the steam from the hot water to rise inside the bowl of each glass.
3. As each glass is steamed, remove it from the wire mesh and wipe dry with a lint-free cloth, being careful to hold stemware only by the stems and tumbler-style glassware at the bottom of the glass to minimize fingerprints.
4. Fill the wire mesh with more glasses. Repeat until all glasses have been steamed. Disassemble chafing dish.

Many restaurants have circular glasswashers in bar areas so those glasses never need to leave the bar area. Many restaurants are also installing circular glasswashers in key service areas, allowing the bussers and servers to load, wash, and unload glassware in their station. These eliminate the need for glassware to go back to the kitchen and warewashing areas, save time, and reduce breakage.

Sometimes bussers are required to load the glasses into special racks, bring them to the glasswashing machine, and then retrieve racks of cleaned glasses.

Glassware can be a continuing problem. Glasses that are milky looking as the result of a defect in the washing cycle should not be offered to the dining room. Unless the washing procedure is improved or the machinery repaired, the dining room service staff must either steam the glasses (described above) or rewet and polish them, as described here:

Technique: Rewetting and Polishing Glassware

1. Fold several 1-yard squares of clean cheesecloth four times end to end, making 9-inch square pads.
2. Fill a clean, sanitized vessel with very hot water—as hot as can be tolerated by bare hands.
3. Place the glasses to be polished, the cloths, and the bucket in a clean working area.
4. Remove the clean but water-spotted glasses from the rack.
5. Dip each glass in the hot water, holding the glass by the bottom of the stem or the bottom. Immediately remove it, and polish vigorously with the cloth. Place the glasses, inverted, back in the rack, and wipe their bottoms.

Flatware

Bussers share in the responsibility for clean flatware. How flatware—dirty or clean—is handled by the service staff can affect its cleanliness. Most operations provide a separate vessel with a special chemical in it for soaking soiled flatware so that food particles do not stick to the flatware or between the tines of forks. Egg residue can be especially difficult to remove once it has hardened.

In some operations the soaking containers are heated, which improves the performance of the chemical. Other operations, especially those which assign specific silverware to individual stations, require the service teams to keep buckets of solution on their stations for soaking soiled flatware. If the flatware has been properly soaked in the station and properly washed in an efficient machine, polishing should seldom be necessary.

If the flatware requires daily supplemental care there are various methods that can be employed. There are two specialized cleaning machines for flatware.

1. A tumbler washer, which is used with a special soap for the cleaning and polishing of already clean flatware after every use.

2. A burnishing machine, essentially a revolving drum lined with rubber and filled with metal pellets, which is used for deep polishing on an occasional basis.

    Lacking mechanical assistance, the servers are obliged to complete the cleaning of the flatware by hand. Two methods are described below for polishing tarnished silverware.

❖ *Technique:* Polishing Silverware

Method 1: Using Silver Polish

When the silverware is removed from the warewashing machine, it must be towel-dried, then cleaned with a silver polish:

1. Polish the flatware with the cleaning compound.
2. Rinse, removing the compound.
3. Polish to a high sheen with a soft dry cloth.
4. Redip in hot water and polish dry to remove any residue.

Method 2: Quick-Dip Tarnish Remover

A quick method to remove tarnish from silverware:

1. Place in a pot or other metal container, for example, a silverplated coffee pot or stainless water pitcher, the following:

Hot water	about 1 qt
Ball of crushed aluminum foil	about 4″ strip
Lemon juice	about 1 lemon
Salt	about 3 Tbsp

2. Stir
3. Dip the tarnished silverware into this solution
4. Allow to steep for 1 to 3 minutes
5. Remove and polish
6. Repeat if necessary

Preparing Flatware for the Dining Room

To gather flatware for use in the dining room, take it directly from the warewashing station, still wet, and wipe each piece dry, eliminating the possibility of water stains. Have a large oval tray lined with a clean napkin ready to place each piece of dried flatware on as it is wiped, and an extra dry napkin (or clean cloth) or two available for drying.

With one hand holding a napkin (or clean cloth), grab a few pieces of wet flatware (the "holding hand"), and with the other hand holding another clean napkin or cloth, take flatware one piece at a time and dry it. At no time should bare hands touch the flatware, as then fingerprints will result, defeating the whole purpose of wiping it clean!

If the flatware is already dry, and spotted with water marks or fingerprints, then a flatware cleaning station should be set up, either at the station in the dining room if before service and there are no customers present, or at an area in the back of the house where there is sufficient space to do the following procedure.

1. Obtain a large oval tray and place a clean napkin or cloth on the tray. Flatware should always rest atop a clean napkin on a tray, in case there is any dirt or residue on the tray.
2. Fill the tray with clean but spotted flatware. Fill a pitcher with hot water. Gather a few clean napkins or cloths and proceed to work area.
3. Dampen one napkin, which will be used to wipe water stains and fingerprints off the silverware.
4. With the other hand, lined with a clean napkin, grasp a bunch of silverware (the holding hand). Using the damp napkin, wipe each piece clean and place in a napkin-lined receptacle or drawer if you are working at the sidestand. Otherwise, place atop a clean napkin on a large tray.
5. Continue wiping pieces of flatware until a sufficient quantity has been prepared for service. Quietly stock the sidestand per the house procedures.

Cleaning Other Service Articles

In any type of operation there are numerous supplemental service articles. The gourmet dining room may contain several large silver gueridons or wagons; the coffee shop or fast-food restaurant may have 20 or 30 napkin dispensers, several dozen straw holders, and condiment stands. Generally, these articles are the responsibility of the dining room staff to keep clean and filled.

Silverplate and Copper

Silverplate and copper serviceware can be cleaned using commercial silver- or copper-cleaning products, according to the manufacturer's directions. These paste products are often rubbed onto the surface and rinsed thoroughly, or sometimes the compounds are allowed to dry and are then brushed from the article with a soft brush. Then polish the article with a dry chamois.

Glass Cruets

Glass cruets and water jugs present a considerable problem in hard-water areas. A commercial deliming agent can be used, or the glass vessels can be filled with a mixture of hot water and either bird shot or sand and vigorously shaken until crusts and discolorations are gone. Should they remain, treat with household ammonia and hot water. If this does not work, mix one teaspoon of muriatic acid to 8 ounces of water and add to the vessel after the ammonia mixture has been drained.

Stainless Steel

Stainless steel should be cleaned daily with a detergent product specifically suited to it, and treated weekly with a deliming agent to prevent the build-up of haze and film.

Plastic Trays

Plastic trays can be cleaned with soap and water, or with a metal polish.

Painted Articles

Painted articles—for example, napkin dispensers—can be washed in lukewarm water with mild soap. Periodically, service personnel might consider repainting them using canned spray paints.

Stocking Sideboards, Booster Stations, and Sidestands

One of the most important jobs of dining room preparation is stocking sideboards, sidestands, and booster stations. A sideboard is simply a cabinet standing against a wall of the dining room or pantry which contains supplies needed during the meal service. It may be in the kitchen, or in the public space. There are two types: open and closed. The open sideboard displays all the articles it contains, and therefore is easier to use. The closed sideboard—essentially a cupboard fitted with doors and drawers—is less efficient but more elegant and is generally used in the public spaces.

A booster station has the same function, but it is found in the center of the room; that is, among the tables or booths. Some booster stations, in large high-volume operations, also double as pantries. They have cabinets for holding warm breads, ice, running water, electrical outlets, storage drawers, and cupboards. Sidestands are stands built along the sides of a room which hold supplies needed by the staff during service—extra plates, coffee, silverware, and a loading and unloading area for trays of foods and beverages.

These areas must be stocked before service if they are to be of maximum use during service. The professionalism of a server or team can easily be judged by the thoroughness of the preparation for service. If a hamburger is delivered to a table, but it takes another 20 minutes to deliver the ketchup, the server or team was not prepared!

Table 1.1 is a fairly exhaustive checklist containing items that most operations need and use, and some that apply only to certain operations. It is meant as a guide, as source material to be customized. The "wardrobe items" are typical of deluxe service restaurants, while the "portioned food items" are typically found in high-volume operations. This model can be adapted to specific needs, and an inventory level or par stock of each item can be added according to the requirements of a particular operation.

After the items necessary for a sidestand have been gathered, they must be arranged for easy access. Usually each operation will have predefined places for certain items in each sidestand, so all are identical. If standards are maintained, when one station runs out of something, the bussers or servers know exactly where to look for it in another sidestand without looking through all the drawers, shelves, and so on.

Figure 1.1 shows how a drawer in a sidestand might be stocked, whether it is one wide drawer, two drawers, or three drawers adjoining each other across the front of a sidestand. The idea is to provide a uniform system of stocking the sidestands throughout an operation so anyone can find anything in any sidestand. Once an operation decides upon an order, it should be posted and everyone on the staff should be advised of the house's standard arrangement.

The theory behind the placement described is to place the most-often-used items—for example, appetizer forks, entree forks, and entree knives—in the most accessible drawer or position. The least-used items—for example, iced tea spoons, cocktail forks, and steak knives—are placed in the least-accessible drawers or positions. Those in-between items—for example, teaspoons, bread-and-butter knives, and soupspoons—are placed in a moderately accessible position.

It is much neater if the spoons and forks are nested. This is especially true for the plate of flatware brought for tableside service when guests are present. For this, line a plate with a napkin. Neatly fold the napkin into a square, with a "pocket" showing. Place clean, polished flatware into this pocket with the "eating" end enclosed in the pocket, and the handles pointing out.

A standard plate might have a few of each of the following: appetizer/dessert forks, teaspoons (for coffee and tea service), soupspoons, and steak knives. Items infrequently needed—for example, cocktail forks (for shrimp cocktail), fish knives (for fish entrees), and entree knives (for guests who drop their knife on the floor or use it with an appetizer)—can be added to the flatware plate and taken to tables as needed.

TABLE 1.1 Sidestand Checklist

Flatware

Soupspoons	Entree dish knives
Bouillon spoons	Butter knives
Dessert spoons	Salad forks
Iced tea spoons	Entree dish forks
Teaspoons	Steak knives

Wardrobe Items

Ashtrays	Cake slicers
Bread baskets	Pickle forks
Butter dishes	Cheese slicers
Asparagus tongs	Crumbers
Sugar tongs	Flower vases
Bone mustard spoons	Fruit stands
Grape scissors	Doilies
Nutcrackers	Rechaud stove and pans
Finger bowls	Champagne coolers
Sugar bowls	Petit four stands
Lobster picks	Oil and vinegar cruets

Miscellaneous Items

Salt shakers/cellars	Pencils/pens
Pepper shakers/mills	Service cloths
Matches	Toothpicks
Corkscrew	

Food Items

Coffee	Lemons
Tea	Salad dressings (bottle or portion)
Decaffeinated coffee	Sugar
Chocolate	Sweetener
Breads	Mayonnaise (jar or portion)
Crackers	Jams (serving vessel or portion)
Ketchup (bottle or portion)	Nondairy coffee creamer
Mustard (jar or portion)	Red pepper sauce
Steak sauce	Vinegar
Olive oil	Red pepper flakes
Parmesan Cheese	

Single-Service Items

Place mats	Coffee stirrers
Paper napkins	Bibs
Doilies	Packaged miniature towels
Straws	Coasters
Disposable forks	Butter chips
Disposable knives	Ashtrays
Disposable spoons	

FIGURE 1.1   Sample of silverware placement in sidestand drawer.

Positioning Tables and Chairs

Once the dining room is clean and the sidestands are stocked, it is time to position the tables where they belong and the chairs around the tables. This is important because if the tables are not in position before service, the chairs will not be in position. If the tables and chairs are not in their proper places, when service begins and the dining room fills with guests, there may not be room enough between certain tables for the service personnel to squeeze through, let alone walk comfortably. Therefore, it is important to place the tables and chairs where *you* want them, so you have plenty of room to get between tables, keeping the aisle ways clear.

Position the tables where they belong using a floor plan. If one is not readily available, ask your manager for one. Check tables for sturdiness. If they are wobbly, fix them now, placing bits of cork or wood wedges under the wobbly leg or section of the table.

Position the chairs around the table. Tables with an even number of chairs should have chairs positioned opposite each other, and equally spaced around the table when the table is round. If the table is a square four-top, the chairs should be opposite each other and centered along that side of the table. See Figure 1.2.

❖ PREPARING FOR THE GUESTS' ARRIVAL

Before the first customer arrives for any meal, the dining room personnel must prepare themselves and the area to serve the customers. Specifically, the table may have to be covered with a cloth or a cloth substitute; china, glassware, and flatware have to be set according to the tabletop design of the restaurant; and table accessories have to be placed. The proper menu must be brought to the dining areas, and dining room personnel must respond to daily menu changes by equipping sidestands, booster stations, and tables properly.

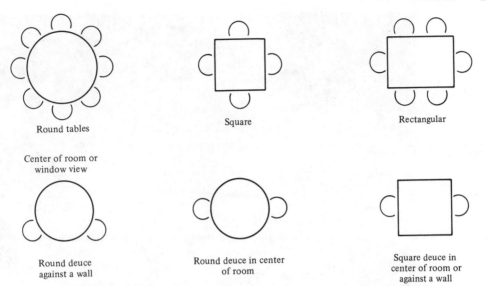

FIGURE 1.2   Chair placement around tables of various shapes.

Napery

Luxury or upscale restaurants usually use cloth tablecloths—of linen, cotton, rayon, or other fibers. Table linens add an air of luxury and soften the sound level, keeping the restaurant quieter. Before the cloth is laid, another cloth of heavy material, usually felt or foam rubber, is placed on the table to reduce the noise of placing plates and cutlery on the table during service. This "silence cloth" also is more comfortable for guests' elbows.

Any cloth laid on a table should be clean, pressed, and without holes, rips, or visible darns. If it is colored or has a pattern, it should appear new and not faded. It should lie with edges straight and parallel to the floor.

Technique: Placing a Tablecloth on a Table, Using Linens with Commercial Laundry Folds

1. Make sure the tabletop is clean.
2. Make sure the table is standing firmly, is level, and is balanced. Often tables with four legs can be balanced by placing a piece of cork under the short leg. Pedestal tables can be balanced with a piece of cork, or they can be turned over and the nut and bolt holding the base to the top can be tightened.

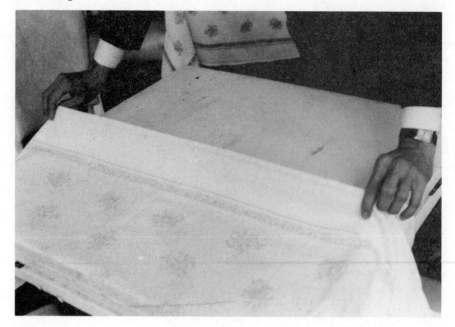

(a)

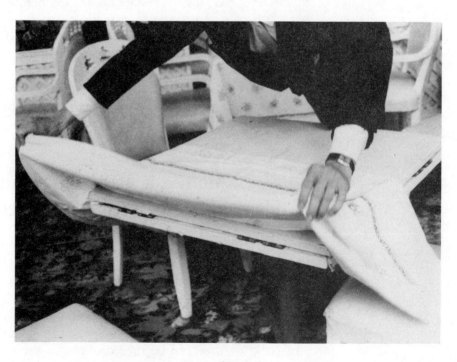

(b)

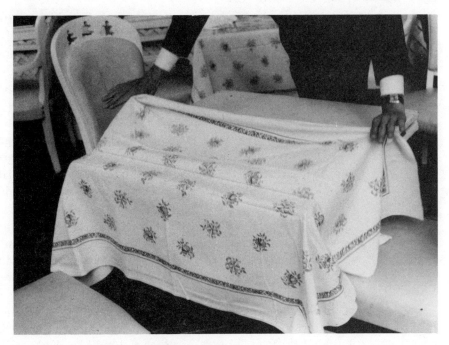

(c)

PLACING THE CLEAN LINEN (a) Position the folded cloth on the tabletop; (b) Drop the top edge over the edge of table; (c) Pull the hem edge toward yourself.

3.   If silence cloths are used, spread the cloth (which is often felt) over the tabletop.
4.   Smooth any creases in the silence cloth and adjust it so that it rests evenly on the table.
5.   Some operations cover the silence cloth with an undercloth, usually a white tablecloth, so that the table does not have to be completely stripped during service. If used, spread the undercloth over the silence cloth (generally it is only slightly larger).
6.   The top cloth, the decorative cloth the guest sees, goes over the silence cloth or the undercloth. It has two sides: the "right side" or face, which has the design if there is one, and which is sometimes shinier, and the "wrong side" or hem.
7.   If the tablecloth has been laundered by a commercial firm, it will be folded in four sections like a screen. One long side contains a hem, a double fold, and a hem; the other has two double folds. Place the two double folds on the far side of the table, keeping loose "edges" toward the center of the table.
8.   Take the top flap, a hem, between the thumbs and index fingers. Drop it over the far side of the table. Smooth the corners.
9.   Find the remaining hem edge; it should be the bottom section of cloth. With the thumbs and index fingers, gently pull the hem section toward yourself, over the top of the table, allowing the hem to drop over the side of the table.
10. Position the cloth on the table, with all the edges even and parallel to the floor, creases smoothed, cloth centered. *Note:* The *hem edge* should always be down, facing the floor.

Technique: Placing a Tablecloth on a Table, Using Linen with On-Premise Laundry Folds

When the tablecloth was not commercially laundered but instead was washed on the premises, it will probably not be folded as a screen but folded lengthwise and then in half and in half again. One side will contain four double folds; another of the four sides will contain one thick fold.

1.   Place the tablecloth in the near left corner of the table with the four double folds to the right and the single fold to the top.
2.   Lift the top flap (a double fold) and place it on the table.
3.   Lift the next flap and place it on the table. The table is now half-covered.
4.   Open the cloth like a book and cover the rest of the table.

Half Tablecloths

In some very formal restaurants, at lunch and supper, tables for two are covered with a special half tablecloth that leaves some of the tabletop exposed. Spread this cloth across the length of the table for a rectangular table, or position it equidistant from the sides on a square table. The hem side goes down. The edges of the cloth are the same distance from the floor, parallel to the floor.

Place Mats

Position place mats and doilies in the exact center of the "cover," the place the guest will occupy, 1 inch away from the edge of the table.

Cloth Napkins

Cloth napkins are part of many restaurants' tablesetting. They add a touch of luxury, give a third dimension to the tabletop, and give a decorative effect. Napkins are available in a wide assortment of colors, also adding color to the dining room. Many restaurants adopt one fold—a prescribed house fold, which every member of the service staff should know. Some restaurants use several folds, depending upon the dining room or banquet. A better-trained staff is required if several folds are used.

Napkins can be placed in one of two areas, generally speaking: in the center of the place setting, or to the left of the place setting. The most common is to the left of the forks (or at the left of where the forks will go) with the open edges at the lower left. When they are centered, they are placed exactly in the middle of each place setting. If a service plate is used, napkins are often centered atop the service plate. The bottom edge of the napkin should be 1 inch from the edge of the table regardless of the fold.

When a napkin is used with a place mat (the napkin can be cloth or paper), the bottom edge of the napkin should be approximately 2 inches from the edge of the table (1 inch above the place mat), and approximately one-third of the napkin should extend beyond the left side of the mat.

Occasionally napkins are rolled and placed in glassware. While dramatic, this may leave lint in the glassware, and is not a suggested napkin placement for upscale dining.

Paper Napkins

Paper napkins are available in every conceivable size and in a variety of textures. There are even paper napkins which resemble cloth. When the napkin is dinner size (17-inch square) and two-ply, facial quality, it can be treated like a cloth napkin; that is, it can be placed on the table.

Dispenser napkins should not be used except in dispensers. Put the dispenser on the wall side of the table in booths, and in the center of other tables. Before the guests arrive, fill the dispenser with clean napkins and wipe the dispenser.

Table Accessories

Table accessories should do just that—accessorize. In fine dining or high-check-average restaurants, minimal accessorization is the rule: Only what is needed for the course is on the table during that course. For example, during the appetizer and entree courses, salt and pepper should be on the table; during the dessert course, salt and pepper should not be on the table, but cream, sugar, and sweetener should be. Only accessories such as fresh flowers should be on the table during the entire meal, and ashtrays in smoking sections.

Where there are service staff or time constraints, such as at high-volume restaurants, the table may be set with all the accessories that have been anticipated for the whole meal and for any number of menus. The object is to save the service staff time by having sugar, sweetener, mustard, ketchup, and the like at hand.

A checklist of table accessories follows. This checklist should be modified according to your operation's particular standards. Accessorization should be centered or balanced to avoid overburdening one side of the table.

Checklist of Table Accessories

Ashtray
Matches
Salt
Pepper
Straws
Sweetener
Flowers
Pickles
Cream
Table tents (cardboard advertisements folded like tents)
Napkin dispenser
Bottled sauces
Menu stand (which may contain salt, pepper, and sugar)
Oil and vinegar cruets
Crackers
Coffee whitener

Flatware

Flatware for place settings must be immaculate and polished. Once these basics are covered, the rest is detail. Immaculate and polished flatware excludes that with the following:

◆ Fingerprints.   It defeats the purpose to polish flatware then touch it with fingers!
◆ Water stains.   Running the flatware through the warewashing machine and letting it "drip dry" leaves water marks.
◆ Bits of food particles.   Even if the dried egg yolk has been sterilized, no one wants it!

The rules to remember when handling flatware follow.

◆ Always handle flatware at its "waist," not at the top, which will go into the guest's mouth, nor at the bottom, where fingerprints will show.
◆ Always use a cloth napkin or clean cloth when handling flatware to avoid getting fingerprints on it.
◆ Use a clean lint-free cloth or cloth napkin to wipe down wet flatware to prevent water marks. Only water makes them, only water removes them!
◆ When resetting or replacing flatware at a table with guests present, carry the flatware in a cloth pouch or folded napkin envelope atop a salad plate; remove the flatware from the pouch and place it for the guest's use. This is very good dining room technique and maintains the illusion of cleanliness and sanitary conditions throughout the restaurant.
◆ Place pieces of flatware parallel to each other, and perpendicular to the edge of the table. A flatware setting should be opposite its mirror image if an even number of covers are placed at one table. In other words, the entree fork of the person facing north is opposite the entree knife of the person facing south. See Figure 1.3.

Technique: Laying Place Settings

1. Lay tables neatly and geometrically.
2. Make all tables in the dining area appear identical.
3. Place covers (individual place settings) so that they face each other across the table when possible. This is generally when an even number of places are being set, or when more than four places are being set.

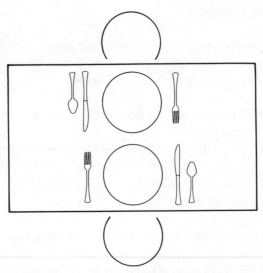

FIGURE 1.3   Flatware alignment on a table.

4. When two places are set at a round deuce along a wall, place them so that the guests face the center of the dining room and are sort of "next to" each other. See Figure 1.4.
5. Set covers between table leg areas.
6. Allow 24 to 30 inches from plate center to plate center between covers.
7. On a square table, lay the flatware at exact right angles to the edge of the table. On a round table, either "square" the flatware to each place setting or follow the rim of the table (with all flatware pointing to the center of the table).
8. Place flatware at least one-quarter inch and not more than $1\frac{1}{4}$ inches from the edge of the table. Align all the bottom edges of the

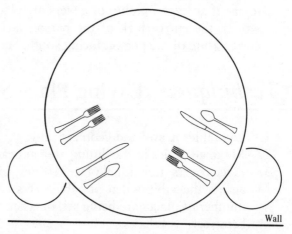

FIGURE 1.4   Flatware alignment at a round deuce along a wall.

flatware exactly the same distance from the table edge for square or rectangular tables.

9. Place the first piece of flatware three-quarters of an inch from the edge of the main dish plate. For example, if a 10-inch plate is being used, the flatware on either side of the plate should be $11\frac{1}{2}$ inches apart.

10. Place decorative "lay" plates in the exact center of the cover, even with the bottom of the flatware.

Laying Flatware

The different pieces of flatware should be positioned as follows:

◆ Spoons go on the right of the cover and to the right of any knives, with the front up (concave side up).

◆ Knives go on the right, with the cutting edge facing the center of the cover.

◆ Forks go on the left, with the tines (points) facing up, with the exception of cocktail or oyster forks, which are placed at the extreme right of the cover beyond the teaspoons. Alternatively, they may be laid across the right of the service or lay plate with the fork underneath the lip of the cocktail glass or oyster service.

◆ Dinner knives and dinner forks (main utensils) are placed next to the plate and on the right and left side, respectively, and the rest of the service is then placed on the appropriate sides in order of use. Flatware used first is on the outside.

◆ Butter spreaders are placed across the top edge or on the right side of the B&B plate, with the handle either at right angles or parallel to the edge of the table. The cutting edge of the butter spreader is turned toward the butter plate. Sometimes when a sharp steel-bladed serrated knife is used for the meat course, a smaller straight-sided silver knife is placed at the right of the meat knife for butter.

◆ Iced tea spoons are placed on the right just before they are needed.

◆ Parfait spoons are placed on the right just before they are needed.

◆ Dessert forks are placed just before they are needed. Or, dessert utensils, typically a dessert fork and dessert spoon, may be placed above and centered over the entree plate, the handle of the fork to the left and the handle of the spoon to the right. The spoon is above the fork if the fork is the longer of the two utensils; if the spoon is a true dessert spoon, and larger than the dessert fork, then the spoon is below the fork. The longer utensil is on the bottom, the shorter on top. See Figure 1.5.

◆ Dessert knives are placed just before they are needed.

◆ Breakfast and luncheon forks and spoons, when no knives are set, are placed to the right, with the forks closest to the plate in order of use, and the spoons to the right of the forks in order of use.

FIGURE 1.5 · Banquet flatware and glassware setup.

Chinaware and Glassware

China must be immaculate. It should not have cracks or chips, and if there is a pattern on the china, it should be vibrant and clear—not faded. When you place china on the table, center the design toward the guest. If there is food on the plate, the placement of the design will not matter unless there is a design present on the rim of the plate by which the servers can tell the proper way to present the plate to the guest. If there is a way to position the plate with the design facing the guest, position it that way. These small points are often noticed and remembered by guests—not all guests, but those who do notice that the service is exceptional will certainly be back.

Glassware must also be immaculate—with no fingerprints, streaks, water marks, chips, or cracks. For the proper cleaning of flatware, china and glassware, see the above section "Cleaning Serviceware."

Position specific plates and pieces of glassware as follows:

♦ Bread and butter plates are placed at the left of the cover. If there is sufficient space on the table, the top rim of the B&B plate should be to the left of and parallel to the top of the tines of the entree fork. Otherwise, place the B&B plate directly above the tines of the entree fork.
♦ Butter chips are placed to the left of and on a line with the water glass, toward the center or left side of the cover.
♦ Coffee cups are set with the top of the saucer in a line with the top of the last piece of flatware on the right. The handle of the cup should be to the right and slightly angled (pointing to about 4 o'clock).
♦ Water glasses are placed to the right of the cover immediately above the point of the meat or entree knife.
♦ Wine, liquor, and beer glasses are placed to the right of the water glass in a straight line in order of use. The straight line may be angled, with each successive glass being slightly lower than the one to its left. Or, if three glasses are placed, they might be formed into a triangular pattern, with the first one to be used closest to the guest, and the water glass the top left glass. Or, the smallest glass may be placed to the right and the rest aligned in order of size. See Figure 1.5.

- ◆ Liqueur glasses or port wine glasses, when they are set for banquets, are placed above the line of table wine glasses.
- ◆ Salt and pepper shakers for banquets are placed between covers in a line parallel with the bases of water glasses.

Covers for Specific Services

Each operation should establish a specific tabletop setting or requirement for each meal period, and these standards should be maintained. Diagrams of each tabletop setting and when it is used should be created and posted for all employees.

For example, a high-volume operation might set no cover (have no tablesetting) for breakfast, or only a place mat, napkin, and teaspoon, while in the evening it might set a place mat, napkin, entree knife, entree fork, and two teaspoons. Some examples follow.

High-Volume Fast Breakfast Set a place mat and put a teaspoon in the center of it. Place a napkin under the fork if there are no dispensers.

High-Volume Full Breakfast Place a cup and saucer, water glass, and juice glass on the right side of each cover. Place napkin and fork to the left of the cover, knife and teaspoon to the right.

Banquet Breakfast or American Plan Breakfast Set a napkin, fork, knife, and two teaspoons. Put a coffee cup to the right of the spoons. Place a butter plate parallel to the main plate, with the butter knife on the right side, parallel to the main fork. Put jam pots at the top of the main plate. Put the sugar bowl behind the cup. If an open-topped sugar bowl is used, lay a sugar spoon to the right of the bowl.

High-Volume Lunch or All-Day Service Place an entree fork, entree knife, and two teaspoons on top of a napkin (no service plate).

High Volume After 9 P.M. Place a fork, knife, and teaspoon at the place setting (no service plate). Put a napkin under the fork if there is no dispenser.

American Plan Lunch Place a fork on top of a napkin. Set an appetizer plate or underliner, knife, soupspoon, and teaspoon (no coffee cup).

Banquet Set the entire service according to the menu. The first utensil to be used should be on the outside—the right-most or left-most utensil. The next to be used should be the next closest to the outside. The main course fork and knife should be closest to the plate or inside of the setting. Dessert fork and spoon are usually placed above the place setting, with the handle of the fork pointing left and the handle of the spoon pointing right.

French a la Carte Lunch or Dinner Set a fork, hors d'oeuvre plate, knife, and B&B plate. Put a butter knife on the butter plate. Put a napkin in the center of the hors d'oeuvre plate.

Formal French a la Carte Dinner Set two forks, a silver or decorated lay plate, a main dish knife, and a bouillon spoon. The second fork is a smaller fish fork. Put a butter knife on the butter plate. Lay the dessert cover above the plate, fork handle pointing left, spoon handle pointing right.

American Plan Dinner Set two forks, a B&B plate, a knife, and a bouillon spoon (not a soupspoon).

Accompaniments for Specific Menu Items

The daily "specials" menu which supplements the standard menu in many operations may require additional serviceware, garnishes, or accompaniments. For example, according to the restaurant's policy, certain dishes will require another plate or "underliner" beneath them when they are presented to the guest. If an item that is served in a round casserole is on the menu on a particular day, the dining room staff will have to stock a supply of the appropriate underliners in the sideboards, booster stations, or pantry.

Particular food items stimulate requests from guests for garnishes, sauces, or utensils which one should anticipate by having the items available (or set on the table in banquet or American plan service) and by having portion service vessels when they are needed. For example, fried fish may increase requests for tartar sauce. If it is available, serve it attractively: in individual-portion cups, relish dishes, mustard crocks, or atop a piece of lettuce. Table 1.2 suggests some food accompaniments that are often requested. In addition to the traditional or common combinations such as pancakes and syrup, some of the rarer requests are listed, so you will be prepared. You can't afford to lose time searching for a condiment during the rush of service and then looking for something to put it in.

❖   # PREPARING GARNISHES AND FOOD

Service personnel have a role in food preparation and food garnishing. For example, dining room personnel routinely cut lemon wedges for iced

TABLE 1.2   Checklist of Food Accompaniments

Item	Accompaniment
Baked beans	Ketchup; chili sauce; pickles
Beets	Vinegar
Boiled beef	Ketchup; horseradish sauce; chili sauce; steak sauce; mustard
Broiled beef	Steak sauce of any brand; mustard; ketchup
Cheese	Toasted crackers; water biscuits
Chow mein	Soy sauce
Fish	Lemon; tartar sauce; ketchup
Fowl	Cranberry sauce; currant jelly
French fries	Ketchup; vinegar
French toast	Syrup; honey
Fruit	Sugar; lemon
Ham	Mustard; horseradish
Hot cakes	Syrup; honey; jams and jellies
Hot chocolate	Whipped cream
Italian food	Grated Parmesan cheese
Lamb	Mint sauce; mint jelly; currant jelly
Melons	Lemon; lime; salt; pepper
Pork	Applesauce
Roast beef	Steak sauce of any brand; mustard; ketchup; horseradish
Shellfish	Lemon; cocktail sauce; mayonnaise; ketchup; chili sauce; red pepper sauce
Soup	Grated cheese; croutons
Tomato juice	Lemon; horseradish; steak sauce
Waffles	Syrup; honey; jams and jellies

tea; prepare lemon halves for fish and seafood dishes; prepare butter curls or pats; and garnish plates with sauces, relishes, and condiments. In some operations they prepare the garnishes themselves; in most they at least transfer them from the commercial container to a dispenser or serving dish.

Service personnel may also be involved in the preparation of vegetables, and even entrees. The advent of preportioned, single-portion entrees compatible with microwave reconstitution has literally turned servers into "cooks" at some establishments.

Garnishes

The dining room staff needs to ensure that garnish items are ready and available when needed. It is too late to look for potato chips or pickles when customers are waiting for their sandwiches.

Typical garnish sidework includes

♦ The preparation of food garnishes
♦ The transfer of some food garnishes
♦ The transfer of some preparations from large storage or commercial containers to dispensers, portion cups, or serving vessels

Butter

Butter is almost always prepared by dining room personnel. In some restaurants the butter is purchased in bulk and "curled" using a butter curler, a special tool. Other operations use butter pots or porcelain ramekins, which are filled with softened or whipped butter—sometimes flavored butters, such as maitre d' butter, dill butter, or chive butter. When butter is purchased in chips or pats, the dining room personnel separate the pieces and arrange them in dishes so that they can be taken one by one as needed or a dish of pats can be placed on each table.

Butter arrangements can be used for decorative effect. For example, butter chips can be piled like tiny tiles to form a cylindrical latticework, or butter curls can be piled into a pyramid shape. Butter in porcelain ramekins can be stamped with the restaurant's logo or monogram.

Sandwich Garnishes

Sandwich garnishes are usually prepared after breakfast, especially in high-volume operations. Most often, servers are asked to portion items such as coleslaw and potato salad into individual-service cups. In some operations the dining room personnel cut pickles into spears. In order to facilitate the service during the noon rush, compound garnishes—for example, apple-orange-grapefruit skewers—are assembled in quantity in the morning.

Lemons

Lemons are generally prepared two ways:

Lemon Wedges   These are usually used with beverages, such as iced tea and hot tea.

1. Using a stainless steel knife, trim the ends from the lemon.
2. Cut the lemon in half the long way.
3. Place the cut side on the cutting board.
4. Cut a wedge of one-third of the half-lemon.
5. Divide the remaining piece into two parts.
6. Cut off the white pith (along the inside, center edge).
7. Remove any visible seeds.
8. Repeat steps 3 to 7 with the remaining half.

Lemon Halves   These are usually used with fish and seafood, or when a customer requests lemon (sometimes with salad greens or french fries).

1. Using a stainless steel knife, trim the ends from the lemon so the halves will stand upright on a plate.
2. Cut the lemon in half crosswise.
3. Remove any visible seeds.
4. Encase in cheesecloth "wrappers" to prevent seeds from falling into food.

Parsley

Parsley requires very little preparation. Thoroughly wash the entire bunch of parsley; drain it and gently pat it dry. Cut the individual flowerettes from the stems. Keep in a stainless steel bowl set in ice until needed. Parsley is usually a garnish for fish and fowl.

Watercress

Watercress is washed while still tied in a bunch. After draining, cut the stems so that about three-quarters of an inch of stem is left on the leaves. Keep in a stainless steel bowl, on ice, until needed. Watercress is usually a garnish for red meats and game.

Condiments and Sauces

Condiments and sauces are rarely prepared by the dining room staff; however, they are often portioned by the dining room staff into glasses, containers, or single-service plastic or paper cups. Some operations use a portioning device which, when its trigger is pulled, drops a predetermined portion into a cup. Other operations fill several dozen cups at once by using two precisely fitted metal plates. The bottom plate holds the cups in holes, while the upper plate has matching holes with tiny lips on its bottom side which just fit into the top of cups. Once the device is assembled, the sauce (e.g., tartar sauce or cocktail sauce) or the condiment (e.g., ketchup or mustard) is spread in the upper plate and pushed into the holes which channel it into the cups, without dirtying the cups.

Ice

Ice buckets (used for wine service) and ice bins (used for iced water, iced tea and coffee, and sodas) may have to be filled before service. Ice is usually the responsibility of the bussers. Often bringing cubed ice to the station is all that is required. At times ice must be crushed in a machine or with a mallet for use in specialty dishes, such as "supreme" cups.

Always use a nonglass scoop—for example, metal or plastic—whenever ice is being scooped. If any glass gets into the ice bin then all the ice must be thrown away, lest a piece get into a guest's drink.

Portion Packs

Portion packs have to be assembled on the station as they are used in the operation, (e.g. portioned jams, mustards, salad dressings, sugar, salt, and pepper).

Toast

Commercial toasters may be positioned outside of the kitchen for bussers or servers to toast fresh bread or muffins in.

Microwave Cooking

Many operations supply service personnel with microwave ovens, usually out of sight of the customers—on sideboards, at booster stations, or in the pantry area—for heating certain foods. Often breads, rolls, danish pastries, or pies will be warmed by microwave; soups can be warmed by microwave; customers may ask that baby food or bottles be warmed. This system may extend the shelf life of baked goods to several days since only one portion at a time is heated for service.

Fast-food operations make extensive use of microwaves for heating wrapped sandwiches as customers order them. The cook or server routinely places the sandwich—for example, a hamburger—in the microwave, presses a button marked "hamburger," and removes the sandwich when the buzzer sounds or the "in-use" indicator light goes off.

Reconstituting Prepared Entrees

Multiunit operations sometimes use a central preparation commissary for the actual cooking of foods, and deliver them portioned, frozen, and perhaps as complete "meals in a dish" to units which defrost and heat them in the shipping containers to serving temperature. Most 6- to 8-ounce main dish portions in sauce—for example, beef stew, macaroni and cheese, chili con carne—require between 55 and 70 seconds to heat from refrigerator temperature to serving temperature in a microwave oven. A chart indicating the proper reconstitution times for food items used in the establishment should be posted near the oven.

When the items are frozen, a short period of microwave defrosting, followed by a "rest" of 1 minute, followed by the heating cycle, is recommended to defrost then cook.

Technique: Operating a Microwave

1. Keep the machine clean. Dirt impedes the functioning of the unit and disrupts cooking times.
2. Use only approved packaging or vessels for microwave cooking. Plastic wares, ceramic wares, paper, and china without a metal rim are satisfactory. Metal utensils and metal foil should never be used in microwaves as they can damage the machine.
3. Do not overload machines. Recommended heating times apply to measured quantities. If more food is put in, increase cooking times.
4. Do not shunt or bypass door switches.

BEVERAGES

Beverages—iced tea, coffee, hot chocolate—are routinely prepared by the service staff in many establishments. In others, they are prepared by the kitchen staff. Each restaurant must determine responsibilities for various beverages at each location. It may be a mixed responsibility; for instance, the coffee urn in the kitchen may be maintained by the kitchen staff while the two-pot or four-pot burners at the stations are maintained by the service staff.

Coffee

The best-selling beverage in most operations is coffee, and being known for fresh, good coffee is one of the best word-of-mouth endorsements a restaurant can have. Usually poor coffee results from a build-up of residue in the coffee urn; from improper use of the equipment or improper preparation of the coffee; and from not making fresh coffee often enough, allowing it to stale. Poor coffee is rarely the result of the blend of coffee or the quality of the equipment.

Regardless of the coffee-making methods a restaurant uses, the Coffee Brewing Institute is available to all to assist with information, suggestions, and instructions. Contact the National Restaurant Association for the address and phone number.

Technique: Making Coffee in an Urn

There are two types of urns in general use: automatic and manual. Automatic urns spray a measured quantity of hot water (200°F, plus or minus 5°) on coffee spread in a filter. Making coffee in a manual urn requires you to pour a measured amount of water over the coffee.

Automatic Machine Method

1. Drain the water from the side of the urn to be filled. Make sure hot water is available.
2. Rinse the urn until the liquid from the "coffee pour" faucet is clear. Some establishments have a wire brush to be whisked around the inside of the urn.
3. Place a single-use filter paper and riser in the urn, or place a wet urn bag and a metal "riser," if required, in the top of the urn.
4. Evenly spread a portion pack or a "pound" of ground coffee in the bag or filter. (Many operations order 14-ounce pounds.) It is important to spread the coffee evenly. For automatic machines, move the sprayer arm over the coffee. Cover the urn and press the "1-pound brew" button.

Manual Machine Method

1. For manual machines, prepare the coffee grounds and filter or bag as described above. Draw hot water, using a coffee pourer. (In practice, a 1-gallon pourer is usually filled to half or three-quarters full to make handling easier.)
2. Pour the first measure of hot water over the coffee grounds, using a circular motion.
3. Draw another measure and a third or fourth for a total of between 2 and $2\frac{1}{2}$ gallons:

$$\tfrac{3}{4} + \tfrac{3}{4} + \tfrac{1}{2} = 2$$
$$\tfrac{3}{4} + \tfrac{3}{4} + \tfrac{1}{2} + \tfrac{1}{2} = 2\tfrac{1}{2}$$

4. When all the water has filtered through the filter, remove the coffee grounds.
5. On machines with a mixer, switch to "mixing cycle." Otherwise, draw 1 gallon of coffee from the urn and pour it rapidly into the urn to mix the coffee. Do not pour brewed coffee through the grounds; it may pick up a bitter taste.
6. Empty the urn bag and wash in hot water, without soap or detergent. Rinse it in cold water and leave it to soak in clean cold water.

Technique: Making Coffee by the Pot

Many operations use automatic brewers which make one or two pots of coffee at a time.

1. Run a pot of water through the machine without any coffee.
2. Place a single-use paper filter in the filter holder.
3. Make sure the machine has been on long enough to be hot.
4. Spread a portion pack of coffee in the filter paper.
5. Place the filter unit in the slot under the sprayer head.
6. Place a clean glass or metal pot under the filter outlet.
7. Switch to the "brewing cycle."
8. When the coffee has completely drained from the filter, remove the pot to a heater.
9. Pour one cup of coffee—more or less—from the pot and pour it back in the pot to mix the coffee.
10. Remove the filter holder. Discard the filter and spent grounds.

Technique: Making Coffee by the Vacuum Method

Some operations use "vacuum coffee makers," which resemble an hour-glass.

1. If the unit requires a filter cloth, wet the cloth in cold water and tie it over the filter. If the unit requires filter paper, place the filter paper in the upper bowl. If the unit requires a glass rod, place it in the upper bowl.
2. Place a measure of coffee in the upper bowl.
3. Fill the lower bowl with cold water.
4. Bring the water in the lower bowl to a boil.
5. Insert the top and twist to ensure a tight seal.
6. When the water has risen to the upper bowl, remove the unit from heat.
7. Allow the coffee to filter into the lower bowl.
8. Return the coffee to a warmer; remove the upper bowl.

Espresso and Cappuccino

Some restaurants offer true espresso and cappuccino coffee, which is drawn from a specialized machine which forces steam through the coffee grounds. Others make strong, espressolike coffees using stove-top "espresso-makers." Both are detailed below.

Detailed instructions, similar to the following, should be prepared and distributed to everyone in an operation, so everyone is thoroughly advised of the proper procedure for making espresso and cappuccino.

Technique: Making Espresso and Cappuccino via the Traditional Method

Espresso

1. Have lemon twists and saucers at the sidestand.
2. Go to the cappuccino/espresso machine.
3. Take an espresso cup (they are very tiny). Fill it with hot water from the coffee machine. Set it aside to warm.
4. Take the ground coffee holder by the handle and, hitting it against the side of the garbage can, remove the old coffee grinds. Run holder under hot water to remove any remaining grinds.
5. Place the ground coffee holder under the coffee dispenser. There is one for regular espresso and another for decaf espresso, if the house has both. They are usually different colors so as to be easily distinguishable.
6. Pull the lever (usually twice), filling the ground coffee holder.
7. Place the ground coffee holder under the packer, and pack the grounds, applying pressure, with your other hand, from above. *Be sure to pack the coffee tightly!*
8. Wipe the rim of the ground coffee holder to ensure a good seal.
9. Place the ground coffee holder into its receptacle on the cappuccino/espresso machine.
10. Pour the hot water out of the espresso cup. Place the cup under the ground coffee holder.
11. Pull the lever down. This activates the steam, forcing it through the ground coffee, creating espresso.
12. The espresso cup will fill with espresso, then foam. When the cup is almost full, pull the black lever up to stop the flow of steam through the coffee grounds. (Some operations have machines that work with a button and stop automatically. Customize the procedure to the machine.)
13. Serve on a small saucer atop a regular saucer, taken from the sidestand. Place a lemon twist on the small saucer. Serve.

If There Is No Foam

♦ Coffee grounds *weren't packed enough*.
♦ Top of the holder was not cleaned off, preventing a *good seal*.

Cappuccino

1. Fill a cappuccino coffee cup one-half full with cold milk.
2. Pour the cold milk into the steamer container at the cappuccino/espresso machine.
3. Fill the cappuccino cup and a creamer with hot water; set them aside to warm.
4. Holding the steamer container under the steam nozzle, steam the milk, moving the container vertically to distribute the steam throughout the milk, creating lots of foam on top.
5. Pour the hot water out of the coffee cup, and replace with the steamed milk, spooning the foam on top.
6. Sprinkle cocoa powder atop the foam. Set aside.
7. Empty the creamer. Make espresso as described above, placing the empty, warmed creamer under the ground coffee holder to collect the espresso.
8. Take the coffee cup with the steamed milk and the creamer with the espresso to the sidestand.
9. Pour the espresso into the steamed milk, straight through the center of the foam. When you pour from the creamer spout, only a small "hole" will be made, which can be camouflaged with cocoa powder. Serve.

Hint Rinse out the steamer container with cold water before steaming the milk, and if possible, use fresh, cold milk. More foam is produced with a cold container and fresh, cold milk than with a warm steamer container, warm milk, and/or old milk.

Technique: Making Coffee by the Filter Method

Other restaurants offer cafe filtre (by whatever name), which is made from dark roasted coffee (espresso beans ground to an espresso grind) in individual pots. These pots consist of the actual serving pot with a detachable filter and a coffee compartment, and an upper vessel.

To Make Filtered "Espresso" Coffee

1. Fill the coffee chamber of the canister with dark roasted ground (espresso) coffee. Screw the filter to the canister.
2. Place the upper vessel upside down on a table and fill it three-quarters full with boiling water.

3. Insert the canister in the upper chamber with the filter up.
4. Place the inverted serving pot on the unit (that is, with the spout up).
5. Invert the entire device so that the serving pot is in the proper position when the coffee is served.
6. When the water has drained through the filter, and the top chamber is empty, remove it.
7. Cover the serving pot.
8. Serve the coffee.

Tea

Tea by the Cup

In most operations tea is served by the cup. If tea bags are used, house policy should determine whether pots of hot tea are made in the kitchen for use throughout the dining room; whether tea bags are placed in cups in the kitchen, with hot water added there as well; or whether the guests place the tea bag in the cup at the table, with the hot water added there also.

Valid arguments for each of the above methods are described below; however, the preferred method is to have the guests place the tea bag in the cup so they can control the strength of the tea.

Guest Places Tea Bag Argument

"Guests should have the option of deciding how strong or weak their tea will be, and they can control this only if they make their own."

Procedure

Serve a warm cup, saucer, teaspoon. (Warm the cup by filling it with boiling water and allowing it to remain for a minute or so; then pour out the water.) Serve the tea bag on a separate small plate—perhaps a B&B plate. Serve the boiling-hot water in a separate vessel. Ask the guest, "Shall I pour?" This is the cue for the guest to place the tea bag in the cup, at which time the hot water is poured over the tea bag by the server. The guest will remove the tea bag to the small plate it arrived upon when the tea is brewed to the proper degree. Milk (not cream or half-and-half), lemon wedges, sugar, and artificial sweetener are traditionally served with tea, unless the guest requests otherwise.

Server Prepares Cup of Tea Argument

"The tea is best if the tea bag is placed in the cup at the source of the boiling water and allowed to brew."

Procedure

Warm the cup by rinsing it with hot water and allowing it to rest for a minute or so. Pour the hot water down a drain. Place the tea bag in the cup (hot water should always be poured over the tea). Fill it almost to the rim—about one-half inch from the top—with fresh boiling-hot water. Serve a lemon wedge, sugar, artificial sweetener, and milk separately.

Loose Tea Service

If you are serving loose tea, brewed in the pot, take a separate nonmetallic (preferably porcelain china) loose tea strainer and tea strainer holder, as well as a warmed tea cup and saucer, the hot tea, and the usual accompaniments, to each guest having tea. Before pouring hot, brewed tea from the pot, the guest places the tea strainer in the warmed tea cup, then pours the hot tea into the strainer. The tea passes through the strainer into the cup, leaving any loose tea leaves trapped in the strainer. The guest then places the strainer in its holder (placed above and to the right of the teacup), where it remains until the guest desires a refill.

For even more luxurious service, guests are given a choice of loose teas and brew it themselves. A portion of the chosen tea is placed in the tea strainer, which is then placed atop the cup, with the strainer section dipping into the cup portion. Hot water is brought to the guest, and the guest pours the hot water over the tea leaves, brewing the tea in the cup to the desired strength. Then the strainer, with the trapped tea leaves, is removed to the strainer holder. With this method, additional water is readily available (in the tea pot) for a second cup of tea, but the tea leaves have not been brewing in the hot water all the while. Guests can brew a second cup to their desired strength.

Tea by the Pot

Tea is sometimes offered in pots that use either tea bags or loose tea. Warm the pot with boiling water. Discard the water. Place the bag or a measure of tea in the warm pot. Fill the pot with boiling water, allowing the tea to steep for a few minutes. Serve a second pot of plain boiling water to the guest so the tea can be diluted to the desired strength.

Iced Tea

Iced tea is made in one of four ways:

1. From liquid tea concentrate from a commercial source
2. From liquid tea concentrate prepared on the premises from loose tea or tea bags

3.   From powdered tea concentrate
4.   From a dispenser using powdered tea

Liquid Tea Concentrate   Liquid tea concentrate is made by using tea bags, loose tea, or a large commercial iced tea bag. Use one-fourth the amount of boiling water necessary to make hot tea (i.e., use 6 cups of water to brew 24 tea bags). Brew the tea for 7 to 10 minutes. Remove the tea bags or strain. Do not refrigerate the concentrate.

The liquid concentrate can be either unsweetened or presweetened. If it is to be presweetened, the sugar or sugar substitute should be added while the concentrate is still hot, to ensure that the sugar dissolves completely.

To prepare an individual portion, fill the glass one-fourth or one-third full with liquid tea concentrate. Add a bit of cold water to the concentrate so it will not be too strong. Then fill the glass with ice and additional water as necessary. Garnish with a lemon wedge, a sprig of fresh mint, and a straw—or whatever the house policy dictates.

Powdered Tea Concentrate   Powdered commercial concentrate is available unsweetened or sweetened, or either way with lemon flavor added. To prepare an individual portion, mix 1 teaspoon of concentrate with half a glass of cold water. Stir. Add ice to fill the glass, topping off as necessary with cold water. Garnish and serve.

Powdered concentrate can also be used in a dispenser, where the dispenser is filled with the concentrate and the machine is hooked up to a fresh cold water supply. Fill a glass with ice, place it under the dispenser, and push the start button. The machine measures the amount of concentrate and water that are released, combines them, and squirts the tea into the glass on the dispensing pad.

Hot Chocolate

Hot chocolate is usually prepared from powdered concentrate in a specially designed hot chocolate machine. The powder is poured into a container at the top, the machine is hooked up to a hot water source, and preproportioned amounts of hot water and powder are mixed in the machine and dispensed into a cup, placed below the dispensing spout. Alternatively, hot chocolate individual-portion packets are available, to be mixed with 1 cup of water, stirred, and presented to the customer.

Should neither of these methods be available, heat milk, mix it with chocolate syrup from the fountain or dessert area, and top this with whipped cream. This method is detailed below. Any of these presentations can be garnished with tiny marshmallows or whipped cream on top.

Technique: Preparing Hot Chocolate

Ingredients

2 Teacups   3 Tbsp Whipped cream
1 Teaspoon   2–3 tsp Chocolate syrup
$\frac{7}{8}$ Cup milk

Method

1. Fill 1 cup with cold milk, to within an inch of the top of the cup.
2. Place the cup of milk in the microwave, and warm for 50 seconds. When buzzer sounds, remove the cup. (Or heat on stove until milk is scalding.)
3. Add chocolate syrup to the hot milk. Stir thoroughly.
4. Spoon whipped cream on top. (If necessary, use second cup to procure whipped cream, then spoon from second cup into hot chocolate milk cup.)
5. Place second teacup, if used, and teaspoon at dishwashing area.

In summary, the busser has a lot of things to do to get ready for service. An abbreviated list follows:

1. Clean the dining room: Sweep; polish glass, mirrors.
2. Position tables where they should be.
3. Position chairs around tables. Chair backs should be 24 inches from the edge of the table, as they would be with people sitting in the chairs. This will ensure sufficient space for service personnel to pass between chairs when customers are seated.
4. Stock sidestands, booster stations, service areas.
5. Clean coffee urns; make beverages for service.
6. Check flatware, glassware, china for chips, cracks, cleanliness. Steam-clean as necessary.
7. Check for menus, checks, and the like.
8. Set tabletops.

ONCE CUSTOMERS ARRIVE: BASIC RESPONSIBILITIES DURING SERVICE

Bread and Butter

As your customers enter, greet and seat them, observe how many guests there are, and double-check this number against the seating card to see if anyone else will be joining the table. Proceed to the kitchen and procure bread and butter for the guests at that table. If more than one table was seated at once, get bread and butter for all tables in the station seated at approximately the same time.

Follow house procedures for getting bread and butter. One method for getting bread is detailed here.

1. Take one clean napkin for each table that needs bread, and go to the bread station. Tell the bread person how many people bread is needed for, or obtain the bread or rolls yourself.
2. Wrap the bread or rolls in a napkin using the house fold (perhaps with the bread in the center, edges folded over and meeting in the center, and ends tucked under), and place bread or rolls in a basket.
3. If the bread and rolls are not kept in a warmer drawer, place the bread and the basket in the microwave and warm for 10 to 30 seconds, depending on the amount of bread in the basket.
4. While the bread is heating, gather butter curls (or chips or whatever the restaurant uses). Butter curls go into a monkey dish, or other dish, which should be chilled. Use the proper number of butter curls or chips—don't waste butter! (Generally figure one curl or chip per person, plus two.) If more butter is needed, it can be brought later—many people do not eat bread or butter.
5. Take the warmed bread, in the napkin in the basket, and the butter, in a chilled dish, to the sidestand. Take both the bread and the butter to the table.

Water Service

If the house policy is to serve water automatically, serve one glass to each person at the table. Otherwise, serve water on request. If one person at a table requests or is served water, water should be served to all guests at that table.

Water should be ice cold, and served in a glass with ice. Refill as often as necessary, without guests' requesting you to do so, until the dessert course, at which time water is served only on request.

Coffee and Tea

Captains, servers, and bussers—everyone on a team—serve coffee and tea when a customer requests it. General tea service follows the guidelines discussed on pages 36–37; specific coffee and tea service techniques are detailed in Chapter Two.

Clearing a Table During Service

As the meal progresses, dishes and flatware from previous courses must be removed. Whether they are removed to a bus box or a tray or are arm-carried to the kitchen is unimportant—the same technique is necessary. When there are only a few dishes, handling them is simple. When a greater number of pieces and glassware and flatware are involved, efficiency must be combined with good taste.

The technique described below is standard. It is used regardless of whether the busser or server is right- or left-handed. It is time to clear a course when everyone in the party has finished that course, unless management dictates otherwise or there are extenuating circumstances. Extenuating circumstances might include an elderly guest who is much slower than the rest of the guests or a host or hostess who is constantly jumping up from the table. If it is the policy of the house to do so and the next course is ready to be served, the person with the unfinished course would be asked if he or she wants the unfinished dish placed on the side to be finished during the next course or would prefer to have it removed.

The guest then has the option of finishing the dish during the next course or having it removed and going on to the next course with the rest of the party. Meanwhile, the remainder of the guests are cleared and prepared for the next course.

The technique, used universally, regardless of the type of service (American, French, or Russian) is as follows:

Technique: Clearing a Course

1. When it is time to clear a course (usually when all the guests have finished that course), stand at the right side of the first diner to be cleared. This should be a woman if any are present at the table.
2. Extend your right hand to the diner's plate, gripping the plate at approximately 3 o'clock keeping on the plate any cutlery the diner has left on the plate. Grasp the plate with your index finger and middle finger under the plate and the thumb tightly clasped to the top edge, not in any food.
3. Withdraw the plate, around the guest, keeping the plate below eye level until out into the "aisle space."
4. Transfer the plate to your left hand, using the same grip.
5. Place forks next to each other on the plate, tines outward, with your left thumb on top of the base of one fork.
6. Place the knife under the bridge (curved part) of the secured fork, with the sharp edge away from the server. If the knife (or other utensil on the right side of the guest) was not used but should have been used for that course, reach to the table again and remove it

and other utensils that should have been used. Place them on the plate, under the bridge of the fork.

7. Move forward (clockwise around the table). If the first guest has a fork that should have been used on the table, reach in with the right hand from the left side of the guest and remove it. Otherwise, position yourself at the right side of the second guest to be cleared, and still holding the first plate, remove the second plate from the second guest in the same manner.

8. Place the second plate on your lower left forearm.

9. Support the plate on three points: the lower forearm (not wrist), the thick part of the thumb of the left hand, and the upturned little and ring fingers of the left hand. Both plates should be parallel to the floor. The plate furthest from you may lean in slightly toward the closer plate.

10. Remove the knife and fork (or whatever flatware was on the plate) from the second plate to the first. Place them next to the original flatware—the fork next to the first fork and over the knife, the second knife (and any spoons) going under the bridge of the fork.

    If knives or spoons that should have been used but weren't are on the table, reach in with your right hand and remove them quietly.

    Always remove the soiled plate first, then the clean flatware that should have been used but wasn't. Customers don't mind looking at clean, unused flatware; they do object to dirty or finished plates sitting in front of them.

11. Move as much out of the line of sight of the guests as possible, using aisle space to scrape excess food from the plates and place the cutlery on the further plate.

12. Scrape any large pieces of food from the second plate to the first plate. For faster clearing, if the food remains are squashable (rice, mashed potatoes, salad greens), squash them by putting the next plate directly on top. If the food remains are not squashable (e.g., bones), then scrape.

13. Proceed to the next guest.

14. Repeat steps 7 to 13.

15. When all the plates have been cleared, remove the lower plate from your left hand (now loaded with flatware and debris) and place it on top of the stack of clean plates on your left forearm.

16. Grip the stack with both hands and proceed to the tray on the bus stand, the bus box, or the dish room.

17. If you are stacking on a tray, stack like-size plates atop each other, keeping the "garbage" plate on top. Make separate stacks for each size plate. If additional room is necessary on the tray, place a stack of smaller-diameter plates atop a stack of larger-diameter plates.

Keep the weight of the plates in mind—someone's got to lift the tray after its loaded!

18. Flatware should be piled on one side of the tray.

Detail Notes on Clearing a Course

♦ Clear unused forks, B&B plates, and side dish plates from the left side of the guest, after removing the entree plate. Don't reach in front of a guest to retrieve cutlery, glassware, or china.

♦ Clear all china from a small table in one trip. If the table is large, remove entree plates and flatware first, then make a second trip around the table to remove B&B dishes, side dishes, bread, salt and pepper, and other plates that are not essential for the next course.

 ## *Technique:* Clearing the Table

1. Clear the dishes and flatware as described above.
2. Remove glassware from the right side of a guest, using your right hand, traveling in a clockwise direction around the table. Handle stemware by the stem; handle tumbler-style glasses by the bottom $1\frac{1}{2}$ inches of the glass.
3. Place all glassware on a beverage tray rather than taking it from the table in the hand (more glasses fit on a tray and it looks more professional), unless the operation does not use beverage trays. If a large table is being cleared, an oval tray may be used for glassware.

    If glassware and china must be combined, then place glassware between stacks of dishes (stemware) and around the perimeter of the tray (tumbler-style glasses).
4. Stack stemware and unsteady (top-heavy) glassware in the center, if possible, since if stemware is on the perimeter of the tray and a corner is negotiated quickly, the glasses may fall. Place tumbler-style glassware, which is steadier, around the perimeter of a tray.
5. Take the tray or trays of dirty glassware, china, and flatware to the kitchen immediately. Cover all trays going to the kitchen with at least one napkin for aesthetic purposes.

    If possible, use one or more of the napkins from the table you've just bussed so it is not necessary to use clean napkins to cover dirty dishes.
6. Remove salt and pepper shakers, B&B plates, and the bread and butter when the entree plates are cleared.
7. Leave table with only the tablecloth, if there is one, and any appropriate accessories—for example, fresh-cut flowers, an ashtray if the table is in a smoking section, and a candle if it is night.

8. Crumb the table between courses and always before the dessert course, if only for show. To use a crumber, slide the straight edge of the crumber from the center of the table toward the edge, gathering the crumbs in the concave hollow of the crumber. Scrape the crumbs onto an appetizer plate, which is held just under the edge of the table. Don't permit crumbs to fall onto the floor.

9. If the guests have left, change the tablecloth (if the restaurant uses them) using the technique described later. Soiled tablecloths should be rolled into a ball and carried under an arm, not placed on a tray. If table linens are placed atop a tray, there is a chance that the weight of the tablecloth will cause a glass to move and drop off the tray. Or because of the height of the linens atop the servicewares, the linen might roll off the tray, drop to the floor, and unroll, creating a safety hazard.

When a rectangular small tray is used, use essentially the same procedure, except that two or more stacks are made on the tray: one or more of cleaned (scraped) plates, the other of a plate full of debris and flatware. The flatware should be on the side of the tray, in a pile.

Loading a Bus Box

Occupied tables (with guests seated) are usually cleared using an oval tray. After guests have left, however, there is a choice: Clear tables either with an oval tray (more formal settings) or with a bus box, which is carried by hand or in a specially fitted cart accommodating two or three boxes.

Bus boxes are often divided into two compartments, one approximately three times the size of the other. Silverware is accommodated either in the smaller compartment or in a canisterlike container that fits the side of the box. Proper loading of the bus box ensures that the table will be properly and promptly cleared for the next customer, that no dishware or glassware will be broken, that no silverware will be lost, and that the bus box can be unloaded efficiently in the dish room.

It is important to load the bus box completely—that is, to the maximum weight you can carry or to the maximum number of dishes that can be fit into a box, to reduce the number of trips to the kitchen. The technique for doing this follows.

❖ *Technique:*   Loading a Bus Box

1. Approach the table either with the cart or with the bus box held in your left arm as though it were a rectangular tray. Place the bus box on the bus stand unless it is on a cart.

2. Remove the largest plates first. Using a fork, scrape food scraps and paper goods into a corner of the box or the waste compartment.
3. Stack the plates in the bottom of the box, along the middle third. Place silverware along one side of the box or in a separate compartment.
4. Nest cups and small bowllike dishes on top of the stacked large plates.
5. Place glasses, stem or base down, on one side of the box, opposite the silver.
6. Place small, flat dishes—for example, salad plates and B&B plates—on edge, bottoms against the walls of the bus box.
7. Place articles like cream pitchers on top of plates or in cups.
8. Do not place anything in glasses except other glasses if they are stackable.

Resetting a Table During Service

Resetting Flatware

Occasionally it is necessary to replace or reset flatware during service: Perhaps a guest used an entree utensil for an appetizer. Perhaps a guest is having fish or steak and a special knife must be brought to the table. Perhaps a utensil fell or was knocked to the floor.

Each of these instances requires that a member of the service team replace the appropriate flatware. In the case of the improperly used utensil, the utensil used is removed from the table when the course it was used with is removed. In addition, the utensil that should have been used is also removed.

From this point, the placing of the flatware is the same procedure for all three instances. Clean, polished flatware is brought to the table in a hygienic, appealing manner. One technique is to nest the flatware, forks against forks, spoons against spoons, upon a clean, folded napkin. The napkin is usually folded in a large square shape, often with a pocket for the flatware, with the eating ends protected by the pocket. The napkin, in turn, is placed upon a plate for support, usually a salad or entree plate. See Figure 1.2 for an example.

Hold the plate in your left hand and approach the guest requiring the flatware. In order to replace a piece (e.g., a fish knife for the entree knife), remove the entree knife (or other piece) and placed it upon the napkin, then place the fish knife (or needed piece) on the table in the appropriate position.

When placing spoons or knives approach from the right side of the guest and replace the flatware on the right side; when placing forks, approach from the left side of the guest and replace them on the left side. In other words, don't reach over the guest.

If a utensil has dropped to the floor, put the replacement flatware on the table first, *then* pick up the soiled piece of flatware, not placing it on the napkin/plate with the clean flatware, but keeping it in the right hand. Proceed to the sidestand or warewashing area and drop off the soiled piece to be cleaned. Return the plate with the clean flatware to the sidestand.

Resetting Covers

Resetting a table during service requires some advance preparation. Prepare complete covers or sets of the operation's basic setting before the meal. For instance, an appetizer fork, an entree fork, an entree knife, a B&B plate, and a napkin might make up the cover. Place the flatware and glassware on top of the chinaware and cover it with a clean napkin. During service, carry the complete covers to the bus stand or booster station nearest the table and set them quickly after the cloth has been changed.

Changing a Cloth During Service Without Baring the Table

If you've ever seen a tablecloth being flapped in the dining room over a table ready to be reset, you know what not to do! Placing a tablecloth on a table should not resemble a bullfight, or hanging out the laundry. These actions disturb guests, creating a distraction at nearby tables.

The procedure described below is for changing tablecloths during service in a classic, dramatic, yet very understated manner. It is a coup de grace for those who can do it. When done properly, the tablecloth is changed with style—smoothly, quickly, and with a minimum of disruption to guests. This method keeps the accessories on the table during the changing of the cloth, not putting the fresh flowers on a chair where they might get knocked over and wet the chair, and not putting the ashtray on the chair where it might leave ashes.

This procedure is for changing a tablecloth that has been professionally laundered and folded into fan or Z or accordion folds, with the design, if any, folded to the inside of the cloth. It cannot be done with a cloth folded in any other way.

Technique: Changing a Tablecloth on a Square Table During Service (Using Linens with Commercial Laundry Folds)

1. Completely clear the table, except for standard accessories, such as flowers. Place the clean tablecloth, folded, on a clean chair seat. Standing in the center of one edge of the table, move accessories to a near corner (right or left near corner). Reach over the far edge of the table and grasp the far edge of the soiled tablecloth (at the hem) between the thumbs and index fingers of each hand, hands spread at least the width of the table. Pull the top edge of the soiled tablecloth toward you, folding it onto itself, exposing about 6 or 7 inches of the bare table.

   A portion of the soiled tablecloth should now be doubled back onto itself, with a hemmed or selvage edge on top. The edge should be at or just past a horizontal "center" line, with the edge closer to you than to the far edge of the table. All of the crumbs, ashes, and so on are on top of the soiled tablecloth (the part toward you) or "inside" the folded-over portion of the tablecloth (the part away from you).

2. Place the fan-folded clean cloth at the top of the table, atop the folded-over portion of the soiled cloth. Have a "short" end facing you. Open the clean cloth horizontally across the far edge of the table, keeping a hemmed edge on top and facing you and keeping all other folds in place.

   The clean cloth should now be folded into quarters lengthwise and draped across the far edge of the table, atop the folded-over portion of the soiled cloth. The edge of the clean cloth closest to you should be along the horizontal "center" line of the table but *not covering* the edge of the soiled cloth, which should be directly below it, with the edge showing. The "far" edges of the clean cloth should be at or even hanging over the far edge of the table (if a deuce) or an inch or so away from the far edge of the table, toward you (if a four-top or larger).

   Hints: Keep edges on top and facing you! Keep edges visible at all times!

   Place the clean cloth atop the folded-over portion of the soiled cloth only. No portion of the clean cloth should be touching the "right" side of the soiled cloth, as that is where crumbs; cigarette ashes; spilled drinks; and drops of puddings, sauces, and gravy are, which would soil the clean cloth before it was even unfolded!

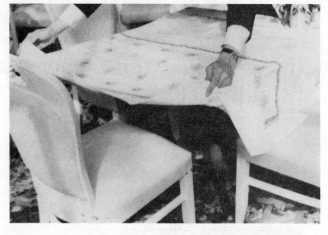

(a)

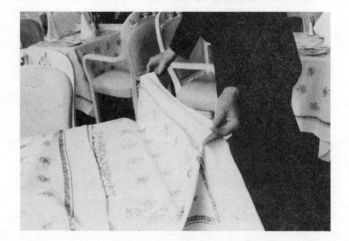

(b)

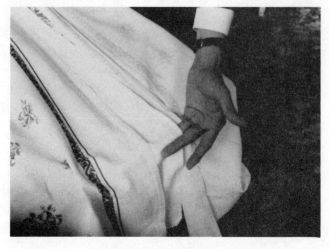

(c)

(d)

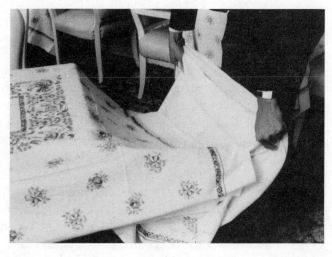

(e)

REPLACING THE SOILED LINEN WITH CLEAN LINEN (a) Drop the top edge over the edge of the table; (b) Bring the bottom edge up to table height; (c) Grasp the second edge; (d) Step back from the table holding all three edges, just before releasing the top edge; (e) After dropping the top edge, bring your hands together, keeping all crumbs inside the folds of the tablecloth.

3. Take hold of the top hem edge of the clean cloth (along the horizontal "center"), at the table edges, one hand at either side of the table. Grasping this top layer by the selvage or hemmed edge, lift it slightly, and lay it across the far side of the table edge, dropping it over that far edge of the table.

4. Smooth the far edges and corners of the clean tablecloth, so it lies properly over the edges of the table and is not wrinkled or turned up.

5. Pull the top edge of the clean cloth towards you, stopping about an inch *before* reaching the edge of the soiled table linen. Be sure you can see *both* edges—the edge of the clean cloth on top, and the edge of the soiled cloth, which has been doubled back upon itself, underneath the clean edge.

    One inch to $1\frac{1}{2}$ inches of the edge of the soiled cloth must be visible along the "center" of the table. That cloth must be showing in order to be grasped later (step 7).

    If the fold of the new cloth is at the far edge of the table, or within 6 inches of that far edge, pull it toward you. Double-check to ensure that 6 inches or so at the far edge of the table have only one layer of cloth, and that it is the clean cloth.

6. Move accessories (flowers, ashtrays) from the near corner of the table (where they are atop the soiled tablecloth) to the far side, on those 6 inches of single-layer cloth. Center them in the middle of the table, atop the clean tablecloth. The accessories must be resting on only one layer of the clean cloth.

    Check to be sure that none of the accessories are atop or resting on the fold of the soiled tablecloth, which is underneath the clean cloth, about 6 inches back. Feel for the fold with your fingers; make sure nothing is on it. There must be only one layer of cloth underneath the accessories—the clean cloth. These accessories, if any, will "anchor" the clean tablecloth for the next step.

    This is the most difficult step: You will be opening and spreading the clean cloth across the table while simultaneously removing the soiled cloth, without allowing the crumbs to drop onto the floor.

7. With arms extended horizontally, reach down and grasp the *near* hemmed edge of the soiled tablecloth (the edge closest to your knees). Keep your arms extended horizontally, to the sides, and about 2 or 3 inches beyond the width of the table (about 36 inches wide). Grasp the bottom tablecloth edge (keeping your hands about 36 inches apart) using the little finger of each hand on the bottom and the ring finger on top. Close those fingers, holding the tablecloth edge in place in each hand.

8. Keeping your arms horizontally extended, bring them up to almost tabletop height. Holding the bottom edge between the little finger

and ring finger of each hand, slide the ring finger, little finger, and tablecloth combination under the "top" edge of the soiled tablecloth, which had been folded back from the top. Slide it under the cloth along the sides, below tabletop height, to ensure getting all the crumbs inside the tablecloth.

9. Grasp the top of this selvage edge with the middle fingers of each hand (each hand is performing the same action, the right hand on the right side of the table, the left hand on the left side of the table).

10. Holding both the top and bottom edges of the soiled tablecloth with the little, ring, and middle fingers of each hand, grasp the selvage or hemmed edge of the clean cloth with the index finger (under) and thumb (on top) of each hand.

    Do not grasp the folded edge of the clean tablecloth; leave it free.

11. Lifting your hands upward, toward the ceiling, to a height of about 12 to 14 inches (no more than that), gently shake the layers of cloth side to side, loosening the clean cloth. When the tablecloth layers are loose, pull your arms (still extended horizontally) toward yourself, toward the near end of the table, holding onto all three edges.

    This action will pull the clean tablecloth across the table (anchored by the accessories, if any) while the soiled tablecloth is being removed. Since both edges of the soiled tablecloth are being held, all of the crumbs will be caught in the center, folded edge of the soiled tablecloth.

12. Step backward one step as the clean tablecloth is pulled across the table, dropping the edge of the clean tablecloth (which was between your index fingers and thumbs of each hand). Hold onto the two edges of the soiled tablecloth in each hand; if either edge is dropped, so are the crumbs!

13. Bring both hands together with the edges of the soiled tablecloth. Grasp all edges in one hand, and rapidly roll the tablecloth into a ball; use it to quietly brush the crumbs off of chair and banquette seats. Then place the rolled soiled table linen on a chair seat temporarily.

14. Smooth out any wrinkles. Fine-tune placement of the clean tablecloth.

    · Is it centered?
    · Are the edges parallel with the floor?
    · Are there holes, rips, or stains on the cloth? If so, change it again.
    · Move accessories to the center of the table, or wherever the operation dictates.

15. Place soiled tablecloth under your arm and take it to the used linen receptacle.

Technique: Changing a Tablecloth on a Round Table During Service

Use the technique just described with the following exceptions:

♦ For deuces, follow the preceding technique.
♦ For "statler" tables or six-tops: Use two square tablecloths if there are not round table linens available. In this case, place one on the bottom and the second with the points (corners) being placed in the middle of each side, so there is sufficient overhang on all sides of the table (there should be a minimum of 12 inches overhang on all tables).

> In other words, cover the first cloth with another. Place the first with its fold lines north to south and east to west. Position the second linen with its fold lines going northeast to southwest and southeast to northwest.

♦ On large round tables (eight-tops and larger), use a large, preferably white undercloth, and the house linen (with special color or design on it) as a top cloth.

> Between seatings, change only the top cloth unless liquids or sauces have been spilled, in which case both cloths will have to be changed.

Technique: Changing a Tablecloth on a Rectangular Table During Service

Use the above technique with a rectangular cloth, if available. Otherwise, use two square tablecloths, side by side, with one cloth fully extended and the center edge of the second (the top one) being folded over. This way, if there is a design on the linens, the designs will complement each other and meet in the center. Each should be centered on its imaginary "half" of the table (right half and left half).

These should give you some ideas of techniques for unobtrusive changing of tablecloths while resetting tables in the dining room during service. If your tablecloths are not folded professionally, and these techniques will not work, use the same theory and develop your own technique (no flapping, no full extension of the tablecloth, no "bullfights").

❖ SUMMARY AND OVERVIEW

In summary, attention has been given to the two major components of a busser's job: duties before service and duties during service. Below is a sample overview of those tasks that bussers typically do from the moment they report for a shift through the service of that shift. It should be customized for your operation, and can be used as a handout to each new busser employee. Overviews such as this can be developed also from the server and captain chapters—this is a guide for your use!

Busser Duties and Responsibilities

◆ Find station for the shift
◆ Gather supplies

  · Silverware—steam it so it's clean: no fingerprints
  · Coffeepots—three: coffee, tea, decaffeinated coffee
  · Creamers, sugars
  · Ashtrays, matches
  · Linens, napkins
  · B&B; appetizer, dessert plates

◆ Set station

  · Clean out and wipe down sidestand
  · Return used utensils, plates, bad condiments, dirty ashtrays

◆ Stock sidestand

  · Water glasses, pitchers
  · Linens, napkins
  · Ashtrays, matches
  · B&B plates
  · Appetizer, dessert, salad plates
  · Silverware:
    —Appetizer forks   —Entree forks
    —Cocktail forks   —Entree knives
    —Steak knives   —B&B knives
    —Teaspoons   —Soup, serving spoons
  · Condiments
    —Mustards
    —Olive oil—in glass cruet, *filled,* not rancid
    —Vinegar—in glass cruet, *filled*
    —Salt and pepper shakers, clean and filled

—Pepper mill
—Cayenne or red sauce
—Steak sauces
—Ketchup, with caps and clean necks, inside and out
—Mint jelly
—Sugars, artificial sweetener packets
—Orange marmalades—breakfast and brunch only
—Strawberry preserves—breakfast and brunch only

◆ Set tables in station

· Line up tables where they should be
· Line up chairs at tables, 2 feet from the edge of the table
· Put clean linens on tables, edges straight and parallel to the floor; no rips, tears, darns

◆ Set tabletop

· B&B plates—go to the left of the forks
· Silverware—cleaned (put silverware on a beverage tray, atop a clean napkin; touch only by the sides, never by the top)
· Jar or vase with flowers (in center of table, unless it is a deuce along a railing or window; then create an illusion of privacy by placing the flowers on the outer edge of the table, near the aisle)
· Ashtrays with matches (smoking section only; one ashtray per two people)
· Napkins (cone fold: dining room 1; pleat fold: dining room 2; fan fold: banquet rooms)
· Lantern with candle (P.M. shifts, dinner only)
· Salt and pepper shakers (one set per table; make sure they are filled and wiped clean; salt on the right; pepper on the left as you look at the table).

◆ Ready station extras

· Icebuckets—2
· Water pitchers, filled with ice water
· Lemon wedges, twists
· Pens—ballpoint, black or blue ink, retractable
· Table crumber

Details of Busser Job

◆ Silverware

· Steam using hot water, in an ice bucket. Dip the silverware into the hot water. Hold the silverware in a clean napkin in left hand.

· Using a clean napkin, wipe each piece of silverware with right hand, and place on the table linen.
· Use only clean silverware. If it is tarnished, dirty, or bent, do not use it. If it is fingerprinted, or water-stained, clean it using the steam/water method.

♦ Table linens

· Use only bright, not faded, linens on the tops of tables.
· Use faded linens, or those with tiny defects, as underliners on tables requiring two linens.
· Locate clean, folded linens.

♦ Coffee, tea, coffeepots, teapots

· Located_____
· Take three—one for coffee, one for decaffeinated coffee, one for tea.
· Fill coffeepots as often as necessary.
· When a customer requires coffee, check the coffeepot. If it is luke-warm, get some fresh, *hot* coffee.
· Tea bags and loose tea are located . . .

♦ Creamers, sugars

· Sugars are found_____
· Check and fill sugar containers with both sugar packets and artificial sweetener packets.
· Creamers are found_____

♦ Ashtrays and matches

· Ashtrays are found_____
· Ashtrays must be clean and without any stickers. If there are stickers, peel them off before placing on a table.
· If the ashtray is chipped or cracked, throw it away.
· Use ashtrays only on tabletops. Do not use them to level-off tables or to prop doors open. They crack, and then glass fragments splatter all over the floor.
· Quietly change ashtrays during service, as often as necessary—when used and between courses.
· Matches are found_____

♦ Linens

· Make sure any design on the linen is centered on the table, edges parallel to the floor; not faded, ripped, torn.

♦ Napkins

· Napkins must be folded uniformly.

- Use one napkin shape per room. Fold extras to have during service, so time is not lost in resetting tables.
- Napkins with holes or stains should be used as service cloths in the dining room (e.g., opening wines, under the hot platters when serving Russian style, around coffeepots or water pitchers to prevent drips).

◆ B&B plates

- Stock the sidestand with several stacks. Wipe each one before placing it in the sidestand. If chipped or cracked, discard.
- Find them_____

◆ Appetizer or dessert or salad plates

- Stock sidestand with several stacks. Wipe each one before placing it in the sidestand. If chipped or cracked, discard.
- Located_____

◆ Condiments

- Located_____
- Make sure the jars are clean, wiped, and have lids.
- Ketchup: Wipe top 1 inch of ketchup bottles, inside and out. Make sure lid is on top.
- Mustards
  —Grainy mustard
  —Smooth mustard
  —Spicy smooth mustard
- Oil and Vinegar: Make sure glass cruets are filled and wiped. Smell olive oil to make sure it is not rancid.
- Salt and Pepper: Make sure filled and clean. Extra salt and pepper located_____
- Steak sauces, etc.: Make sure outsides are wiped off and necks of bottles are clean. If any are less than one-half full, "marry" two bottles so all guests receive relatively full bottles of condiments.

◆ Ice buckets

- Two per station.
- Fill half full with ice.
- Just before service, add water to two-thirds full.
- Stands and buckets are located_____
- Ice machines are located_____

◆ Water pitchers

- Two per station.
- Fill with ice from ice machines.
- On return trip to the station, stop at sink, fill with water.

◆ During service

- · Water service—automatic refills
- · Bread and butter service
- · Clear plates as guests finish
- · Coffee and tea service—automatic refills
- · Change and reset table when guests leave
- · Proper tablecloth changing—no bullfights
- · Bus trays to kitchen—napkin covering all trays

Two

S·E·R·V·E·R

Servers are people persons, persons whose job it is to provide good food and good service, and to make sure guests enjoy their stay at the restaurant. Servers are professionals whether they work in a diner or a white tablecloth operation. Because owners are seldom visible to the public, dining room personnel often represent the operation to the customer. Therefore the service provided (or lack thereof) during a meal is of pivotal importance to the quality of the dining experience. Likewise, the server's attitude, efficiency, and skill communicate as much about the operation as they do about the server.

Servers are sales representatives. Their job consists of three major aspects—representing the operation to the public, selling foods and beverages and the dining experience to the guests, and then delivering what they promised! Since in operations utilizing captains it is the primary responsibility of the captain to sell, the discussion of selling, and how it fits into the service industry is presented in the chapter on captains.

This chapter is primarily devoted to the third major aspect—delivering what was promised to the guests, or service skills. The skills detailed in this section are those of the front server (who has the most contact with the guests and works primarily in the front of the house) and the back server (who has the most interaction with the kitchen or "back" of the house, gathering foods to be brought to the front). Some operations divide these skills into two separate jobs; some combine them and one person does everything. Adjust your service to the requirements of your restaurant.

A job description for servers follows. First we've covered the basic duties that pertain to all servers; then we've broken the descriptions down further, with separate sections detailing the duties of the front server and the back server, should they be two positions in your restaurant.

This section is written for operations utilizing an electronic point-of-sale food system. When concrete examples are used, they are based upon the NCR 2160 food system, which is one of several equally good electronic systems available today. Also, this section is written for operations utilizing American-style service, that is, serving food from the left and clearing from the right (detailed below). Many situations are described which may or may not pertain to your operation. Use the portions that do apply, and ignore the operational areas that do not. Examples of ways to do certain tasks are included to illustrate one method of performing those tasks, and should be customized or changed to suit each individual operation.

We cover professional mechanics first—handling serviceware, tray handling, and equipment—then outline all the steps involved in service (from the servers' point of view) from the moment guests arrive. We close the chapter with an explanation of various styles of service.

JOB DESCRIPTION: SERVER

Job Summary

The server is responsible for the complete service of food and beverages, catering to all guest needs. The server works closely with the captain and busser in order to provide guests with an enjoyable dining experience. Specifically, it is the server's job to do the following:

- Serve and clear food and beverages quietly and professionally, in a timely manner, and using proper serving and clearing techniques.
- Ensure the setting of proper silverware *before* the arrival of the food item requiring such silverware.
- Enter food orders into the electronic point-of-sale terminal and communicate special orders in person to the kitchen.
- Obtain drinks (front server) and food (back server), assisting other members of the team.
- Maintain good grooming and personal hygiene.
- Keep the station clean, keep sidestands cleared of soiled dishes and glassware, and keep the station stocked with necessary supplies.
- Communicate, cooperate, and coordinate actions with the team members, and all other members of the front and back of the house to ensure professional customer service.

Duties and Responsibilities Prior to Service

- Be ready to work, in uniform and well groomed, on time.
- Check for personal supplies:

· Corkscrew
· Retractable ballpoint pens (black or blue ink)
· Table crumber
· Tablet or note pad
· Checks and/or dupe pad

◆ Determine assigned station from the schedule. Double-check with the manager on duty for last-minute changes, banquets, large parties, group sales, sick-calls, and so on.
◆ Check station and supplies: Are place settings, table linens, and chairs clean and neat? Is sidestand clean and stocked?
◆ Linens, flatware, china: Are they clean and polished, without water-marks, fingerprints, or stains?
◆ Pieces of flatware on tables must be parallel to each other and perpendicular to the edge of the table (square/rectangular tables).
  Cutting edges of knives must be pointing to the *left*.
  Top of the B&B plate should be even with the top tines of the entree fork, if to the direct left of the entree plate, or above the fork and to the left of the entree plate, allowing room for a salad or vegetable plate to the immediate left of the entree plate.
  On tables with an even number of place settings, entree fork and entree knife of opposing place settings must be in line with each other, directly across the table.
◆ Sidework (e.g., folding of napkins) must be completed *before* the start of service.

Front Server Responsibilities

◆ Assist the captain with meeting, greeting, and seating of guests when this is required.
◆ Take the beverage order if the captain requests. Enter beverage order into the electronic point-of-sale terminal. Obtain beverage dupe and then, with the dupe, the drinks, serving those drinks to the table within 10 minutes of the beverage order being taken.
◆ Serve beverages from the right side of a guest, using your right hand, traveling clockwise around the table, if possible.
◆ Hold stemware by the stem; hold tumbler-style glassware by the bottom $1\frac{1}{2}$ inch of the glass so there are no fingerprints on the upper half of any glass.
◆ Check with customers who have empty beverage glasses whether another round of drinks or another bottle of wine or champagne is desired. Remove empty glasses and replace with clean ones if necessary.
◆ Take food order if captain requests.
◆ Enter the order into the electronic point-of-sale terminal.
◆ Preset necessary silverware (e.g., soup spoons, steak knives).

◆ Pick up and serve cold appetizers. Wait for back server to bring out any hot appetizers, so all appetizers are served together at each table.

◆ Enter additional food and beverage orders into the electronic point-of-sale system (e.g., second or third round of drinks, desserts).

◆ Serve food as soon as it is brought from the kitchen. Serve ladies before gentlemen. Serve hot food before cold food.

Serve food from the *left* side of the guest, using your *left* hand (American style). Exceptions: Soup—serve from the *right,* with the *right* hand. Clean Plate—serve from the *right,* with the *right* hand.

◆ Clear dishes when all guests have finished a course, and glassware as guests finish (or per house policy). Do not remove water glasses.

Clear dishes and glassware from the *right* side of guests, using the right hand. Exceptions: Items placed on a guest's left side (e.g., B&B plates, vegetable, plates, unused forks). Clear these from the *left* side of the guest, using your *right* hand, not reaching in front of the guests.

◆ Be attentive to guests' needs (e.g., water and coffee refills, replacements for dropped napkins, refills of wine or champagne, freshly ground pepper or condiments).

◆ Change ashtrays often—between courses, or as used.

◆ Pick up and serve desserts, cappuccino, espresso, after-dinner liqueurs, and so on.

◆ Check and recheck tables during service. Remove empty plates and glasses; remove and replace ashtrays as needed.

◆ Always take something back to the kitchen—never go empty-handed!

◆ Keep the sidestand neat and the top clear; this ensures that there will be a landing area for the next person bringing out a tray of food or supplies from the kitchen.

◆ Close out checks on the electronic point-of-sale terminal. Process credit card transactions, utilizing correct credit card procedures (see "Credit Card Procedures," Appendix B).

◆ Be courteous, maintain a professional attitude, and act professionally throughout service, no matter how busy you are.

Back Server Responsibilities

◆ Know how to enter food and beverage orders into the electronic point-of-sale terminal, and do so in coordination with the front server. (Usually the front server enters the orders into the terminal; however, the back server must know how to, serving as the backup person.

◆ Pick up food items for the team, in conjunction with the front server. (Front server concentrates on beverages; back server concentrates on food items.)

◆ Pick up hot food and entrees in the kitchen, following kitchen proce- dures. (Front or back server can pick up cold appetizers—whoever has time to do so.)

◆ Pick up cold foods before hot foods (e.g., salad entrees before hot entrees, sour cream before the baked potato). This keeps hot items hot!

◆ Pick up all of one table's covers at the same time. If you are picking up food for more than one table at one time, carry no more than the house limit on one tray. For example, if the house limit is eight, observe the *eight-cover rule*. Pick up either one table's food, however many covers, or all of two or three tables' food or eight covers, whichever comes first. Partial tables may not be picked up. In other words, either three deuces or two deuces and one four-top may be picked up, but *not* three four-tops.

Only back servers pick up hot foods to avoid confusion in the kitchen. Pick up all cold foods first, then proceed to the hot food area. Once in the hot food area, stay there and collect all hot foods. Then go directly to the dining room. Don't leave the hot area to pick up cold items or else the hot foods will cool.

◆ If it is the house policy, fire all grill items, or even the whole order. To fire:

1. Enter the order into the point-of-sale terminal (unless front server has already done so).
2. Proceed to the kitchen; obtain a *fire dupe;* complete it, time- stamp it, and give it to the grill cook. (Or, call out the order, preceding it with "Firing.")
3. Include station number and table number.
4. Clarify before service who's doing the firing—the front server or the back server. If both enter fire dupes or begin firing, the cooks won't start any items for that team for fear of duplication.

◆ Clarify with the front server who's doing what so you can act quickly. An example: Appetizers should be served within 5 to 10 minutes of being ordered. Know what is needed, and from which stations. Once the order is entered, get an oval tray; go to the cold station and pick up the cold appetizers; then go to the hot appetizer station and pick up the hot appetizers. Then get back to the table to serve the guests.

Another example: If the back server takes a dessert order (which usually the captain or front server would do), before he or she goes into the kitchen to retrieve the desserts, the captain and front server must be told that the dessert order has been taken, that it is being filled, and what each guest has ordered so the appropriate silverware can be placed in front of each guest before the desserts arrive.

A lack of communication results in repetitive disturbances to the guests—in other words, poor service.

♦ Check and recheck tables during service. Remove empty plates and glasses; remove and replace ashtrays as needed.
♦ Always take something back to the kitchen—never go empty-handed!
♦ Keep the sidestand neat and the top clear; this ensures that there will be a landing area for the next person bringing out a tray of food or supplies from the kitchen.
♦ Be courteous, maintain a professional attitude, and act professionally throughout service, no matter how busy you are.

BASIC SERVICE SKILLS AND EQUIPMENT

Personal Equipment

Every server uses certain items during the course of a shift that are fairly standard, and in most restaurants, provided by the employee. Standard items that you need to provide, maintain, and have available for use every shift include the following:

Pens or pencils.   Preferably *retractable-tip ballpoint* pens with black or blue ink. Fountain pens may leak or run out of ink, and when the caps get lost, they bleed all over shirts and pockets. Pencils blur and cannot be read easily, and the records are subject to being changed (and so are not permanent).

Corkscrew.   Preferably a "waiter's" corkscrew, which folds into a compact pocketknife shape. It contains a knife for cutting the foil capsule at the top of each bottle, a "worm" for pulling the cork, and a lever for leverage. Once folded, it fits easily into a pocket without causing bulges or being bulky. "Wing-tip" corkscrews are too bulky to carry in your pocket; the "ah-so" type of corkscrew is an acceptable second choice, although harder to cut the foil cap with. Many use the ah-so in conjunction with the waiter's corkscrew—the waiter's to cut the foil and the ah-so to remove the cork, especially an old, crumbly cork.

Tablet or other paper.   There should always be some form of writing material available to jot notes for customers needing directions to the theatre, a state park, or whatever.

Table crumber to crumb the table.   If the restaurant is less formal (without linens), a clean damp cloth to wipe the tabletops with when crumbs accumulate and after guests leave, before new guests are seated.

Handling Serviceware

In the hospitality industry, serviceware is a shorthand term encompassing glassware, flatware (silverware, plasticware, silverplate), and china. How serviceware is handled is of primary concern to everyone: the servers, the customers, and the operator. Servers want to serve as efficiently as possible without messing up the food on the plates or spilling the beverages; the customers want hygienic handling of the food, plates, and glassware, as well as an attractive presentation; the operators want as little breakage as possible.

In order to meet these three objectives, there are several techniques that should be used when handling serviceware. Many of the specific techniques are detailed in this chapter and in Chapter One; however, a summary of the important points to remember is listed below.

China

- ◆ Place dishes on the table and remove dishes from the table using the four fingers of your hand, putting the four fingers under the lower edge of the plate, and resting the thumb along the upper edge and outer rim of the plate, *not* on the inner surface or flat border of the plate!
- ◆ Lower plates to the table, and place them where they should be positioned, one-half inch from the edge of the table—do not slide them into position.
- ◆ Place full dinner plates with the main item facing the customer, unless the chef has suggested alternate placement.
- ◆ Practice holding plates level with your arm fully extended so you can place dishes in front of guests sitting at the far side of booths.
- ◆ Use underliners and B&B plates when appropriate.
- ◆ Place coffee and teacups with the handles to the right, and slightly angled—pointing to about 4 o'clock from the customer's point of view.

Silverware or Flatware

- ◆ Handle carefully—no fingerprints!
- ◆ If it is tarnished or dirty, don't use it. Return it to the kitchen.
- ◆ Carry large quantities of clean flatware, polished or not, on a tray lined with a clean napkin or service cloth and covered with the same. Clean flatware should never be placed directly on a tray.
- ◆ In the dining room, carry small quantities of clean, polished flatware on a napkin-lined plate, the napkin folded to create a pocket for the silverware. Nest spoons and forks against each other. Never use bare hands.

♦ Be as quiet as possible when handling flatware—it makes a lot of noise, and guests would rather hear themselves talking to each other than flatware clanging.

♦ Handle flatware on the sides, at the waist, the narrow portion of the flatware, both for hygienic reasons and so fingerprints won't show. Under no circumstances should the part of the flatware that comes in contact with the customer's mouth be touched by your hands, nor should the base be handled (fingerprints will show, looking sloppy and unhygienic).

♦ "Steam" silverware to remove water marks before placing it on a table. (See Chapter One for details.)

♦ Place flatware on a tablecloth, cloth napkin, paper napkin, or place mat when possible, and not on a bare table surface.

Glassware

♦ Carry clean, empty stemware and glassware on a beverage tray. In banquet service, clean stemware can also be carried upside down, with the stems between the fingers of the left hand, the bases above the fingers, and the globes below.

♦ Always handle stemware by the stems.

♦ Handle tumbler-style glasses by the bottom $1\frac{1}{2}$ inches of the glass.

♦ Never handle glasses by the rims or stand them on their rims. The rim is the weakest part of a glass.

♦ *Never put fingers in a glass* when clearing a table. Clear stemware by the stems and barware by holding the bottom half of the outside of the glass.

♦ Clear glassware onto a beverage tray. Don't pick up glasses from a table and carry them in your hands unless beverage trays are not used in the operation.

Water Glasses

♦ Refill water glasses without lifting them from the table, if it is possible to do so. Lift water glasses to fill them, or remove them from the table, only when necessary. Otherwise, simply take the water pitcher to the table, and refill the glasses.

♦ Keep water glasses filled—don't ask if more water is desired. Exception: with dessert. When dessert is served, discontinue water service, unless a refill is asked for.

Ashtrays

♦ Ashtrays, if used, must be replaced throughout service, quietly. Replace them as used, and between courses. How?

Place a clean ashtray atop the used ashtray, upside down, and *quietly* remove both from the table with the right hand. Place your right hand behind your back. Move your left hand behind your back. Transfer the bottom ashtray (the used one) to the palm of the left hand and cover the top of the ashtray with the fingers of the left hand so the ashes cannot fly out of the ashtray. Return the right hand to the table with the clean ashtray, placing it quietly on the table. This method ensures that ashes from the dirty ashtray do not blow into someone's food or drink.

❖ TRAY HANDLING

Foodservice professionals use transporter systems—trays, tray stands, and bus boxes—to move the foods, beverages, and servicewares from the kitchen to the guests and, later, from the guests back to the kitchen.

There are two basic types of trays used in foodservice: those used for beverages and those used for foods. Beverage trays are usually circular, 11, 14, or 16 inches in diameter, and often have cork or other nonskid surfaces. Food trays are usually oval in shape and much larger, approximately 19 by 24 inches or 22 by 27 inches, and often have nonskid surfaces. There are also rectangular food trays, often used in cafeterias or other fast-food establishments.

As a general rule, beverages are served and cleared from beverage trays; food is brought to the dining room either on the hand and arm or on a tray, and served to the guests by arm service.

When you are clearing, collect glassware on beverage trays, or, if a large number of glasses are to be cleared, collect glassware on one large oval tray and china and flatware on another large food tray. Separation of glassware and china facilitates faster processing at the warewashing station and reduces breakage.

❖ BEVERAGE SERVICE FROM A TRAY

There are several techniques that must be mastered in order to serve beverages from a beverage tray to guests at a table. These will allow you to be graceful, maintain a balanced tray, avoid reaching over guests (except in banquette or booth situations), and avoid spills. Using the beverage service techniques detailed below, you can even smile doing all of the above.

Loading and Carrying a Beverage Tray

There are two basic rules for beverage tray use, regardless of the type or style of foodservice utilized by your operation:

♦ Carry beverage trays in the *left hand.*
♦ Keep the tray balanced.

Beverage trays are carried in the left hand so beverages can be served with the right hand. Beverages are placed at the guest's right side, in front of the right shoulder, to facilitate the guest's reaching for the glass with his or her right hand. This convention developed over the years as a way of serving the majority of the population, who are right-handed. Beverages are cleared from the *right* side of the guest, using the *right* hand.

Whether serving or clearing, whether the server is right-handed or left-handed, regardless of the type or style of foodservice utilized in the operation, beverage trays are carried in the left hand and beverages are served by the right hand, from the right side of the guest.

Technique: Loading and Carrying a Beverage Tray

♦ Rest the beverage tray atop your flat left palm, wrist, and lower left arm, with your fingers spread apart. Keep you forearm parallel to the floor, with your elbow next to your body.
♦ Place the heaviest glasses along the axis of your arm, or on the part of the tray closest to your body.
♦ Place tall glasses or champagne flutes (any glasses that are top heavy and likely to tip over) in the center of the tray, and surround them with short "on the rocks" glasses or tumbler (highball) glasses, which are steadier.
♦ As the tray is loaded, shift your hand underneath the tray to keep the tray balanced. Load the center, then the portion along the axis of your arm, so your forearm bears much of the weight of the tray and glasses.
♦ If you are loading warmed cups and saucers for coffee and/or tea service, stack the saucers and place them in one pile, in the center of the tray. Place the cups around the stack of saucers. Sugar and creamer should also be on the tray, unless they are kept on the sidestand or are already on the table.

Technique: Serving Beverages

- ♦ Serve ladies before gentlemen unless there are more than six people at the table. If there are more than six guests present, the house should determine the policy: Either serve all ladies before gentlemen, or begin serving a lady, then move clockwise around the table serving sequentially, regardless of the sex or age of the guest.
- ♦ When serving a beverage, stand to the guest's right side, with the beverage tray on the left hand, parallel to the floor.
- ♦ Grasp the glass to be served with your right hand. If it is a stemmed glass, grasp it by the stem, keeping fingerprints off the bowl. If it is a tumbler-style glass, grasp it at the lower 1½ inches of the glass, keeping fingerprints off the top portion of the glass.
- ♦ With your *right* foot, take a step toward the guest, placing your right foot between two chairs.
- ♦ Lower your body by bending your knees (keeping your back straight) while reaching forward with your right arm, which is holding the beverage to be served to that guest. Your left arm, holding the tray of remaining beverages, should swing outward, behind the guest, and over the aisle space, always staying parallel to the floor.
- ♦ If the reach to the guest is not far, you don't have to reach forward far with your right arm, nor back into the aisle far with the beverage tray. However, if it is a far reach to a guest (e.g., inside banquette positions), extending both arms (in opposite directions) provides that extra reach. This minimizes the number of times a drink must be handed to a person other than the intended, asking one guest to pass the beverage to another guest (a service gaffe).
- ♦ Place the glass at the right side of the guest, at the tip of the entree knife if one is set.
- ♦ Bring both hands back to the "starting position," your left hand holding the tray directly in front of your left shoulder and your right hand reaching for the next glass to be served. Simultaneously raise your body to a standing position with both feet together, in the aisle.
- ♦ Walk *forward* (in a clockwise direction) around the table to the next guest to be served, serving ladies before gentlemen.
- ♦ Stop to the right of the next guest to be served, and repeat the serving sequence. When all ladies are served, serve the gentlemen.

Serving Alcoholic Beverages

The service of alcoholic beverages is reviewed in Chapter Three (it is covered in detail in the second guide in this series). However, some of the most important points to remember are listed here as well:

♦ Be sure the guests are of legal age to consume alcoholic beverages. If you're not sure, ask for identification.

♦ Cocktails usually have specified garnishes and glassware. Be sure to follow the house policy in this regard.

♦ Beer served in a bottle should be poured at the table. Pour against a side of the pilsner glass (or other glass) to minimize the head of foam.

♦ When pouring beer or any beverage from a bottle, do not let the bottle touch the rim of the glass (the weakest part).

♦ When pouring wine, pour only 3 to 4 ounces per person. A typical 6- or 8-ounce wine glass will be only one-third to one-half full—that is a correct pour.

♦ Refill wine glasses the same way: A 3- to 4-ounce pour (one-third to one-half full in a standard wine glass).

♦ Offer another bottle when the first one is almost finished. (A 750-ml bottle—the standard wine bottle—should provide six 4-ounce servings or eight 3-ounce servings.)

♦ If not using tablecloths, use cocktail napkins under glasses with alcoholic beverages in them.

Serving Nonalcoholic Beverages

Coffee and Tea

Coffee service in very elegant restaurants may entail the following: server's placing a warmed cup and saucer before each guest having coffee and pouring the coffee from a pot resting on a silver tray that also has lump sugar, a sugar tong, and a pitcher of cream. In this situation, the servers inquire how each guest would like the coffee served and prepare each cup individually in front of the guest.

However, in most restaurants this level of service would be prohibitively expensive—in terms of the time required for training and practice sessions, the maintenance of cup warmers and silverplate equipment and a high enough staff-to-guest ratio to provide timely refills.

Therefore, it is the normal coffee and tea procedures of most restaurants that will be the focus here. Coffee is generally poured at the table from a decorative coffeepot into a preset cup resting on a saucer. In a fast-food restaurant, the coffee may be poured directly into the cup, then presented to the customer (on a saucer). Cream or half-and-half, sugar, and artificial sweetener accompany coffee, with a spoon or stirrer.

Tea may take either milk (not cream) or lemon, or both of these. Often customers enjoy additional hot water to make a second cup of tea or to dilute tea that was brought to the table with the tea bag already placed in the hot water and that may be too strong. The best procedure (detailed in Chapter One) is to bring the tea bag separately, on a small plate (e.g., B&B plate), allowing customers to brew the tea to their preferred strength at the table.

For most restaurants, the following is acceptable coffee and tea service. Some of the steps may not apply to all operations. The procedure for each restaurant should be customized to fit the ambience of the restaurant, the level of service provided, and the customer's expectations.

♦ *Technique:*   Serving Coffee and Tea

(See Chapter One for additional information.)

1. Warm the cups with hot water from the coffee urn before bringing them to the table.
2. Ensure the coffee in the pot is hot (and fresh).
3. If there is a microwave oven available, warm the milk or the cream. Be sure it is not in a metal vessel.
4. Place a warmed cup upon a saucer *on the tray*, then serve them as one piece to the right of the guest, with the handle of the cup positioned at 4 o'clock. Move clockwise around the table to the next guest needing a cup and saucer. Place other needed accessories on the table at this time.

   · Individual tea bags for tea drinkers, with the tea of their choice being properly placed on a B&B
   · Individual tea strainers if loose tea and individual tea strainers are available
   · Lemon wedges and/or milk for tea drinkers, whichever each requested, or both
   · Creamer(s) for coffee drinkers
   · Sugar and artificial sweetener

5. Pour the coffee or tea into each cup at the table. If individual coffee- or teapots are used, leave them to the right of and above the coffee cup or teacup. Be sure extra hot water is available for tea drinkers, who often want it diluted (if the tea bag was in the water when served and is too strong for the guest), or for a second cup.
6. In a very formal restaurant, change cups when more coffee is offered; do not pour fresh coffee on cold coffee.
7. If coffee must be poured away from the table, stack the saucers on the tray separately, so that any spillage remains on the tray and is not served to the customer in the saucer. Pour the coffee into the cup. Place the cup on the saucer and serve them as one unit to the guest.
8. If it is necessary to remove the cup from the table to refill it, transport the cup on the saucer, as one unit, to just past the edge of the table, and refill. Never lift just the cup. Exceptions: mugs, which do not use a saucer under them. Also, do not walk the cups

and saucers back to the service station. Once they are served to a guest, that guest's cup and saucer should remain on the table or in sight of the guest. This ensures that cups do not get mixed up and returned to the wrong guest!

9. Ensure each guest has a clean teaspoon on the table before the coffee or tea is poured.
10. Fill coffee cups only three-quarters full, unless the customer specifies "black."
11. If loose sugar is used, make sure there is a clean spoon expressly for the sugar.
12. Ensure that granulated sugar is available when iced coffee is served. Lump sugar dissolves too slowly.

Dispenser Beverages

The manufacturers of beverage dispensers build them to be operated in a certain way. For example, a milk dispenser handle should be lifted fully when the milk is dispensed so that it foams slightly in the glass.

Soda dispensers are adjusted to dispense a drink that requires a full glass of ice cubes. That is, the carbonation is high enough and the syrup-to-soda-water ratio concentrated sufficiently to allow for the melting of the ice as it chills the beverage. If insufficient ice is put into the glass, the drink will be too sweet and too bubbly. Soda dispensers must also be opened fully. Unless the handle is completely raised or completely depressed, the machine will dispense either too much soda or too much syrup.

Soda "guns" must have the buttons depressed completely to activate the flow of the soda. Each operation should have a chart somewhere in the bar area depicting which letter represents which soda, allowing servers and new service personnel to find quickly the button they need for dispensing the correct soda.

Carbonated Beverages

Carbonated beverages should have ice placed in the glass. Open the bottles at the table (if a leisurely dining establishment) to assure the guests that the beverages are fresh and untampered. Serve one straw to each guest ordering a soda or carbonated beverage.

Fruit Juices

Fruit juices should be chilled. Pour canned juices—such as grapefruit, cranberry, or apple juice—into a nonreactive plastic, stainless steel, or glass pitcher with a cover or a stopper, then chill. Otherwise, when chilled, the canned juice may react with the inside of the can, spoiling the juice.

Water

Serve water chilled, preferably in chilled glasses, and to everyone at a table once one guest has requested it.

The easiest method is to determine the number of guests at a table, grab that number of glasses from the sidestand, place them on a beverage tray, and pour prepared ice water into the glasses from a pitcher of ice water. If an ice bin and water dispenser are at the sidestand, fill the glasses with ice cubes (using a metal or plastic ice scoop—never place glass into a bin of ice), then fill each glass with water from the dispenser, rather than using the pitcher of ice water.

A variation is to take the chilled glasses from the sidestand, and add fresh ice cubes and then ice water (from a pitcher containing ice and water). Another variation is to place ice cubes in glasses at the sidestand before the "rush" and then add ice water when the customer is seated. Alternatively, you can pour the water at the table into preset glasses or just-placed clean, empty glasses.

Preparing Fountain Specialties

At restaurants that serve ice cream, many exciting specialty dishes and beverages can be created capitalizing on the fun nature of ice cream preparations or fountain specialties. These are usually high-priced specialties, which add to check totals, and to the service team's tips!

Sundaes, milk shakes, sodas, and ice cream floats do require extensive preparation, but if the dining room personnel need only dip their own ice cream, these are not overly time-consuming and are fun to have on a menu.

Techniques in how to dip ice cream and how to make each of several fountain specialties follow.

Technique: Dipping Ice Cream

1. Remove the dipper or disher from the well containing running water.
2. Strike the dipper sharply on a heavy sponge to shake off water.
3. Take the first cut at the very edge of the ice cream container.
4. Cut out the scoop of ice cream; do not lean on the dipper.
5. Remove one layer of ice cream at a time; do not dig into the center of the container and make a V.

Sundaes

Sundaes contain many tasty ingredients: ice cream, fruit or fudge sauce or syrup, whipped cream or marshmallow cream, chopped nuts, and stem cherries. The choice of syrup and ice cream is the customer's except when a special sundae is being promoted. Exact portioning will vary with the operation, but it is likely that a standard scoop will be used and syrup pumps will be adjusted to a standard portion.

Technique: Making a Sundae

1. Place one or two scoops of ice cream in the sundae dish (or as many scoops as are in that particular sundae).
2. Ladle a portion of sauce, syrup, or fruit over the ice cream (generally 1 to 1½ ounces).
3. Dispense whipped cream over the ice cream, spiraling the cream to a peak on top of the ice cream mound.
4. Sprinkle 1 teaspoon of nuts over the whipped cream.
5. Top with 1 stem cherry.

When soft ice cream is used, the procedure is the same, except that the ice cream is dispensed from the machine into the serving dish.

Banana Splits

The usual ingredients for a banana split are a ripe banana; vanilla, chocolate, and strawberry ice cream; crushed preserved pineapple; preserved strawberries in syrup; chocolate syrup; whipped cream; chopped nuts; and a stem cherry.

Technique: Making a Banana Split

1. Trim the ends of the banana.
2. Cut the unpeeled banana in half lengthwise.
3. Peel the halves.
4. Place both peeled halves in a banana split dish (a boat-shaped glass or metal dish, with or without a stem) with the cut sides down and the ends pointed outward.
5. Place a scoop each of vanilla, chocolate, and strawberry ice cream on top of the banana in a straight line.
6. Ladle one portion of crushed pineapple (generally 1 ounce) over the vanilla ice cream. Ladle one portion of strawberries over the straw-

berry ice cream. Ladle one portion of chocolate sauce over the chocolate ice cream.

7. Dispense a band of whipped cream along the scoops of ice cream.
8. Sprinkle the entire dish with 1 teaspoon of chopped nuts.
9. Place a stem cherry in the center of the whipped cream.

Floats

Floats contain a carbonated beverage and ice cream or sherbet. The choice of beverage and ice cream flavor is the customer's. Fountain specialities that contain soda water—for example, ice cream sodas and floats—are almost impossible to deliver to the customer with as much foam as they had when they were first made. If the drink is left standing for any length of time its appearance deteriorates drastically.

To prevent this, gather all other beverages and desserts first. Then, just before going to the dining room, "top" the drink with fresh soda water, and immediately serve to the customer. Remember to provide straws and a parfait spoon for floats and ice cream sodas!

Technique: Making a Float

1. Fill the glass three-quarters full with soda. Do not add ice.
2. Add a scoop of ice cream to the glass.

Ice Cream Sodas With Syrup

Ice cream sodas with syrup contain milk (or in some operations half-and-half or cream), syrup, carbonated water (the fizz for the soda), and ice cream. The customer chooses the syrup and ice cream flavors.

Technique: Making Ice Cream Sodas with Syrup

1. Dispense or pour $1\frac{1}{2}$ ounces of milk or cream into an ice cream soda glass.
2. Add syrup (generally $1\frac{1}{2}$ ounces).
3. Mix the ingredients by rotating the glass slowly under a fine stream of carbonated water from the fountain, directed at the side of the glass. Fill the glass three-quarters full.
4. Scoop one portion of ice cream and place in the glass.

5. Fill the glass with carbonated water.
6. Place second scoop of ice cream in the top of the glass.
7. Top with whipped cream.
8. Place a cherry on top of the whipped cream.

Note: This may be made with only one scoop of ice cream, or with more than two. The general procedure remains the same: Mix the milk or cream with syrup, fill the glass with carbonated water, top with ice cream and garnish.

Ice Cream Sodas with Fruit

Ice cream sodas can be made with fruit (generally either pineapple or strawberry) and with a corresponding syrup. When a particular syrup flavor is not available, vanilla syrup is used.

Technique: Making Ice Cream Sodas with Fruit

1. Dispense or pour 1½ ounces of milk, cream or half-and-half into an ice cream soda glass.
2. Add a 1-ounce portion of syrup.
3. Add one ounce of fruit.
4. Mix the ingredients by rotating the glass slowly under a fine stream of carbonated water from the fountain, directed at the side of the glass. Fill the glass three-quarters full.
5. Scoop one portion of ice cream and add to the glass.
6. Fill the glass with carbonated water.
7. Place a second scoop of ice cream in the top of the glass.
8. Top with whipped cream.
9. Place a cherry on top of the whipped cream.

Milk Shakes

Milk shakes contain milk, syrup, and ice cream. How they are made varies according to the operation. One version is to make them in the same way as floats; that is, some of the ice cream is mixed with the milk and some is added to the beverage in the glass. More often, all the ice cream is mixed with the milk.

Technique: Making an Ice Cream Float or Milk Shake

1. Dispense or pour 4 to 6 ounces of milk into the mixing container or "can."
2. Add a portion of syrup (generally 1½ ounces).
3. Scoop and add two (three for a milk shake) scoops of ice cream. (For an ice cream float, use only one scoop.)
4. Place the mixing can on the milk shake mixer. Blend until smooth. Do not overblend.
5. Pour the shake from the can into a glass.
6. Serve. For a float-style shake, float the remaining one or two scoops of ice cream on top. Serve.

Thick Shakes

To make a thick shake you need a soft ice cream machine. Or else you can use the method described above but with three scoops of ice cream that is relatively soft, so as not to burn out the motor of the mixer. If using hard ice cream, the ice cream temperature should be 26°F to 29°F for easy mixing.

Technique: Making a Thick Shake Using a Soft Ice Cream Machine

1. Dispense or pour 2 ounces of dairy product (milk, cream, or half-and-half) into an ice cream mixing container or "can."
2. Add a portion of syrup (generally 1½ ounces).
3. Add a portion of soft ice cream or three scoops of softened hard ice cream.
4. Mix only until the ingredients are blended.
5. Pour the shake into a glass. Serve.

Freezes

Freezes are a combination of noncarbonated drink and sherbet blended together to form a thick slush, which is then topped by a scoop of sherbet.

Technique: Making a Freeze:

1. Dispense or pour 4 ounces of noncarbonated drink into the mixing container or "can."
2. Add one to two scoops of sherbet.
3. Place the mixing can on the mixer.
4. Mix the ingredients until they are smooth. Do not overbeat.
5. Pour the freeze into a glass.
6. Top with a portion of sherbet.

In summary, there are several basic rules for serving beverages.

♦ Serve and clear from the right, using your right hand, moving clockwise around the table if possible.
♦ Serve ladies before gentlemen unless there are more than six at the table. For more than six guests, follow the house policy: Either continue with ladies before gentlemen, or begin serving a lady, then move clockwise around the table serving sequentially, regardless of the sex or age of the guest.
♦ Hold stemware by the stems; hold tumbler-style glassware at the bottom $1\frac{1}{2}$ inches inch of the glass.
♦ Don't reach over customers.
♦ Don't put fingers inside glassware when clearing. Handle glassware when clearing as when serving—by the stems or by the bottom $1\frac{1}{2}$ inches of the glass.

❖   FOODSERVICE FROM A TRAY

Foodservice has many similarities to beverage service. Both foods and beverages have to get to the guest at the proper temperature—hot foods and beverages hot, and cold foods and beverages cold. Both must arrive and be presented to the guest looking attractive—no spilled coffee on the saucers, no sauce or drips on the edges of food plates, on which the food should be arranged attractively.

But there are also differences in the two types of service involving primarily the state of the matter involved. Food is generally solid or in puree form (except for soups and some sauces), while beverages are liquid. Therefore, whereas a tray of beverages must be kept level at all times, there is more "play" in a tray of food, which can be allowed to tilt to some degree without its affecting the placement of the foods on the plates.

Larger trays of food than of beverages can therefore be negotiated through dining rooms and aisle ways, and generally, they are larger. Much more food (and weight) is placed on a food tray. Consequently, it is very important to lift and carry these heavily laden trays properly in order to avoid back injuries, spills, and accidents.

Techniques for loading, lifting, carrying, and unloading food plates onto and off trays and bus boxes are described below.

Loading a Food Tray

There are two types of food-carrying trays in general use: large oval trays and smaller rectangular trays. Large oval trays are the most common, with two sizes in popular use. They are used when there are sidestands, bus stands, tray jacks, or tray stands available to place the tray upon before serving the customers. Most operations that serve full dinners or large parties use large trays and some sort of a stand. Often plate covers are used atop each plate, which serve as a base for another plate, allowing for the stacking of dishes on the tray. When dishes are stacked, many more plates can be carried safely—usually up to 16 covers.

Small rectangular trays, or tea trays, are widely used in high-volume, limited-menu operations, as well as in self-service operations such as cafeterias. They are often used when the use of all available space for seating leaves no room for bus stands or booster stations in the middle of the dining area.

Technique: Loading a Tray

1. Make sure the tray is clean, top and bottom.
2. Unless the tray has a nonskid surface of cork or other similar material, place a damp service cloth on the inside of the tray to prevent articles from sliding.
3. Often equipment, hot items, and cold items are all loaded. The general order of loading is

   · Equipment
   · Cold foods, plates
   · Hot plates
   · Hot foods

   Position on the tray is not determined by order of loading, but by the need to

   · Balance the tray
   · Separate hot and cold foods
   · Preserve the food's attractiveness

4. Load larger, heavier pieces toward the center of the tray.
5. Load lighter, smaller pieces toward the edges of the tray.
6. When plate covers are used, stack hot dishes on hot dishes; cold dishes on cold dishes. When stacking meats of differing degrees of doneness, stack the least done on the bottom, the well-done meats on the top.
7. Do not place cups on saucers or soup bowls on underliners, but pile all saucers and underliners separately.
8. Place spouts of coffeepots and teapots inward, but away from food and plates.
9. Balance the tray.
10. Keep uncovered dishes away from the side which is near your hair.
11. When stacking dishes with covers, do not stack more than four high or attempt to carry more than 16. (It is possible to carry four stacks of five each, but covered dish columns lose rigidity as they increase in height.)
12. Leave one hand free to open doors, make a path through customers, and carry a bus stand or tray jack if needed.

Lifting an Oval Tray

Since a tray loaded with silver service or a full complement of covered dishes can weigh in excess of 60 pounds, it must be lifted properly if physical injury or stress is to be avoided.

Trays should be carried above the shoulder that is on the opposite side of the door hinges. That is, if the kitchen door is hinged on the right side, as many are, the tray should be carried on the left hand, above the left shoulder, leaving the right hand free to open the door and hold it open while passing through. Otherwise, if the door is simply kicked (as with swinging doors), it may come back too fast, knocking against the tray, jarring the food, and causing plates to fall off.

❖   *Technique:*   Lifting an Oval Tray

1. Make sure the tray is properly loaded.
2. Position the tray so that one broad side of the oval extends 5 inches off the shelf or table on which the tray rests.
3. Place your left hand (or the hand that will support the tray) under the edge of the tray in the middle of the extended broad side.
4. Grip the right-hand, narrow side edge of the oval tray with your right hand.

5. Bend down completely (to a squat position), using your knees and keeping your back straight, positioning your left shoulder under the tray.

6. Pull the tray slightly toward your shoulder with your right hand so your left hand can slide under the tray's bottom, centering itself. Twist your torso slightly, moving the tray until it is centered over your shoulder, supported by your left hand (which is virtually in the middle of the tray) and steadied by your right hand (which is steadying the front rim).

7. Stand up, using your thigh muscles and keeping your back straight, holding the tray above your shoulder. If the tray is very heavy, rest it slightly on your shoulder, so your shoulder bears some of the weight.

Technique: Carrying and Unloading an Oval Tray

1. Hold and carry the tray above your shoulder, on the flat of the palm of your hand.

2. If the tray is heavy, continue to steady it with your helping hand, not your main weight-bearing hand, and/or by resting it on your shoulder.

3. If many turns have to be negotiated and you are sufficiently strong, the fingers of your supporting hand can be drawn together so that the tray rests on your fingertips and can thus be tilted slightly into the turn.

4. Lower the tray the same way it was lifted. Bend using your knees, keeping your back straight, steadying the tray with your helping hand. Twist your torso toward the bus stand or booster station when the tray bottom is level with it and slide the tray onto it.

5. If a tray stand is being used, place it where the food is to be unloaded and open it using the hand that carried it, keeping the tray balanced on the other shoulder. Be sure the stand is steady before lowering the tray.

6. Unload dishes from the center or alternately from opposite sides, keeping the tray balanced at all times. If plates are unloaded from only one side, the tray will tip over.

Rectangular Trays

A rectangular tray, being smaller and generally not as sturdy, cannot usually be loaded as heavily as an oval tray. Even so, they can become quite heavy. A full breakfast for two people on a rectangular tray can reach 25 pounds.

Rectangular trays, especially those with handles, can be carried in front of you, with a hand on either side, but this may create stress on your lower back. A better way is as follows.

Technique: Carrying and Unloading a Rectangular Tray

1. Make sure the tray is balanced.
2. Slide the tray broad side forward onto the left forearm, so the tray is longitudinal, along the axis of the arm.
3. Hold the upper left arm close to the body.
4. "Lock" the left elbow.
5. Grip the far rim of the tray with the left hand, if the length of the tray and arm length permit.
6. When serving, with the tray still in the carrying position, unload it first from one side and then from the other in order to maintain the balance.
7. If the tray is loaded with covered dishes in two piles (A and B), it is necessary to remove cover A-1 and place it on top of pile B, and then to serve dish A-1. Then it is necessary to remove covers A-1 and B-1 and place them on top of cover A-2 to serve dish B-1, and so on, so that the tray's balance is maintained.

SERVICE BASICS: SERVING A WHOLE TABLE

The preceding techniques must be mastered in order to provide competent, efficient, professional service to individuals. However, people usually sit in groups and must be served as a group, which requires rules for serving groups of people. Knowing how to serve one person is not enough.

Who gets served first, and how groups of people (two or more) are served are explained by the "Service Basics." Optimum service results from following four rules, which are detailed below. If you remember and practice these rules, combine them with the other techniques described herein, and provide service that is friendly, courteous, and prompt, customers are bound to enjoy their visit.

- ◆ Service basic 1: Ladies before gentlemen
- ◆ Service basic 2: Old before young
- ◆ Service basic 3: Hug your customers
- ◆ Service basic 4: Walk forward

These four basics may seem easy, but in the dining room they are difficult to remember and practice consistently. Many bussers, servers, and captains need to think about them, to practice, practice, and practice some more until they become automatic. It usually takes a few months, so don't get discouraged if they don't become automatic overnight.

Ladies Before Gentlemen, Old Before Young

Ladies before gentlemen means just that. Serve ladies before serving gentlemen. Children are served with ladies. Combine this with the next basic, old served before young, and you'll see you should serve older ladies before young ladies; older gentlemen before young gentlemen. If there is a young woman and an older man, the woman is served first.

Hug Your Customers

"Hug your customers" is a shorthand way of saying "Don't reach in front of customers" and "Face your customers as you serve them."

When serving a glass of water, for instance, it is incorrect to serve it from the left side of a guest, reaching across to place the glass at the right side, at the tip of the guest's knife. It is also incorrect to serve a beverage on a guest's right side using your left hand, as this creates the image of "turning your back" to the guest. The server in this instance is facing another guest or table or even aisle space, but not facing the guest being served.

If you "hug the customer," your serving hand will be extended along the side of the customer, reaching into the center of the table space and not in front of the customer, blocking his or her view. Your other hand will be at your side or behind the customer's back. You will then be facing the customer, giving the customer the option to make eye contact with you, and perhaps ask for an additional item or ask a general question (e.g., "Where's the telephone?"), should he or she desire to do so. In other words, you will be positioned with hands and arms almost encircling the customer, as if you were about to "hug" the customer!

With this technique you do not reach in front of guests. This allows them to concentrate on what they're there for—food and conversation—certainly *not* watching servers' arms crossing in front of them every few minutes. Their attention can remain, as it should, on the conversation, the food, and the other guests.

Walk Forward

This technique sounds simpler than it is—until it is mastered and becomes a habit. Many servers serve one person, then step backward, backing into the service of the next person. There are two problems with this approach: First, walking backward is slower than walking forward, which slows service; second, walking backward is more dangerous. Since you can't see people or obstacles behind yourself, you can easily back into someone or something, spilling food or beverages.

After serving someone, walk forward—in the direction you are facing. It's faster and it's safer. If you are serving food American style, from the left side of a person with the left hand (detailed below), walk *counterclockwise*. If you are serving food French style, from the right side of a person with the right hand, walk *clockwise* around a freestanding table. Beverages, served and cleared from the right of a guest with the right hand, dictate walking *clockwise* around a table, when possible. In short, *walk forward*.

Exceptions to the Service Basics

Banquettes, booths, pillars, and walls create special situations. Since banquettes and booths are generally approachable from only one side, and since tables by walls and pillars are not totally accessible (as are free-standing tables), "hugging your customer" is often physically impossible.

Likewise, the general rule of "walking around the table in a clockwise direction to serve beverages" works for free-standing tables, but tables that are shoved into corners or next to pillars, booths, and banquettes make it virtually impossible to serve in this fashion.

Rather, service must be performed from a rather stationary point, reaching over the guests in the front to serve the guests in the back. In these special situations

♦ Minimize the disruption to the table. Reach over guests as infrequently as possible, and do not linger over guests.
♦ Extend your arm serving the plate or glass as far as possible, getting the plate or glass as close to the guest being served as possible.
♦ Make every attempt to serve ladies before gentlemen.
♦ Say "excuse me" whenever reaching in front of a guest.

❖ SERVICE: STEP BY STEP

The period of time from the moment the guest walks in the door until the moment the first drink or plate of food is served is critical to the guest's enjoyment of the dining experience, the probability of that guest returning—and the server's tip! Every server should have a standard routine, including a generalized timetable for each step, that is followed for each table. Steps in the professional service of a table include the following:

1. Greeting the guests
2. Seating the guests
3. Explaining the menu
4. Taking the order
5. Writing the order using a seat designation system
6. Transmitting the order to the kitchen
7. Picking up the order from the kitchen
8. Serving the order
9. Checking on the table
10. Presenting check and receiving payment

Steps in the sequence should be established and fine-tuned by management and servers trained in the desired sequence. Some operations want a beverage order taken within 2 minutes of the guests' being seated; other operations want the menu presented first, the specials related, and then, while the guests are mulling over the specials, the server to take the beverage order. Neither method is better than the other; each is for different types of establishment.

A sample sequence is detailed below. The order of tasks can be modified and the details within each step customized to suit your operation.

Greeting the Guests

The guests' first contact is usually with a maitre d' or a host or hostess, who greets them and then escorts them to a table. Someone is needed in a dining room as a "traffic director," balancing the stations so the servers closest to the door are not overwhelmed with too many parties at once, while those distant from the door (or window, or view) are left with empty stations.

In some restaurants, when business is slow, captains or servers will take turns greeting the guests at the door and escorting them to tables.

However, the captain's, server's, and busser's first contact with the guest is generally at the table. Wherever you encounter the guests, remember to *smile*. A genuine smile is the best welcome. A smile states, "I'm glad you're here," without a word being spoken. Even if you are tired, force a smile—after a while it will be second nature.

The maitre d' and service team make the first real impression on a guest. If the staff makes a guest feel welcome; if the staff is well-groomed and efficient; if the restaurant is clean; and if the food is hot, delicious, and attractively served, chances are good that the guests will enjoy their meal and return.

Remember, if the food is terrible, even the best service can't save it, but bad service can ruin otherwise good food. The steps involved in greeting the guests follow.

1. Smile.
2. Make the appropriate verbal greeting ("Good morning," "Good afternoon," "Good evening").
3. Assist guests with coats and packages.

Seating the Guests

In many operations whoever shows the guests to the table seats them. In some operations, the service team members (captain, servers, bussers) seat the guests after greeting them. Regardless of who seats the guests, the same general rules apply.

◆ Seat ladies before gentlemen; older ladies before young ladies.
◆ Give the ladies the best view.
◆ Attend to the guests immediately after seating them. First a smile, then a greeting. Show the guests that they are important and that you're glad they are there.
◆ Smile again. A genuine smile is invaluable, but if you must, fake it.

Technique: Seating Guests

1. Pull out the best seat—for example, the seat facing a window with a view.
2. Offer it to the lady in a party of two or the eldest lady of a larger party.
3. Assist the other ladies with their seats, if the men in the party are not assisting them.

4. At wall tables, pull the table away from the banquette or sofa seat so the women in the party can gracefully seat themselves.

5. Return the table parallel to the wall. Seat the men.

6. If there are not enough chairs for the party, bring the nearest unoccupied chair(s) to the table for the standing guest(s) to be seated. (Later, bring replacement chairs to fill the chair positions at the depleted tables from a readily accessible designated place for extra chairs, if there is one.) If there are not sufficient nearby unoccupied chairs, proceed directly to the extra chair storage location, and bring all needed chairs from there.

7. Suggest a cocktail if it is appropriate to the meal. Suggest another beverage if appropriate (e.g., fresh-squeezed orange juice at breakfast or brunch).

   When suggesting a cocktail, *suggest one.* Don't simply ask, "Would you like a drink?" It is too easy for the guest to say "No" and you won't have another selling opportunity. Instead, sell something specific—"May I suggest our freshly made strawberry daiquiri cocktail? The strawberries are locally grown and delicious."

   If the suggestion approach is used, it suggests to the guests that they should be drinking a strawberry daiquiri, or whatever you suggested. If a guest replies, "No, I don't think so," the guest could be saying no to the strawberry daiquiri, not to a drink. It gives you another selling opportunity: "Well then, perhaps you'd like to try our famous locally processed Glug Beer. It's fresh and unpasteurized, which means it has more flavor than most bottled or draft beers. Would you care to try one, or something else?" This question leaves the guest with two alternatives: to order the suggested beer (or whatever was suggested) or something else. It's much harder to say simply no.

   If the guest objects to alcohol, try bottled waters, virgin drinks, or fruit juices, especially if they are fresh-squeezed. The check can be built quickly with frozen virgin strawberry daiquiris; it doesn't grow fast if the guests are drinking water.

8. Record the beverage orders. (See "Taking the Order.")

9. Present a menu to each guest, ladies first. In operations with high-check averages and folded menus, the menus should be opened as they are offered to each guest. Menus should be presented right-side up, that is, in a position to be read without turning them.

10. Some operations will describe the daily specials at this point, when the menus are distributed.

11. Quietly and unobtrusively remove or add extra place settings as needed.

12. Pour a glass of ice water for each guest.

13. Transmit cocktail or other beverage order to appropriate location.

Explaining the Menu

When the initial beverage order is served, the guests may still be studying the menu or may be talking among themselves. Don't interrupt if the guests are talking unless it is a policy of the house to do so. Wait until there is a natural break in the conversation or return to the sidestand area, waiting for a signal from guests that they are ready to be addressed.

❖   *Technique:*   Explaining the Menu

1. Return with the cocktail or other beverage order, and with bread and butter if it is appropriate to the meal and house policy.
2. When the guests seem ready to order, or if it is necessary for them to order—for example, when the restaurant requires a fast turnover of tables—stand near the table.
3. Stand straight, with both feet on the floor.
4. Explain the specials and menu enthusiastically. Guests usually order whatever is enthusiastically suggested, so make everything sound appetizing and genuinely delicious rather than reciting the information as if by rote.
5. Ask for the order. If a beverage tray is being used, rest the tray on your left hip (if right-handed). Hold it with your left hand, holding the side towel (if used) under the tray with the middle finger of your left hand. Or hold the side towel folded, out of sight, between your left hand and the tray. Or drape the side towel over your left arm.
6. Rest the guest check or order book on the tray, using the tray as a desk. Hold the guest check or order book under the thumb of your left hand to steady it when writing.
7. If a tray is not being used, hold the order book in your left hand, with side towel (if used) folded neatly and draped over your left arm if you are right-handed. If left-handed, reverse.
8. Guests may be ready to order, or they may require some explanation of menu items. Captains and servers should know the menu completely—pronunciation and description of every dish, including ingredients, and method of preparation. Most important, daily specials must be seen and tasted by the staff, so they are able to describe them accurately.
9. Answer guests' questions honestly but without speaking badly of any dish on the menu. Make suggestions according to the merchandising policy of the operation. Sell specials at every opportunity. If there is tableside cooking, sell tableside items if the guests are not in a hurry.

Taking the Order

Taking the order must be done professionally. It is an art to be able to obtain the order both quickly and accurately, and as unobtrusively as possible, while still interacting courteously with the guests. Their primary purpose is to enjoy themselves, so interaction with the service staff should be minimal. If questions are asked, answer them, but don't make an attempt to entertain the guests with stories or jokes unless it is obvious that the guests wish to be entertained.

When taking the order, keep these key points in mind:

◆ Address ladies before gentlemen, unless there is an obvious host who may be ordering for the table.
◆ Circle the table, standing to the right of the person whose order is being taken.
◆ Be quick yet courteous.
◆ Maintain a conversational tone. Even if it's busy and noisy, don't shout and don't ask guests to shout their order. Rather, move closer to each guest, repeating the specials if necessary, and ask for the order in a conversational tone and volume.

In general, for parties of six or fewer, address a lady and take her order, then take the other ladies' orders (and those of children). Then take the gentlemen's orders. For instance, with two couples, take both ladies' orders first, then the two gentlemen's orders, unless the gentlemen are ordering for the ladies as well as for themselves.

For parties of more than six, begin with a lady and circle the table, clockwise, taking orders consecutively, regardless of the age or sex of the person.

General rules for more specific instances include the following:

◆ In a party of two people, a man and a woman in a formal setting, address the man. The woman may have told her order to her companion. In a relaxed or casual environment, address the woman first, asking for her order. Be alert for signs that the man will be ordering for both.
◆ In a party of two people of the same sex, each will order his or her own courses, unless one orders for both. If neither talks readily when asking for the orders, address the elder first, if one member is not clearly the "host."
◆ In large groups, address the host, who will give the group's order, or will turn to the person on his or her right. Begin with that person, then move around the table in a counterclockwise direction, taking orders, ending with the host. Take each person's order sequentially.

Do not take the ladies' orders first, then circle the table again for the men's orders.

♦ When in doubt as to who is the host, begin with the eldest lady in the group and circle the table, taking orders.

♦ When out of "conversational" tone range, circle the table, standing to the right side of the person whose order you are taking. It is totally unprofessional to ask for the order from the far side of the table, forcing guests to shout their orders across the table.

Hospitality means providing service to the guests. Don't ask the guests to make the order-taking process easy for you; you should move around the table, making the order-taking process easy for the guests.

Writing the Order

When writing the order, remember that it must be neat, clear, organized, and able to be understood by others, both in the back and front of the house. Other team members, who might serve the ordered items, must know who gets what, and the kitchen must know what to prepare. Is the steak to be rare or well done? And was it the sirloin steak or the filet? If it isn't recorded properly, the guests will be forced to repeat which steak they ordered, or how they wanted it cooked, or inconvenienced when an item is served by someone asking, "Who gets the steak?"

To avoid these service snafus, here are some general points to remember:

♦ Write clearly, neatly, legibly.

♦ Gather all information needed to complete the order (e.g., degree of doneness of a hamburger or steak, or any of the clarifications listed in Table 2.1).

♦ Note in some fashion who gets what, so there is no need to ask when it is time to serve the food or drinks. Preferably, use the guest position designation system, detailed below, to remember who gets what without asking.

♦ Have a uniform system of designating who gets what for the whole restaurant, so anyone can serve any table.

♦ Indicate ladies' orders in some manner to make it easy to serve ladies before gentlemen.

♦ Designate first and second appetizers in some manner to make service of appetizers easier.

♦ Record the guests' choices on the check following the house procedures. Usually it will be in some sort of summary fashion, using abbreviations and codes which are legible and understood by everyone (the captain, other servers, bussers, the kitchen staff, cashiers). See Table 2.2 for samples of order-taking abbreviations.

TABLE 2.1   Checklist of Order Clarifications

Item	Clarification
Eggs	Style of cooking: scrambled, fried, poached, boiled (how long?)
Fried eggs	Doneness: moist, well-done. Yolks: up, over, blinded, over light
Scrambled eggs	Loose, moist, well-done
Meats	Doneness: blue, rare, medium rare, well-done, end cut
Roast beef	Doneness: rare, medium rare, well-done, end cut
Salad	Type of dressing
Bread	Type of bread
Sauce	On the side
Soup	Bowl or cup
Vegetables	Which one of a choice of vegetables
Potatoes	Which one of a choice of potato styles

Standard abbreviations evolve over time at every restaurant, with some being more universal than others. Examples of some common abbreviations are included in Table 2.2, but remember that each operation will differ. Learn the abbreviations where you work.

Seat Designation System

To avoid the other cardinal sin of restaurant service, asking, "Who gets what?" use the seat designation system. This is a systematic method of ensuring who gets what without asking the guests that question. It is a method that enables you to provide smooth, unobtrusive service, and even better, allows one person to take an order, and another person to serve it.

Choose some point in the room that can serve as a reference point—for example, the kitchen. Mentally number the chairs, starting with the chair closest to (or farthest from) the reference point, and proceeding clockwise around the table: chair 1, chair 2, chair 3, chair 4, and so on. For instance, the chair facing the kitchen may be chair 1. Proceed clockwise around the table numbering the remaining chairs. If there are two chairs or positions that could be number 1 (often the case at large round tables), choose either one, and tell other team members and servers in adjacent stations. This way, any server can be of assistance should the need arise.

Number *all* the chairs, whether someone is sitting there or not. If there are three people at a four-top table, seats 1, 2, and 4 might be occupied. Use those numbers. Should a person arrive and join the party later, he or she would sit in chair no. 3, and his or her food order would have a "3" after it.

TABLE 2.2   Some Standard Order-Taking Abbreviations (with the main menu item written in capital letters, and garnishes, vegetables, and sauces written in small letters)

Menu Item	Abbreviation
Appetizer	
Shrimp cocktail	ShC
Fruit cocktail	FrC
Orange juice	OJ
Tomato juice	TJ
Soup of the day	S
Clam chowder	Chow
Main dish	
Roast beef	RB
Fried chicken	FChix
Hamburger	Burg
Frankfurter	Frank
Chicken pot pie	Chix Pie
Beef burgundy	Bf Burg
Barbecue beef	BBQ
Cheeseburger	C Burg
Chateaubriand	Chat
Filet mignon	Mig
Sirloin steak	SS
Pot roast	PR
London broil	LB
Corned beef	CB
Lamb chops	LC
Pork chops	PC
Ham steak	HS
Sandwich	
Ham on rye; ham on white	Hs, r; Hs, w
Ham and swiss, with mayonnaise	H&S (r,w, etc.), mayo
American cheese, mustard	AC (r,w, etc.) mus
Swiss cheese	Swiss
Tuna sandwich	Tx
Bacon, lettuce, and tomato	BLT
Turkey, lettuce, and tomato	Turk (r,w, etc.), LT
Grilled cheese	GC, or ACE
Steak sandwich	Ss
Salad	
Tossed green salad	Sal
Lettuce and tomato	LT
Chef's salad	CS
Dressing	
Oil and vinegar	ol
Russian	r
Thousand Island	t
Green Goddess	gg

Menu Item	Abbreviation
Sauces	
Sauce on the side	SOS
Vegetable	
French fried potatoes	ff
Baked potato	bp
Baked potato with sour cream	bp,s
String beans	sb
Carrots	c
Peas	p
Baked beans	bb
Onion rings	or
Coleslaw	col
Potato salad	potsl
Mashed potatoes	mash
Beverage	
Coffee	Cof
Tea	T
Iced tea	I T
Iced coffee	I C
Milk	M
Coca cola	Coke
Orange drink	Od
Grape drink	Gd
Skimmed milk	Skim
Buttermilk	ButM
Dessert	
Apple pie	A Pie
Blueberry pie	B Pie
Chocolate cake	C Cak
White cake	W Cak
Danish pastry	Dan
Chocolate pudding	C Pud
Vanilla pudding	V Pud
Chocolate sundae (ice cream first, then syrup)	VanSChoc
Strawberry sundae	VanSStr
Strawberry sundae with strawberry ice cream and syrup	StrSStr
Chocolate ice cream soda (syrup is first, then ice cream)	ChocOVan (O for soda)
Chocolate ice cream soda with chocolate ice cream and chocolate syrup	ChocOChoc or AB (all black)

As the order is taken, place the person's seat designation number next to the food or beverage ordered by that person. Also note any special requirements—for example, extra sauce, or degrees of doneness such as rare, medium, well. See Figure 2.1 for an example. Thus, each guest's food and beverage items have the guest's chair number next to the item.

It is important that everyone in the establishment use the same numbering system and reference point. If there is a uniform system, anyone can serve any table. If there is not a uniform system, only the order taker of a table can be the server of that table. Otherwise, one by necessity must ask, "Who gets what?"

Appetizer Designation System

Often someone or persons in a party will order two appetizers, perhaps soup then a salad, or perhaps a salad then a cup of soup. In either case, a system is needed to clarify the appetizer order.

One commonly used system is the placement of

♦ One asterisk (*) on the food dupe before each first appetizer, if two are ordered.
♦ Two asterisks (**) before each second appetizer.

Note, the asterisks are in addition to the guest position or seat designation number, which is to the right of the items ordered. This method eliminates any confusion that could arise as to the sequence of service—for example, Did they want the soup or the salad first?

Technique: Writing the Order Using the Seat Designation and Appetizer Designation Systems

1. Before writing the order, complete the guest check with whatever information your operation requires: date, table number, server or team name/number, station, number of people in the party, and so on.
2. Use the seat designation system.
3. Don't confuse chair numbers with the order in which to take the food orders. If there are two people, a man in chair 1 and a woman in chair 2, you'd take 2's order first and serve chair 2 (the woman) first.

4. Record the chair number of each guest on the food and/or beverage dupe, to the right of the dish or beverage ordered, as each guest's order is taken.
5. Circle ladies' numbers so their plates can easily be determined and served first without looking at the table, counting chair numbers, and then figuring out what the ladies ordered. See Figure 2.1, a sample order using the seat designation system.
6. As each guest gives his or her order, note which is the first and the second appetizer. Use the appetizer designation system, described above. Ask for necessary qualifications—for example, eggs and meats can be cooked to different degrees of doneness. If you don't ask, the kitchen will either ask or do it their way, which may not be to the customer's liking.
7. Record the guests' choices on the check using abbreviations and codes which are legible and understood by everyone.
8. Know the menu. If a guest orders salmon, the guest knows which item he or she wants. However, if there are three salmon dishes on the menu (broiled salmon, cold poached salmon, and salmon brochette), it is the service team's responsibility to clarify which salmon the guest has in mind. Don't guess, and then serve the wrong one!
9. Summarize the order, especially at large tables. Repeat each order, looking at the person who ordered each item, if possible. This is the last clear chance to avoid misorders.

You should not leave the table until you are certain that the order has been taken correctly. If there is any doubt, repeat the orders to the guests, checking for omissions or other errors. This avoids extra trips to and from the kitchen, shortening the time guests wait to be served.

If it is lunch or dinner and the order has been taken, you might suggest a few wines that would complement the foods ordered, if wine has not already been ordered. Techniques for suggesting wines and descriptions of wines and foods that complement each other are detailed in the second guide in this series.

At this time, check to determine whether the cocktails served need refreshing, and, if so, offer another round of cocktails. If cocktails have not yet been finished, check the table regularly for an opportunity to sell additional drinks or wine.

In summary,

♦ Use the seat designation system: chair number 1 is the seat facing the kitchen (or whatever is designated). Numbers 2, 3, and so on proceed clockwise around each table thereafter.
♦ Circle ladies' seat numbers.
♦ Use asterisks for first and second appetizers.
♦ Use standard abbreviations.

FIGURE 2.1 Sample Order Using the Seat Designation System. This is a sample order taken for four guests using the seat designation system described above. The women are seated in chairs number 2 and 4; the men are in chairs number 1 and 3.

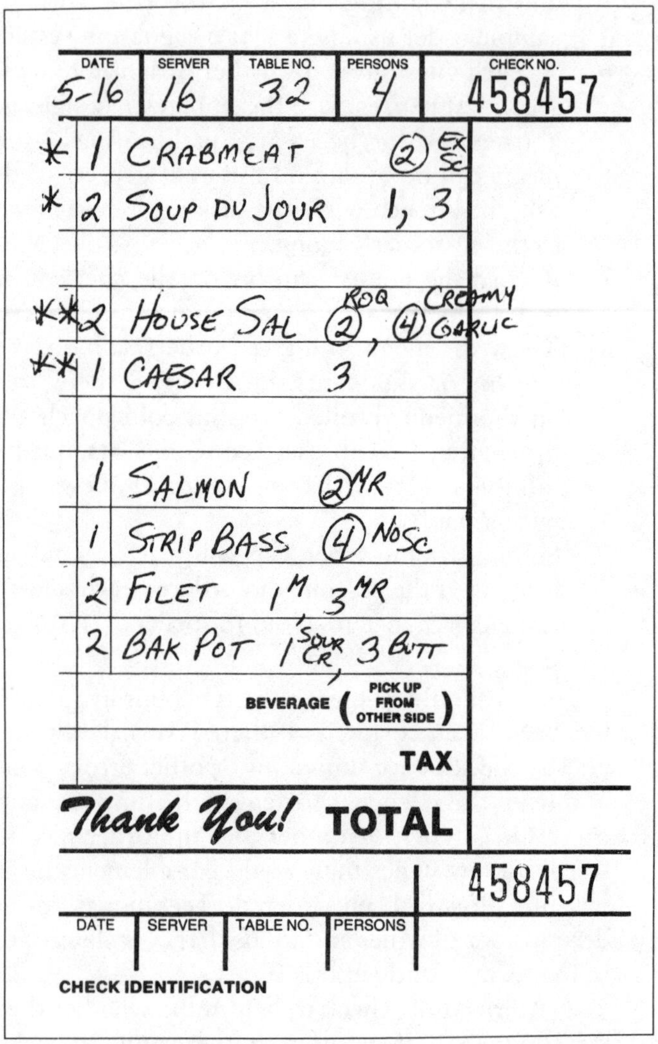

DATE	SERVER	TABLE NO.	PERSONS	CHECK NO.
5-16	16	32	4	458457

* 1 CRABMEAT (2) EX SC
* 2 SOUP DU JOUR 1, 3
** 2 HOUSE SAL (2) ROQ, (4) CREAMY GARLIC
** 1 CAESAR 3
1 SALMON (2) MR
1 STRIP BASS (4) NO SC
2 FILET 1 M, 3 MR
2 BAK POT 1 SOUR CR, 3 BUTT
BEVERAGE (PICK UP FROM OTHER SIDE)
TAX
Thank You! TOTAL
458457
DATE SERVER TABLE NO. PERSONS
CHECK IDENTIFICATION

Key to columns, left to right: first (*) or second (**) appetizer; quantity of item ordered; item; seat number (using seat desgination system); extra instructions.

Sequence of writing the order: Record items first, including asterisks if any, then the chair numbers, then any special instructions.

Items are recorded first for the ladies, numbers 2 and 4. Lady number 4 is not having a first appetizer. Gentlemen number 1 is not having a salad course. Quantities are filled in after the order for the whole table has been taken.

◆ Get all the necessary information, such as degrees of doneness, side dishes, extra or no sauce.
◆ Write legibly.

Writing Different Types of Checks

The information to be recorded and a method for recording that information have been described above. Exactly how that information is recorded is a matter of choice for the operators of each restaurant.

Many small fast-food operations operate with handwritten checks, if any at all, and verbal communication. Many medium-to-large-size restaurants and fast-food chains are using computerized systems that provide menu and sales analysis; payroll information; order-taking functions; transmission of the order to appropriate stations; and the totaling, taxing, and applying of discounts to the guest checks.

Obviously, there are many types of guest checks and systems for writing or taking orders. Some of the more common are described below. Which is best? Any system that works in a given situation.

Guest and Ordering Checks with all Menu Items Listed   When guest checks resembling small menus are used, the general pattern of ordering is main course, beverage, and perhaps dessert. Usually this type of system is not implemented unless fairly simple orders are expected and the menu is limited. If the reverse is true—the menu is complex and large—it may be advantageous for the operation to print "menu dupes" as shown in Figure 2.2. The staff adds the person/chair numbers, degrees of doneness or other special instructions, and quantities of each item to the prepared dupe, but does not have to write out each item name.

This menu dupe or order dupe system saves order-takers time, and provides a copy that is understood by the kitchen staff and other servers as well. It is usually cost-effective as well, since table turnover will increase and the accuracy of orders will lower food cost (by lowering waste caused by poor handwriting and the subsequent cooking of the wrong foods).

The form can be a three-, two-, or one-part order dupe. It is filled out by the order-taker, whether captain or server. On a three-part form, the top form (the original and most legible) is used for entree pickup and service (the most important part of the meal, requiring the most advance preparation and the help of the kitchen). The second copy is used for appetizer pickup and service, and the third copy (the least legible) is kept for backup purposes on the station. A one-part form is used for all service, and not discarded after each course.

The order dupe is the only piece of paper with the seat designation numbers; degrees of doneness for meats and eggs; and special instruc-

DATE	SERVER	PERSONS	TABLE NO.	CHECK No.

No.	ITEM #	ITEM	INSTRUCT.	No.	ITEM #	ITEM	INSTRUCT
						– BRUNCH	2/89
	228	MELON			240	ASSORTED BREADS	
	229	MELON W/PROSCIUTTO			243	HOT ARTICHOKE	
	230	GRAVLAX			247	BROILED SCALLOPS	
	231	CHERRYSTONE CLAM			248	CRAB LOBSTER CAKE	
	232	BLUEPOINT OYSTER			249	SPECL HOT APPTZ A	
	233	SHRIMP (EA.)			250	SPECL HOT APPTZ B	
	234	ASPARAGUS SALAD			335	SPECL HOT APPTZ C	
	235	DUCK TERRINE					
	236	ARTICHOKE – COLD					
	237	SMOKED SALMON					
	238	SALMON PINWHEELS					
	239	TROPICAL FRUIT					
	242	GOAT CHEESE					
	241	MOZZARELLA			251	ONION SOUP	
	226	SPECL COLD APPTZ A			254	N.E. CLAM CHOWDER	
	227	SPECL COLD APPTZ B			255	VEGETABLE	
	334	SPECL COLD APPTZ C					
	266	CHEDDAR OMELET			281	BABY CHICKEN	
	267	GRUYERE OMELET			282	CHICKEN BREAST	
	268	HERB OMELET			283	CHICKEN CREPES	
	269	CRAB/CHIVES OMELET			288	RIB EYE STEAK	
	270	MUSHROOM OMELET			297	SPECIAL ENTREE A	
	271	EGGS BENEDICT			298	SPECIAL ENTREE B	
	272	SCRAMBLED EGGS			299	SPECIAL ENTREE C	
	273	SCRAMBLED W/ BACON					
	275	SCRAMBLED W/TOMATO					
	277	FRENCH TOAST					
	278	CORNED BEEF HASH			305	SWORDFISH	
	279	EGGS CAPRESE			309	SEA SCALLOPS	
					310	SAUTEED SHRIMP	
					312	SALMON	
	257	RISOTTO			313	SPECIAL SEAFOOD A	
	260	FETTUCCINE			314	SPECIAL SEAFOOD B	
	261	1/2 FETTUCCINE					
	264	LASAGNA					
					315	SEAFOOD SALAD	
					327	POACHED SALMON	
					318	CAESAR SALAD	
	329	CHICKEN SANDWICH			319	HALF PORTION	
	331	HAMBURGER			323	SEASONAL GREENS	
	332	CHEESEBURGER			324	GREENS W/ROQUEFORT	
	333	CLUB SANDWICH			325	HOUSE SALAD	
					336	BAKED POTATO	
					337	WITH SOUR CREAM	
	344	CHOCOLATE SORBET			338	FRENCH FRIES	
	345	BANANAS FOSTER			339	FR. ONION RINGS	
	349	NAPOLEON			340	BROCCOLI	
	350	CHOCLATE MOUSSE					
	351	BLACK FOREST CAKE			365	COFFEE	
	352	APPLE STREUDEL			367	DECAFF. COFFEE	
	353	CREME BRULEE			368	ICED COFFEE	
	354	CHEESECAKE			369	TEA	
	355	ICE CREAM SUNDAE			362	HERB TEA	
	356	CHOCOLATE TERRINE			370	ICED TEA	
	357	FASSION FRT MOUSSE			371	ESPRESSO	
	359	FRUIT SORBETS			372	CAPPUCCINO	
	361	RED/SWEET/CRISP			373	HOT CHOCOLATE	
	346	SPECIAL DESSERT A			374	MILK	
	347	SPECIAL DESSERT B			363	DECAF. ESPRESSO	
					364	DECAF. CAPPUCCINO	

FIGURE 2.2   Sample menu-driven order dupe.

tions, such as extra sauce or sauce on the side. The order dupe, therefore, is invaluable for the actual service of the foods and beverages to the guests!

The actual check presented to customers is created separately, whether from a computer system—for instance, the NCR 2160 system—or on a separate check. A computerized system can also be combined with order dupes. After completing the order dupe with the guest, the order-taker may enter the order into a computer. The computer then informs the kitchen which items to prepare. This method controls food cost and inventory and tracks sales. The final check is neat, without ordering notations, and for the purposes of paying the check, that's all the customer needs. For the servers' use, however, the notations are vital.

With this system, dessert service would parallel the dinner service. A new dupe would be utilized, with the top copy, again the most legible, being used for the actual desserts. The second copy would be used for coffee or tea service, and the third copy (the least legible) would stay on the station as a backup copy to be used if one of the others gets torn, coffee-soaked, or misplaced.

A sample of a menu-driven order dupe, complete with PLU (Product Look-Up) numbers for the NCR foodservice computer system is shown in Figure 2.2. Note the space to the left of each item, used for the quantity of each item being ordered. The space to the right of each item is used for special notations—such as no sauce, medium-rare (MR)—as well as for chair numbers (seat designation system), noting who has ordered what items.

Numbered Guest Checks   Numbered guest checks are widely used. In this system, the check used to write the order becomes the customer's check, and the customer's order is usually written out completely—for example, appetizer, main course, beverage, and dessert (when it is ordered)—on the check, including the price of each item. At the end of the meal, it is subtotaled. This system nearly always requires that a kitchen duplicate be created to give to the kitchen, speeding kitchen operations. (Usually a dupe pad, complete with carbon, is provided.) It is also important that the servers write legibly, as the checks can become quite sloppy, especially if guests change their minds and items are crossed out!

Blank Pads   When blank pads are used, the system illustrated in Figure 2.1 can be used, grouping items according to when they will be served during the course of the meal—appetizers first, then second appetizers, then entrees, and so on—and noting seat designation numbers, quantities, and special instructions near the item ordered.

An alternative method is to record the seat references (chair numbers) in a column at the far left of the sheet. Then as many columns as courses are created, left to right, to record the courses for each person. Customer number 1's meal is thus in a horizontal line left to right across the check.

Whenever blank pads are used, a check for the customer is still needed at the end of the meal , which makes for extra work. Also, a summary form must be created for the kitchen unless an electronic point-of-sale system is utilized to record the information, transmit the information to the kitchen, and prepare a guest check.

Two-Part Guest Check   When a two-part check is used, the top sheet (original) may cover only half of the check. The original then serves as a kitchen check, and the duplicate is the customer's. Main courses and other dishes prepared by the kitchen are written in the top half, and items prepared or dispensed by the server are written in the lower half, directly on the duplicate, or customer's copy.

Perforated Guest Checks   When a perforated check is used, the top half becomes the customer's check. Usually the server writes the food order customer by customer in blocks, and then rewrites the main course items in summary form on the lower half, which is the kitchen stub.

Transmitting the Order to the Kitchen

There are three primary methods for transmitting the order to the kitchen: verbally, manually, and electronically. Prior to the mass installation and wide use of electronic point-of-sale terminals, orders on dupes were often rewritten and then carried to the kitchen, or the dupe was given to the kitchen and a final check was rewritten. In some, primarily small, establishments, orders were—and still are—transmitted verbally to the kitchen.

Electronic Order Transmission

With computers and point-of-sale terminals (terminals placed at the point of sale, or in the dining room), orders are entered into a keyboard and transmitted to the controller, which is the part of the computer that processes the orders. The controller analyzes each order, sorting which items are prepared at each station, and sends messages to each station— for instance, the hot line, pantry, dessert station, or bar—telling the cooks (or bartenders) what items are needed from their station for that order.

The messages the controller sends are printed on food dupes or bar dupes, depending on what's being printed and where the printer is located. These dupes are printed in each station (or where the controller has been programmed to print them). Usually, the request for hot food items is sent to a printer near the hot line, and the chef or expediter calls the orders in to the line cooks. Another dupe is printed in the pantry area, and the pantry cooks begin working on those items. A dessert dupe is printed in the dessert area, and the dessert cook begins plating the desserts. Bar dupes are either sent to the service bar area or printed at the station where the servers are entering the order, in which case the servers hand-carry the beverage dupe to the bar and call each order to the bartender.

In other words, an order is entered into a keyboard in the dining room. When the completed order has been entered, it is transmitted to the controller. The controller sends a message to each area, printing out dupes for the cooks in each area. Alcoholic beverage items are transmitted to the bar, pantry items to the pantry, hot items to the hot line, and dessert items to the dessert station. All of this happens without the service staff moving from the dining room or service station (where the electronic terminal is located), and allows them to provide better service to the customers.

This is certainly the way of the future. With the cost of computers and terminals becoming more affordable, the programming and customization of the programs becoming easier, and the terminals becoming more "user-friendly" every year, even small establishments can, or will soon be able to, afford to computerize. Additional benefits include cost control, the monitoring of best-selling items, cover counts per station or server, check averages per station or server, charge tips, and the automatic addition and computation of taxes and discounts.

Some companies that provide electronic point-of-sale food systems include, in alphabetical order:

♦ Micros Systems, Inc.
♦ NCR Corporation, Inc.
♦ Remanco Systems, Inc.
♦ Squirrel
♦ TEC America, Inc.

This list is illustrative, and by no means exhaustive.

Transmitting an order to the kitchen or to the bar electronically requires an electronic system with several parts, including

♦ A "brain" (the controller)
♦ A way to enter the information (keyboard)

♦ A way to verify what's been entered (monitor or screen)
♦ A way to receive the information (printers located at various locations throughout the restaurant/kitchen)

Figure 2.3 is an example of an NCR electronic terminal keyboard, which is similar to the keyboards of most other companies. There is a numeric keypad and keys or "boxes" (the white areas) for the operation to fill in. These areas can be filled with the names of the food items from the menu (e.g., h-burger, cheesebg, ham sand, turkey club, sirloin, T-bone, sole, trout, f fries, baked pot).

A server simply hits the correct button for the food item being ordered—for example, a hamburger. If two hamburgers are being ordered, the server hits number "2" then the "hamburger" button. This is the system at most fast-food operations and other restaurants where there is a limited menu. If the food and beverage offerings are extensive, and there are more items than there are blank keys or buttons, then a system of word buttons plus product/price look-up numbers (PLUs) must be used.

PLUs are numbers assigned to an item, one PLU number per item, and one price assigned to that item. As PLU numbers are used, the computer "looks up" that PLU number and finds the food or beverage item assigned to it, and the price. It then displays the information on a monitor, or screen, and prints that information at printers at kitchen or bar stations and on the check.

If there are different meal periods, the operation can define several keyboards, one for each menu. There could be a breakfast keyboard, a lunch keyboard, a dinner keyboard, a brunch keyboard, and a special-events keyboard. Several blank keyboard overlays are printed with the appropriate items for each meal period. At defined times (when each meal period begins), the keyboard overlays are changed.

Simultaneously, a manager or cashier, instructed on how to program the controller for whichever meal period it is, would reprogram the controller for that meal period—it takes only a few minutes. Then the controller will transmit the correct items for that meal period when each spot on the keyboard is pressed.

The danger of this system is that, if the controller is not reprogrammed at the time that the keyboard inserts (or overlays) are changed, errors will occur—the kitchen might receive a dupe for scrambled eggs when the server punched the hamburger button.

To avoid this pitfall, an operation could program the controller to use PLU numbers for items, and use the keyboard primarily for quantities and modifiers. Figure 2.4 shows a sample keyboard that is based on this method. The keyboard is set up once, and rarely changed. Each food and beverage item is given its own PLU number, and the controller looks up the product and its price from the PLU number.

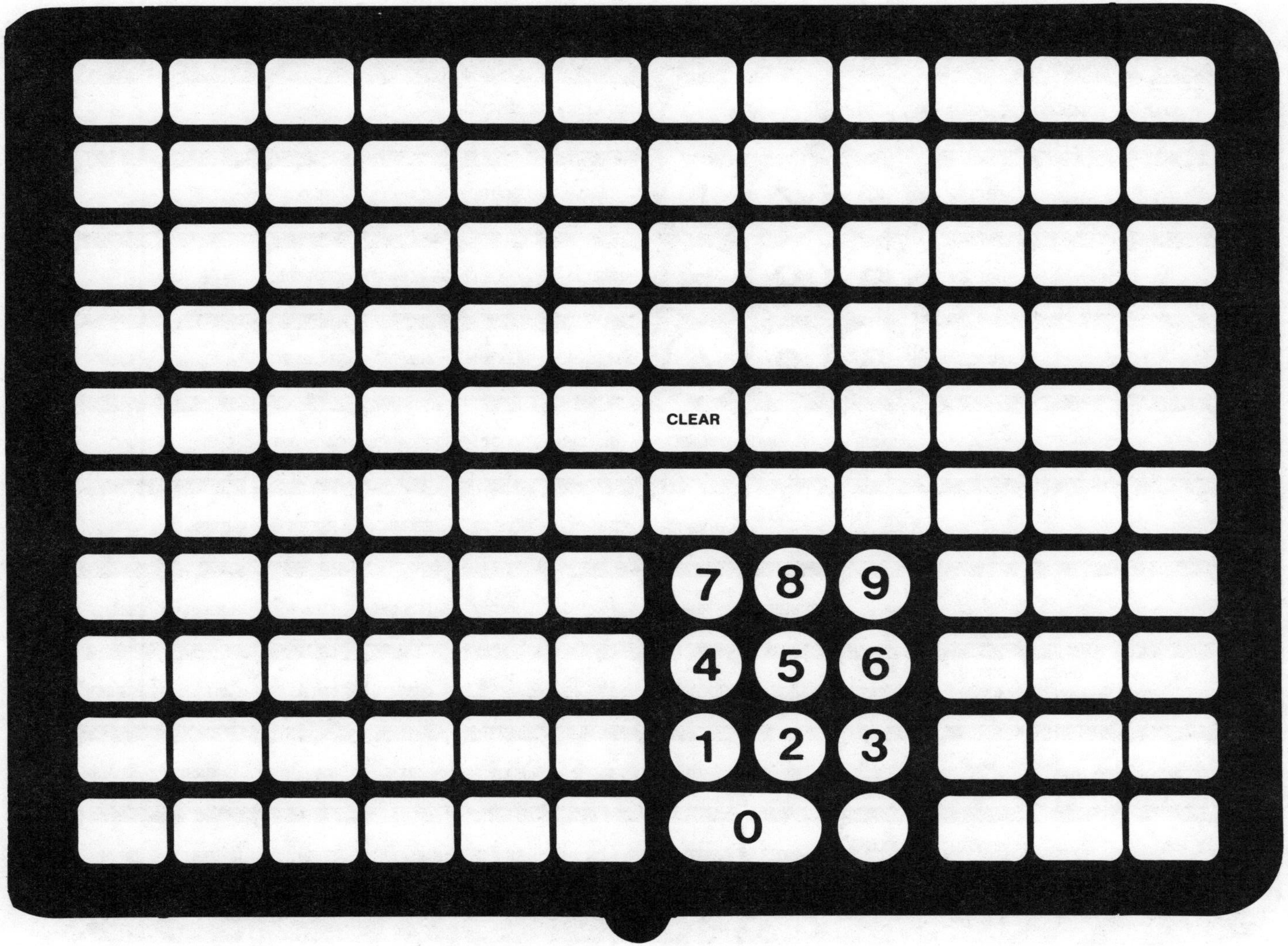

FIGURE 2.3   NCR keyboard.

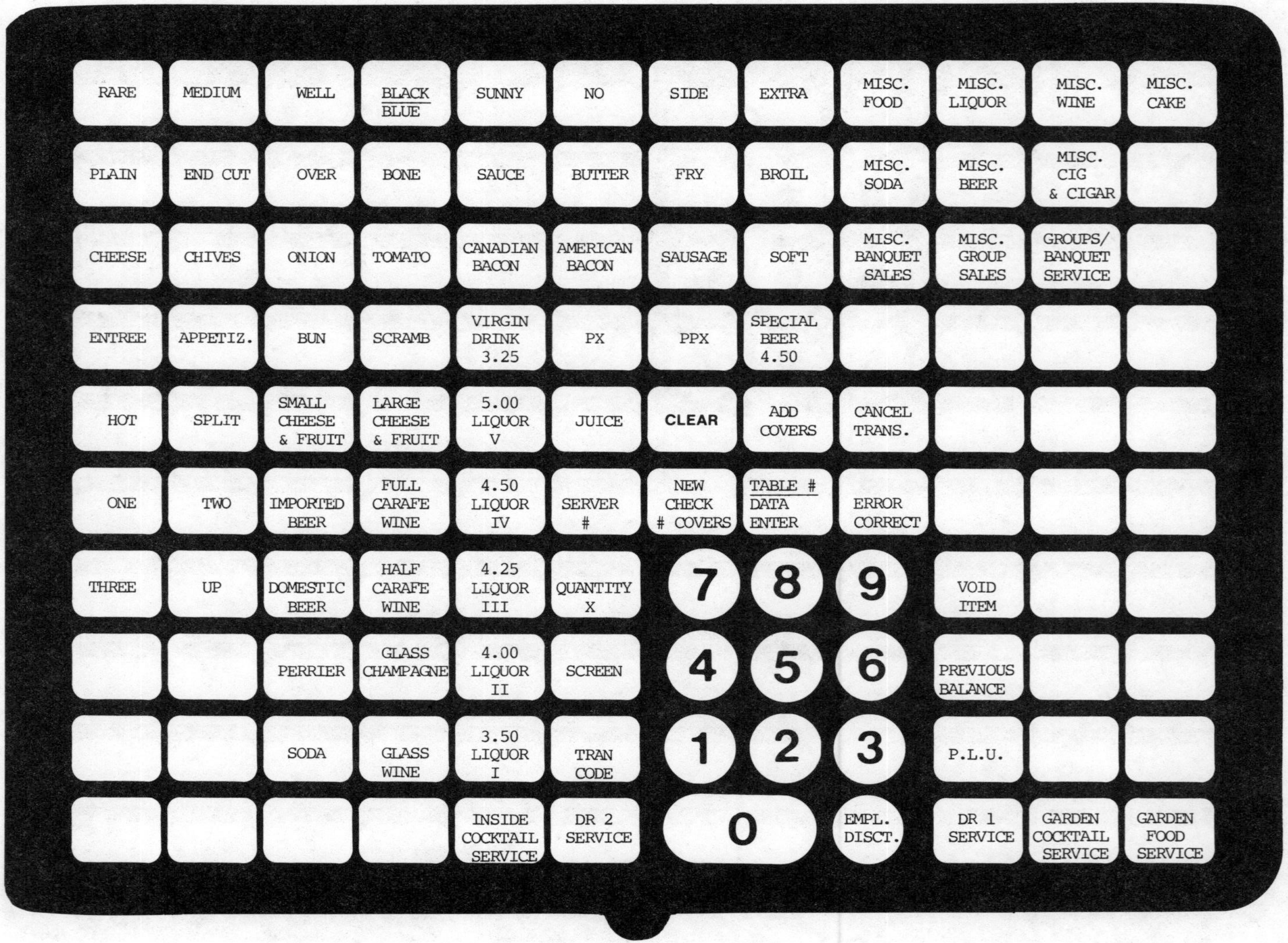

FIGURE 2.4 NCR keyboard programmed for PLU usage.

As a menu changes, items (and PLU numbers and prices) can be quickly added, with no need to delete any for quite some time. Most systems can accommodate 1,000 PLU numbers, representing many more items than the average restaurant offers at one time. PLU numbers can be changed, and new ones can be programmed in quickly to accommodate daily specials. Price changes can be handled by a supervisor, who simply reprograms the price in the controller.

The numeric keyboard is used to initiate the transaction, to define quantities ordered, and to order foods with PLU numbers, which is ordering food items using the number the computer knows that food item by. An example of the exact keys you would hit to open a check and to transmit an order to the bar and kitchen is provided in Appendix A.

Once these sequences are mastered, and most electronic systems are similar, these systems are a fast and highly effective method of ordering food and beverages, and then transmitting those orders to the kitchen or bar. They provide accounting and summary sales data for the operator, and keep track of charge tips for the service staff, making it easy for them to collect those tips at the end of each shift.

But most important, electronic point-of-sale systems enable the service staff to spend more time on the dining room floor, where they can keep an eye on and provide service to guests. For the larger operation, where there is a distinct separation between the kitchen and the front of the house, this is certainly the way to organize the order-taking and transmission operations for optimum performance from the staff, in both the front and back of the house.

Manual Order Transmission

In many restaurants orders are transmitted to the various stations in a kitchen manually—someone carries a piece of paper to the kitchen with the order (or at least those items needed from the kitchen) written on it. Sometimes it's necessary to prepare a kitchen duplicate unless the check is in two parts and produces its own duplicate, or the server prepares a "draft" check that serves as the duplicate. The duplicate system provides a measure of control and facilitates the preparation of many orders simultaneously.

Verbal Order Transmission

In other operations, communication by the server to the kitchen or preparation area is verbal. Sometimes even where the servers prepare a written order at the table, once in the kitchen the server or a designated kitchen employee—the chef, sous chef, or expediter—reads the order aloud to the line cooks, pantry cooks, dessert cooks, and so on. Verbal communication is extremely important. It must be organized rigidly according to a definite, standardized procedure using predefined "short-cut" words to communicate effectively if significant time is not to be lost.

Abbreviated Verbal Communication

Many establishments have and use abbreviated ordering procedures. Especially known for their creative abbreviations are high-volume limited-menu operations, which are more likely to rely on verbal communication alone and need accurate, useful, and short abbreviations.

The "faster" the operation, the faster the communication will be. Short-order items are a good example. Communication concerning these is limited to the necessary words, and the order is stated in a way that follows the cook's sequence in making up the order. For example, in making a tuna fish sandwich, the cook reaches first for the tuna and then for the bread. The order is stated, "Tuna white." Likewise, in making a tuna fish sandwich with a slice of tomato with mayonnaise on rye bread, the order of procedure would be tuna fish, then tomato, then mayonnaise, then bread. The order is announced as, "Tuna tommy mayo, rye." It would disrupt the workflow of an experienced cook if the order were announced as: "A tuna fish sandwich on rye bread, with mayonnaise and tomato."

When no bread is stated, it is assumed that the customer wants white bread. Each order must be complete, and announced once. Table 2.3 offers some examples of abbreviated verbal communication for short orders.

In summary, when an order is transmitted to the kitchen, certain steps must be followed, which are reviewed here.

1. Summarize the order. If an electronic point-of-sale terminal is being used, order all items using proper procedures, modifiers, and PLU numbers.

    If manually written dupes are used, identify the items that are prepared by each station of the kitchen and write those items in summary fashion on a dupe.

    If verbal communication is used, organize the items—appetizers, entrees, and so forth. Know the quantity and special instructions for each item.
2. With a manual system, proceed to the kitchen, or to the cashier if a preregistering system is being used. Hand the check to the expediter or announce the order.
3. With a verbal system, first gather items which are not prepared to order by the kitchen: for example, appetizers and soups, or gather underliners or special plates needed for the order. Once you've organized these items, call in the order.
4. Preface the order with the word "Ordering."

TABLE 2.3   Common Verbal Abbreviations

Item Wanted	Order
Tuna fish sandwich on white	Tuna white
Tuna fish sandwich on white toast	Tuna down
Tuna fish sandwich on rye toast	Tuna rye, down
Tuna fish sandwich with lettuce and tomato on white toast	Tuna LT down
Tuna fish sandwich with tomato and mayonnaise on white	Tuna tommy mayo
Tuna fish sandwich with onion	Tuna slice
Two tuna fish sandwiches on white on one plate	Tuna "21" or Tuna, a pair
Two tuna fish sandwiches on rye toast	Tuna rye down "21"
Two eggs, scrambled, on one plate, well done	Scramble "21" dry
Two orders of scrambled eggs, two eggs each, well-done	Scramble "42" dry
Three eggs, scrambled, on one plate well-done	Scramble "31" dry
What happened to my tuna fish sandwich on white bread?	Echo tuna white

5. State the table number: "Table number ____ ."
6. State the order in a summary form: item and then modifiers—for example, "3 lamb chops, 2 medium, 1 rare."
7. When the customers are ready for their main course, which may be 30 or 40 minutes after the order is announced in the kitchen, return to the kitchen and call: "Fire table number ____" or "Put up table number ____ ." At this point the kitchen begins the final plating of the food, the grilling of steaks, or whatever else is done at the last minute.

Picking Up the Order

Once the food and beverages have been ordered, they must be picked up. Picking up the food items is more complicated than serving beverages as it involves timing and an assessment of each table. Are the guests in a hurry? Do they want to linger over cocktails before the appetizers are served? Do they want leisurely service, and to be able to converse at length between courses? Is it a business meeting?

The timing of a meal depends on many factors, including the type of operation (fast-food? white tablecloth? live music? pianist?), the decor, the pricing, and, naturally, the desire of the guest. Every operation should establish its own guidelines, however, stating the general timetable for each step of service. This and the general timing of orders are reviewed now.

Timing Orders

Servers must be sufficiently familiar with the menu to know the cooking or preparation time of every item on the menu. To prevent guests from being inconvenienced or unduly delayed in their dining, the server transmits the order to the kitchen allowing for the cooking time of the longest-cooking item. For example, if a well-done steak is ordered, which takes 25 minutes to grill, the kitchen must begin cooking that steak as the appetizers are being served. If sautéed fillet of sole is ordered, which may take 5 minutes to cook and plate, the cooking of the entrees can begin as the appetizers are being cleared from the table, allowing 5 minutes or so between courses. Time the "firing" point of the order (when the kitchen begins preparation and plating of the food items for pickup) by the longest-preparation-time food item.

A system must be established between the front of the house and the back of the house to determine who signals when the cooking of the entrees begins. If it is the kitchen (usually based on FIFO, first order in, first order out), an override system must be available for the server to signal to the kitchen to hold the firing for those tables that are lingering over appetizers, or that have ordered second appetizers or another bottle of wine.

Servers must also know which orders can be picked up immediately (no cooking time, no preparation time) and served. This permits the grouping of orders. For example, you might serve one table its cold appetizers (immediate pickup items), getting them ready for only occasional checking, then devote time to the preparation of foods for other tables. Or, serve several tables' beverages together, in one trip, rather than making several trips. Also, orders can be taken from several tables at once. Foods requiring cooking can be ordered, and while those foods are cooking, soups and/or appetizers and beverages can be served to several tables. Bring all of a table's beverages or appetizers in one trip; don't bring drinks or food to some guests at a table and not to the others. Serve one course to everyone at a table at one time.

The advent of the "finishing" kitchen, in which little preparation is done, even of long-cooking items, has made a great many food items almost instantly available to service personnel. For example, refrigerated casseroles take approximately 75 seconds to heat to serving temperature in a microwave oven. Quartz ovens, high-speed broilers, convection ovens, pressure ovens, and pressure steamers have all shortened cooking times tremendously.

Overview of Picking Up an Order

In most operations servers obtain and serve soup, cold appetizers, salads, and beverages themselves. Hot appetizers, entrees, and an occasional hot dessert usually require cooking, heating, or finishing to order.

"Picking up an order" generally means getting those items which must be cooked or plated by the kitchen personnel. When you are picking up food in a kitchen, be as quiet as possible, talking only to the chef or expediter who is trying to get the orders out, and then only regarding the order being picked up.

Points to remember when loading the tray (see section on loading trays for all of the details) include the following:

♦ Stack serving utensils, underliners, and the like on the tray first.
♦ Place cold foods on the tray second.
♦ Place hot foods on the tray last.
♦ Stack hot foods atop hot foods, cold foods atop cold foods.
♦ In stacking steaks of differing degrees of doneness, stack the rarest on the bottom; the most well done on the top (heat rises).
♦ Know before leaving the kitchen which food items will be served to the women at the table. Have those items on top, if possible. Otherwise, have a "landing area," where the men's plates can be temporarily rested while you retrieve and serve the women's plates first.
♦ If the operation does not use plate covers (allowing for the stacking of plates) and there is a large party, "borrow" another server or two to take all food items to the table at once. Everyone should be served at once—not half of the table this trip, and half of the table on another trip to the kitchen!

Steps in Picking Up the Order

1. Collect all serving equipment and cold food accompaniments to the main course—for example, lobster picks and a nutcracker for a lobster dinner, sour cream and chives for a baked potato, and extra plates or underliners.
2. Pick up cold foods—for example, salads.
3. Announce that the order is being picked up ("Picking up table number ____").
4. Pick up hot foods. If Russian (platter) service is being used, pick up and place the plates and then the platters of food.
5. Pick up hot breads or baked goods last, unless they have been previously placed on the table, as they cool quickly.

Serving the Order

When you serve a table of guests, one must be served before another, just as when you take an order. General rules have developed over the years, which should be followed unless your operation has different procedures.

General Rules: The Order of Service

♦ When a man and a woman are eating together, serve the woman first.
♦ When two couples are eating together, serve the woman on the host's right first, then the other woman, the "other" man, and last, the host.
♦ When three couples are eating together, the host and hostess should face each other. Serve the woman on the host's right first, then the woman on his left, then the hostess. Then serve the man on the right of the hostess, then on the left of the hostess, then, finally, the host.
♦ When more than six people are eating together, serve the person on the host's right first, and then serve the guests, moving in a *counterclockwise* direction around the table for food service. (Move *clockwise* for beverage service.)

Alternatively, serve the woman on the host's right, then the woman on his left, then all the guests, continuing to the right regardless of sex.

♦ In other situations, and when it is not apparent who is host or hostess, the following order customarily prevails:

· Old before young
· Ladies before gentlemen
· Children after ladies

Checking on the Table

After service of the beverages and food, it is imperative that you check on the table. Perhaps the steak was cooked too well, or is too rare; perhaps a beverage refill is necessary; perhaps a condiment is needed.

It is your job to be observant, so much so that the guests do not have to summon you to their table for that next round of drinks or extra rolls in the bread basket. If you notice the bread or rolls being depleted, bring more. If you know they're having baked potatoes, have extra butter on the table before the potatoes are served. If the drinks are nearly finished, suggest another round.

The ashtrays must be checked. Food and ashes don't mix: If one is on the table, the other shouldn't be. If your guests are in a smoking section, check the ashtrays often throughout service. If there are ashes, replace the ashtrays as they are used, quietly. Always replace them between courses, if there are ashes in them.

The technique for replacing ashtrays, which was described above, is reviewed here. Using your right hand, place a clean ashtray atop the used ashtray, upside-down, and quietly remove both from the table. Place your right hand behind your back. Move your left hand behind your back. Transfer the bottom ashtray (the used one) to the palm of your left hand and cover the top of the ashtray with the fingers of your left hand so the ashes can't fly out of the ashtray. Return your right hand to the table with the clean ashtray, placing it quietly on the table. This method ensures that ashes from the dirty ashtray don't get blown into someone's food or drink.

After the entree course, or whenever the table has a build up of crumbs in an area, the table must be crumbed. The most often used type of crumbers in restaurants are the long, thin curved pieces of metal. To use it, slide the straight edge of the crumber from the center of the table toward the edge of the table, gathering the crumbs in the concave hollow of the crumber. Scrape the crumbs onto an appetizer plate, which is held just under the edge of the table. Don't allow crumbs to fall onto the floor.

Presentation and Payment of the Check

After service is complete, the check is presented. Although this is detailed in Chapter Three, a brief review is useful here.

At leisurely dining restaurants, the check is usually presented upon request. At fast-food restaurants, or places with a high turnover, or for the breakfast meal, the check is usually presented with the service of the entree, unless dessert is included or usually ordered.

The check should be neat and clean, without coffee spills or ketchup stains. It should be legible, with the total due highly visible; often it is circled. Applicable taxes should have been added, so there are no surprises when the guest gets to the cashier.

The amount of the gratuity, if any, is usually left to the discretion of the guest. If it is added in automatically (as sometimes it is for large parties or at certain restaurants), it should be so noted on the check, and not in the fine print. The gratuity still represents a reward for service, and if none is left, review your service. Don't chase the guests, demanding more.

Checks should be neatly presented. In a more formal restaurant they should be placed face-down on a small plate—for example, a B&B plate. Some operations use "check books" which fold over, with inside flaps, one side for the check and the other side for the guest's cash or credit card. In a casual operation, the check can be placed face-down at one side of the table, in a clean area. Don't place it in a puddle of water from the waterglass, or a spot of oil from the oil cruet! If the guest pays with a credit card, follow the credit card procedures outlined in Appendix B.

As guests leave, bid them "Good morning" or "Good afternoon" or "Good evening." Quickly check around their table for any belongings left behind—a wallet that might have fallen out of a pocket, a lipstick that fell out of a purse, a forgotten package or umbrella or eyeglasses. If any items are found, take them immediately to the area where lost and found articles are kept. If a credit card was inadvertently left on the table, personally hand it to the manager on duty.

Timing of Service

It is imperative that customers be taken care of promptly. The steps in service, described above, must be completed within generally accepted time frames. The exact time frames vary, depending upon the type of service.

For leisurely service, the time span between drinks and the appetizer, or between the appetizer and entree course, may be 10 or 15 minutes, especially if the guests have indicated that they prefer leisurely service. In high-volume establishments, the guest often wants complete service—beverage, appetizer, entree, and dessert—or whatever is ordered, within a short time span, generally less than an hour. An overview of typical steps in a meal and generally accepted times for those steps to take, as well as who generally performs each particular step, is found in Table 2.4.

TABLE 2.4   General Timing of Service

Steps	Timing, Person Responsible, Details
Seating guests at table	
Meeting and greeting	Within 2 minutes of being seated By: server or anyone on the service team
Serving bread & water	Within 2 minutes of being seated By: busser or servers
Presenting menus, wine list	Within 5 minutes of being seated By: server, captain, maitre d'
Taking beverage order	Within 2 minutes of being seated By: server or captain
Explaining the menu, selling specials, add-ons	When menus are presented, unless management dictates otherwise: menu explained at the same time as the beverage order is taken, or, if a server takes the beverage order and the captain explains the menu, within 10 minutes of being seated; specials and add-ons explained at the same time as menus presented. By: server or captain

Steps	Timing, Person Responsible, Details
Serving beverages	Within 10 minutes of being seated By: server or captain
Taking the order	Within 5 minutes of being seated in high-volume establishment Within 15 minutes of being seated or within 10 minutes of the beverage being served By: captain or server
Writing the order	During or immediately after the taking of the order By: captain or server
Transmitting the order to the kitchen	Immediately after the writing of the order By: captain or server
Serving appetizer	Within 15 minutes of being seated except in fast-turnover establishment where total meal should be finished in less than 50 minutes By: service team
Serving appetizer wine	Wine is brought to table before appetizers are served, is opened, presented, and served immediately before or after appetizers are served By: sommelier, captain, or server
Clearing appetizers	When all in the party are finished, unless house rules dictate when each guest finishes By: busser and/or service team
Refilling water	Automatic, without asking, until dessert course By: service team
Serving second course	Within 10 minutes of first appetizer being cleared By: service team
Serving second course wine	With second course service; if a different wine than first course wine service, clean glasses must be set before wine service By: sommelier, captain, or server

TABLE 2.4   (*Continued*)

Steps	Timing, Person Responsible, Details
Clearing second course	When all in the party are finished unless house rules dictate when each guest is finished By: busser and/or service team
Serving main course	Within 10 minutes of first or second course, whichever is the last course served. If no appetizers are served, within 20 minutes of beverage service By: service team
Serving main course wine	Glasses are brought before food service; are presented, opened, and poured immediately after main course service By: sommelier, captain, or server
Clearing all dishes	Clear entree dishes, side dishes, B&B plates, salad plates, salt and pepper, butter, empty wine glasses and bread: only water glasses, filled wine or beverage glasses, clean ashtrays, and flowers, if any, should be on the table By: service team
Clearing condiments	Any remaining condiments (e.g., ketchup, mustard, olive oil) should be removed By: service team
Crumbing table	Using a crumber, crumb onto a salad or B&B plate By: service team
Setting dessert silverware	If preset above entree plate, bring down into position; otherwise, set dessert fork, dessert spoon, teaspoon, and dessert knife (fruit knife), or per management policy By: service team
Setting coffee or tea service	Place cream and sugar, sugar substitute, and milk if tea is being served; set warmed cups and saucers By: service team

Steps	Timing, Person Responsible, Details
Selling desserts	Desserts; specials of the day By: captain
Serving dessert	Within 15 minutes of entrees being cleared By: service team
Serving coffee or tea	With or immediately after service of desserts By: service team
Clearing dessert	When all guests are finished, unless management dictates as the guests finish By: service team
Selling after-dinner drinks	Suggest cordials, liquors, brandy, cappuccino, espresso, etc. By: captain
Serving after-dinner drinks	Within 10 minutes of order By: service team
Refilling coffee and tea	As cups empty: with tea service, have extra hot water nearby; for coffee, have regular and decaffeinated; refill automatically; guests should not have to motion or ask By: service team
Presenting check	Leisurely dining: when requested; fast turnover: when entree served or with coffee/tea refill when guests nearly finished, after asking, "Will there be anything else?" or "May I suggest deep dish apple pie for dessert?"—a cue for guests to ask for more food or the check! By: captain or server
Taking payment	At guests' leisure; house policies regarding forms of payment (e.g., credit cards, house accounts, traveler's checks, personal checks, gift certificates, vouchers) must be known in advance by service staff By: captain, servers

TABLE 2.4   (*Continued*)

Steps	Timing, Person Responsible, Details
Saying thank you	"Thank you, it's been a pleasure serving you" to each party before they depart By: service team
Saying farewell	"We hope you enjoyed your meal; come back soon!" or equivalent to departing guests By: host/hostesses, maitre d', doorman, coat-check personnel, proprietor

STYLES OF FOODSERVICE

Tableservice, like medicine or construction, has its specialties or styles. Restaurants of different types, with different menus, use certain specialized skills in addition to basic tableservice techniques. Sometimes a restaurant will use a combination of two or more styles, one that is for a la carte dining and another for banquets. The major styles are reviewed here.

Major Styles of Foodservice

- ◆ American, or plate, service
- ◆ French, or gueridon, service
- ◆ Wagon service
- ◆ Russian, or platter, service
- ◆ Family service
- ◆ English, or butler, service
- ◆ Buffet service
- ◆ Fast-food, cafeteria, or rectangular tray service
- ◆ Arm service

American, or Plate, Service

Most restaurants in the United States use American (or plate service) as the basic service style, even though they may also employ some other type of service for certain courses or events, such as banquets. In American service the server brings a completed plate to the customer. The food is portioned and the plate is garnished in the kitchen by the kitchen staff. The server simply places the plate in front of the guest. In some operations the server may carry the plates without a tray (arm service), but in most operations either a large tray or a small rectangular tray (tea service) is used to transport the plates to the dining room.

The basic tenets of American service follow.

General Rules of American Tableservice

1. Serve plated food from the *left* of the guest, using your *left* hand, not reaching across or in front of the guest. Move forward, in a *counterclockwise* direction around the table whenever possible.
2. Clear plates from the *right* of the guest, using your *right* hand. Stack them on your *left* hand, wrist, and forearm. Move forward, in a *clockwise* direction around the table whenever possible.
3. Clear B&B plates, side dish plates, other plates, and unused utensils (forks) which are to the left of the guests from the *left,* after picking up the entree plate and other plates on the right side of the guest from the right. Your *right* hand is used to clear.
4. Serve beverages from the *right* side of a guest with your *right* hand, traveling in a *clockwise* direction around the table.

    Note: Soup is considered a beverage and is served and cleared from the right side of a guest, using the right hand.
5. Do not reach across *guests.* If something is to the guest's left, it should be removed from the left. If something is on the guest's right side, it should be removed from the right side.

    Exception: Remove the plates and utensils of two people leaning in toward each other from the "outside," so as not to disrupt their conversation.

    Exception: Banquettes or booths which force you to stretch over and in front of guests to reach those in the back. Be as unobstrusive as possible.
6. Stack plates as quietly as possible, and just behind the guest, out of his or her line of vision. Scrape plates as little as possible, but do scrape what has to be removed in order to stack multiple plates, so you can clear an entire table at one time, if possible.
7. Serve everyone at the table at the same time; clear everyone together as well. Serve and clear as unobtrusively as possible. If the guests are noticeably aware of what you're doing, you're doing it incorrectly, sloppily, or too noisily.

French, or Gueridon, Service

French service entails the partial preparation of food in the kitchen, with the final preparation—the sauce, garnishing, and plating—done in the dining room in front of the guest. Generally the food is prepared in the kitchen and placed in copper sauté pans. Sauces, garnishes, and other ingredients are placed in decorative vessels, often silver goosenecks, sauceboats, or porcelain ramekins. Servers position a gueridon near the table to be served, then bring a tray with the sauces, garnishes, and empty plates to the gueridon. The gueridon is set up, then the sauté pans with the partially prepared food in them are brought to the gueridon, and the items are finished, plated, and served. Examples and detailed information are in Chapter Three.

Classical French service is rarely used except in expensive restaurants (those with high-check averages), as the gueridon and tableside cooking techniques require time, skilled personnel, and tables quite far apart, allowing for the gueridon to pass between the tables. Gueridon service in a modified form, however, is often used in restaurants of all types and price ranges. Gueridons with rechauds (open flames for cooking) are often used for pasta dishes or flaming coffees, prepared tableside. Sometimes gueridons are wheeled out with the makings of a Caesar salad or other cold appetizers, without the rechaud. These forms of modified French service still provide the customer with a "show" and personalized tableside attention, the highlights of French service. This modified style of French service is detailed below, under "Wagon Service."

Some refer to any use of the serving spoon and fork as French service since in French service a serving spoon and fork are used, but this is technically incorrect. Distinctions should be made between the use of the gueridon for tableside cooking using the serving spoon and fork (French service); use of platters using the serving spoon and fork in one hand (Russian, or platter, service); and use of the gueridon for display or plating (wagon service).

General rules pertaining to classical French-style service follow.

General Rules of French Service

♦ Food is finished in the dining room on a rechaud (warmer) or gueridon.
♦ A serving spoon and fork are utilized to plate food. One utensil is held in each hand as you plate the food from the sauté pan to the guest's plate using the gueridon as a work surface.
♦ All food and beverages are served from the right with the right hand.
♦ All food and beverages are cleared from the right with the right hand.
♦ Servers walk clockwise around the tables.

Wagon Service

Wagon service requires the server to finish the preparation at the table, or at least to portion it for the guest. For example, large cuts of meat, like prime rib, might be carved for the guest at tableside, or the guest might be served a portion of salad from a giant salad bowl.

Wagon service differs from French or gueridon service in the level of service provided. French service entails the cooking or finishing of the dish, which often requires carving or sautéing or other skills as well as time with the guests. While the dish is being finished, the server entertains the guests with tales of the history of the dish, or a show such as flambéing crepes suzette or flaming coffee drinks.

Wagon service is quick, while giving the illusion of the French service of the extremely elegant restaurants. It is becoming more and more common in low-check-average specialty restaurants because it can combine a touch of elegance with high productivity and efficiency. Caesar salad is a good example. In French service, a Caesar salad would be made from start to finish tableside, beginning with the rubbing of a wooden bowl with garlic and the crushing of the anchovies. In wagon service, a premade salad (made in the kitchen) would be wheeled to the table in a large bowl, the dressing would be poured on, and it would be tossed and portioned in front of the guests. Examples of wagon service and foods appropriate for this type of service are detailed in Chapter Three.

Russian, or Platter, Service

In some restaurants, and in many banquet situations, the food is placed on a platter with other portions of the same food for the same table. The server then transfers the food from the platter to the guests' plates. Generally, but not necessarily, this type of service is associated with high-check-average restaurants. Platter service demands skill in transferring the food from the platter to the plate without spilling it, spoiling its appearance, or inconveniencing the guest.

The basis of Russian service (serving from a platter) is to use a spoon-and-fork combination in one hand as though it were a set of tongs. But the technique isn't just for luxury restaurants: It may be used in a fast-food restaurant to remove pieces of Danish pastry from a display case, or on a buffet line when serving slices of ham.

Russian-style service is commonly used for banquets and formal sit-down dinners (e.g., weddings) where all guests are having the same meal. Servers often train in teams so they are able to place the plates down in front of guests simultaneously, then begin serving each table simultaneously. This provides quick and professional service, as well as a show for the guests. Likewise, when clearing, team members position themselves to the right of a lady at the first table to be cleared, then when the captain or maitre d' gives the signal to begin clearing, they all begin simultaneously.

Because of the specialized skills and precise nature of Russian service, a quick summary of the rules of Russian service is presented, followed by three areas of discussion:

◆ The basics of Russian service
◆ The techniques needed for Russian service
◆ The steps in Russian service

These tasks may seem difficult to learn at first, and are very precise, but they *can* be mastered. Once learned they seem natural, and add a definite level of sophistication to any meal.

General Rules of Russian Service

- Use serving spoon and fork to serve food from a platter.
- One platter serves that course to one table.
- Serve from the left side of the guest.
- Hold platter along left forearm and hand.
- Move counterclockwise around the table.
- Separate serving spoon for sauce.
- Separate serving utensils for each course.

Russian Service Basics

1. Platters are portioned, filled, and garnished in the kitchen. Each platter contains sufficient portions and garnish for one table. The platter may contain the entree, vegetable, and starch, or only the entree and sauce, if any, with vegetables and starches on a separate platter, to be served immediately following the entree. (The servers trail each other going around the table.)
2. Sauce, if any, is in a gooseneck or sauceboat, and is positioned at the *far end* of the platter, away from the server and closest to the guest's plate.
3. Serving spoon and serving fork are the utensils used to serve the food from the platter to the guest's plate. Each platter or dish has separate utensils; a separate spoon is included for sauce, if one is on the platter.
4. Clean plates are placed from the *right* side of the guest with the *right* hand, traveling in a *clockwise* direction around the table.
5. If a hot course is to be served, hot plates are set; if a cold course is to be served, room temperature or chilled plates are set.
6. Plates are placed immediately before the platters are brought from the kitchen.
7. Service begins with the lady to the host's right, or the eldest lady at the table. Ladies are served first, then gentlemen. If one person is serving a table, it will necessitate circling the table twice. Children, if present, are served at the same time as the ladies.

Technique: Serving One Person Using Russian Service

Now that what Russian service is has been explained, the next step is learning the basic techniques that must be mastered in order to perform this service. They are presented in sequential order, as one would encounter the skills while performing Russian service to one individual. Some of the steps are repeated in the following section, but as this type of service is so very precise, the repetition seemed to be appropriate.

1. Use a fresh serving fork and serving spoon for each dish. Rest the fork in the hollow of the spoon, which is the lower utensil. Potatoes and vegetables require different sets of utensils; a sauce requires its own spoon.

   Two spoons are not used together. A single utensil is never used alone for food items. For delicate items, two forks may be used.

2. Hold platters parallel to the floor at all times. The platter is placed longitudinally along the axis of your forearm—along the length of the arm, so the narrowest part of the platter is placed between the guests.

   The platter extends to the elbow, not above. It is held only by the forearm, wrist, and flat palm of your *left* hand (regardless of preference or being right-handed or left-handed).

3. To serve, begin with a *lady* (all ladies are served first, then gentlemen).

   Stand slightly behind and to the left of the person to be served, your feet together and back straight. Step forward with your *left* foot, into the space between the guests, placing the platter between the guests and over the table space.

4. Lower your body using your legs and keeping your back straight. Your *right knee* will approach the floor if the position is correct, and your right foot will be back, in the aisle.

5. Keep the platter level, parallel to the table. If there is any sauce on the plate (e.g., au jus with roast beef), it will spill onto guests and/or the table if not absolutely level.

6. Lower the platter until it is approximately *1 inch* above the plate to be served, and overlapping the rim of the plate by about an inch or so (this prevents drips from landing on the tablecloth or guest— any drips or spills land either on the platter or on the plate—there is nothing else in between).

7. Don't allow the platter to rest on the guest's plate, or try to serve from a platter held higher than 1 inch above the guest's plate. If the platter is held too high and something spills onto the guest's plate, it will splatter onto the guest's clothing. Always keep platters 1 inch above the guest's plate when serving. This is very difficult to do and will take practice.

8. Place the lower utensil (the spoon) deep in the palm of your right hand (utensils are always in the right hand, as the platter is always in your left hand, regardless of right-handedness or left-handedness).

9. Hold the lower utensil with your little finger, curling your finger somewhat around the base of the utensil. Let the utensil pass under your ring finger, and across your middle finger, at about the first joint.

10. Grip the upper utensil (fork) between your thumb and index finger of your right hand about midway between the tines and the base of the fork. The tines of the fork should rest in the hollow of the spoon. The bases of both utensils should be in the back of your palm, near your little finger, one atop the other.

11. Make pincer movements by raising and lowering the upper utensil with your index finger and thumb, and by raising and lowering the lower utensil by moving the middle finger up and down.

12. Grasp the item with the utensils, scooping it into the hollow of the spoon for support. The upper utensil, the fork, is used to steady the item en route to placement on the plate, so it will not roll off the spoon or lower utensil.

13. Keep the tines of the fork always facing up. While it may be easier to "stab" the food and put tine marks in it, it is unacceptable for fine service. Use the back of the tines to steady the food.

Mastering the first two areas—knowing what to do and how to do it (the skills)—prepares one for the third and final requisite area of knowledge needed to perform Russian-style service professionally: How to serve a whole table.

Technique: Serving a Whole Table Using Russian Service

1. Check to ensure clean hot or cold plates have been placed.
2. Uncover the platter.
3. Drape a clean folded (quarters, lengthwise) napkin or service cloth along your left arm and hand to insulate your arm and hand from the hot platter. The napkin or service cloth should not extend beyond the platter, but be totally covered by the platter, running from the elbow to the palm. Excess, if any, can be folded at your palm end, giving added insulation to your hand area.
4. Place the serving spoon and serving fork in position on the platter (nested into each other, in an easily accessible position).
5. If a sauceboat is on the platter, place it at the far end, away from you, and toward the guest. A separate spoon is inserted into the sauceboat, with the handle of the spoon resting in the pouring spout.
6. Present the platter to the host of the table, from the host's left side.

Move counterclockwise, to the host's right, to the first female guest's left side to serve.

7. Step forward with your left foot and lower your body using your legs, keeping your back straight, until the platter is 1 inch above the plate rim.

   Keep the platter level at all times by keeping your back straight and not bending from the waist to lower the platter, else any juices on the platter run to the end of the platter near the guest and spill.

8. With your right hand, pick up the utensils and serve the items. If sauce is desired by the guest, pick up the second spoon (in the sauceboat), make sure it is filled with sauce, and sauce the item, being sure to nape it, and not cover it with sauce. Replace the sauce spoon in the sauceboat.

9. Position the food on the plate, using the face of a clock as reference points:

Meat	4 to 7
Garnish	3
Starch	12 to 2
Vegetable	8 to 10

10. Replace the utensils on the platter. Rise, keeping your back straight, and lift the platter above and between the guests' shoulders, never lifting directly over a guest's head. Rock your weight back onto your right foot, bringing the platter and your left foot back into aisle space.

11. Proceed forward, in a counterclockwise direction, around the table to the next unserved female guest. If all females are served (or none are present), serve the men at the table.

12. If teams are used (two or three servers serving one table), they should be evenly spaced around the table so each serves one-half (if there are two servers) or one-third (if there are three servers) of the ladies. Each begins serving a lady, then moves to the next unserved lady, and so on. When all ladies (and children) have been served, the gentlemen are served.

Family Service

Family-style service involves placing large bowls or platters of food items on the table, and allowing the guests to serve themselves. The increase of limited-menu specialty restaurants has encouraged the use of family style service for several courses, especially in the South. Courses typically served family style include soup, salad, vegetables, entrees, and dessert, which is just about the whole meal.

Some establishments serve only the soup or salads family style, while others serve all of the courses family style. Servers often portion the soup into the soup tureen or the food onto the platter in the kitchen, which makes them responsible for making the food attractive to the customer, including the garnishing, before placing it on the table.

Some restaurants serve the main course on a plate (American style), or from a platter or wagon style with side dishes family style. Other restaurants serve the whole meal family style, especially if the entree is southern fried chicken with white gravy, or other traditional family-style dishes. Many restaurants in the Amish country around Lancaster, Penn., and in the South serve family style, and are as well known for that style of service as for their food.

English, or Butler, Service

English, or butler, service is a combination of Russian, or platter, service, and family, or "serve-yourself," style. English service consists of arranging prepared food on trays with handles. These trays are held by a butler, who, beginning with the lady to the right of the host, circles the table counterclockwise, stopping at the left side of each guest. At each guest the butler positions the tray so the guest can serve himself or herself, using serving utensils provided on the tray. The following list highlights the basics of butler service.

General Rules of Butler Service

♦ Plates should be preset on the table. *Clean plates* are served from the *right* side of guests, using the *right* hand, traveling in a *clockwise* direction around the table.
♦ "Butlers" or servers approach the guests from the *left* side, holding prepared trays of garnished food at a level approximately 1 inch above the rim of the guest's plate, but not touching the plate. The tray or platter must be *level*.
♦ Serving utensils are on the trays or platters.
♦ Guests *serve themselves* from the tray, using the provided utensils, then replacing them.
♦ The "butler" or server moves *counterclockwise* around the table, serving *ladies* before *gentlemen*.

Buffet Service

In banquet service, which may be plate (American), platter (Russian), or buffet service, the emphasis is on organization and efficiency. Servers are asked to serve up to 30 people each at one time, in a room that may be hundreds of feet from the kitchen. Stamina, physical strength, and skilled, experienced hands are necessary to be a good banquet server with plate or platter service. Organization and courtesy are the requisite skills for servers in a buffet line.

Buffet service consists of preparing food in the kitchen and arranging it attractively in large portions (for many people) for presentation to the guests. The food is placed in a line along a "serving table," which might be a straight line, a curve, a serpentine, or several smaller lines. The guests proceed along the buffet line or lines, first picking up a plate, then requesting portions of foods that appeal to them. A guest may try any of the selections, and return to the table for additional portions until that platter or chafing dish or carving station is extinguished.

Buffets can be as elaborate or as simple as the host desires, from spectacular centerpieces and carved ice displays to simple trays of hors d'oeuvres.

Usually servers stand along one side of the line, serving the guests, while the guests travel the length of the food line, picking and choosing the food items they wish to try. With plate or platter service, the server's contact and conversation with the customer are minimal as the server is always moving, running for the next course, or to clear the last one. In a buffet line, the server needs to be attentive, courteous, and polite. Usually there is little conversation, perhaps pointing to and explaining the food in one chafing dish or another, but sometimes the guests will stop to chat.

Increasingly, buffets are being used for banquets to feed large numbers of people where the food choices can be made in advance, and the formality of a sit-down meal is not required. Buffets are particularly effective when it is desired that guests "mix and mingle," having a chance to talk with each other, for instance, at wedding receptions, open houses, and business receptions for customers or introducing new products.

Fast-Food Service

Fast-food service usually refers to self-serve establishments, cafeterias, or places where there is a limited menu and customers are "served" in a matter of minutes. Items are chosen and placed upon a rectangular tray either by the customer or by a server, and the customer moves on— either to a table (if the server loads the food items onto the tray) or to the next station if it is self-service.

"Deluxe" fast-food service is fast service without the rectangular trays, that is, fast table service. It can be a diner or "family" restaurant where high turnover is desired. Unfortunately, often very little attention is paid to service. Getting the food and beverages to the table and served—it doesn't matter how—seems to be the house policy at many establishments.

The largest percentage of tableservice is this type of fast-food service since a large percentage of restaurant business, in terms of customers served, occurs during the lunch period when customers want fast service. The usual lunch period being 1 hour, a person cannot spend more than 45 or 50 minutes in a restaurant. The essence of fast-food service is giving the customer the impression of dining leisurely, while in fact speeding up the food service so the meal can be completed in less than 50 minutes and the server can turn over the table, feeding more people.

Efficient service—that is, efficiency of motion—is of the essence in fast-food dining, whether it is a traditional fast-food franchise or a diner. There can be no lost time. The server must make every trip to the table and the kitchen significant. Setting the table, order taking, serving the food, presenting the check, and clearing the table must proceed automatically and with precision. Orders must be grouped so that several tables can be served at once, and servers don't return to the kitchen empty-handed! While this is true of all service, it is paramount to those in high-volume establishments, taking precedence over correct procedures many times.

Arm Service

Arm service refers to the practice of carrying dishes and even glassware to the table on the arms, without using trays. Arm service can be used in conjunction with tray service (bring the food to the approximate service area on a large oval tray and then serve the tray to the table using arm service) or in lieu of tray service, utilizing American or French style of service at the table.

In operations using arm service, servers generally handle three, four, or more plates at one time. Two or three are held in the "carrying" hand and one in the "service" hand (left hand for American service; right hand for French service).

Some servers become adept at handling up to five main course dishes (two in one hand, two on the same arm, and one in the opposite hand) without disturbing the food on the plates. For American-style service, three or four plates are held in and on the right hand; service is with the left hand. For French-style service, three or four plates are held in and on the left hand, with service from the right hand.

When beverages are served using arm service, generally two or three glasses are carried in the left hand and one or two in the right. However, up to four glasses can be carried in one hand and two in the other. Virtuosos can manage five cups and saucers in one hand and two in the other, although two or three in one hand and one or two in the serving hand is the norm.

When you are handling several plates, glasses or pieces of flatware simultaneously, it is important to do so professionally, efficiently, and hygienically. Arm service can be professional and done in conjunction with American- or French-style service, or it can be helter-skelter, serving any plate in any order. It is this helter-skelter method that gives arm service its bad reputation in many instances, which is not totally deserved.

Arm service leads to poor service only when servers serve any plate, in any order, from any direction, to whoever gets it, rather than planning in advance who gets what entree, who should be served first (the ladies), and so on. Many servers stack plates on their arm as they are readied in the kitchen (rushed by the chef or expediter yelling at them to get the food out of the kitchen) rather than taking the extra time to stack the gentlemen's plates first, then the ladies' plates so as to serve "ladies first, gentlemen last."

In other words, arm service often leads to sloppy service in the interest of expediency. However, sometimes that's all that's required in many food establishments, and the customers can still be served in a fast, efficient, and friendly manner. Anyone who provides more in the way of service is supplying those extras that differentiate great service from just service. And it's not just arm service that takes a beating—any style of service can be performed well or sloppily!

General Rules of Arm Service

1. Stack plates to be served in the reverse order of service:

   · Stack gentlemen's plates first.
   · Stack ladies' plates last.
   · Last plate picked up will be the first plate served.

2. General rules of service *do* apply:

   · Serve ladies before gentlemen.
   · Hug the customer (don't reach in front of or over a customer if possible).

3. If serving American style, stack dishes on the right arm and serve with the left hand, traveling around the table in a counterclockwise direction when possible.

4. If serving French style, stack dishes on the left arm and serve with the right hand, traveling around the table in a clockwise direction when possible.

5. Coffee cups should be stacked in only one layer.

   If cups are stacked directly atop each other, the cup on top will have a soggy bottom from the bottom cup's steam and sloshing, making a mess on the table when it is placed. Also, the cup that was on the bottom may have grease, dirt, or germs from the bottom of the saucer resting on the surface where the customer places his or her lips.

Three

C·A·P·T·A·I·N

The captain is often the first person guests meet and interact with after the front desk personnel (the maitre d', host, hostess, coat-check personnel). The captain sets the tone with the guests for the entire meal. If the captain is sloppy, the chances are the meal service will be perceived as sloppy. If the captain is friendly, yet professional, the chances are that the meal will be perceived as pleasant, and the guests will want to return—the desired end result.

This chapter details how a captain can set the tone to be friendly, yet professional. It also provides techniques for professional service, and ideas on merchandising—selling. Much of a captain's job is selling. Sales are the basis of the restaurant business—selling the food, the wines, the ambience, the service. Then whatever has been sold (ordered) must be delivered.

The moment a guest walks through the door, the selling process begins. The first smile, the first hello to the guests are all part of the sales process. Anyone who interacts with the guest is a part of the selling process. Those who have the responsibility for primary interaction with the guests are those who are also responsible for the sales, the return of guests, the repeat customers, the good word-of-mouth advertising.

A captain may take an order perfectly, flambé steak Diane tableside flawlessly, create impeccable cherries jubilee, but if he or she does not smile, does not make the guests feel welcome, does not sell the guests on the restaurant, then it's all useless—the guests will probably not come back.

Salesmanship involves promoting the food, wines, beers, sodas, ambience, and goodwill of the restaurant, so customers really do want to return again. That's what restaurant service is really all about.

How do you make someone feel welcome? Follow the steps outlined in the Introduction:

♦ Create a positive experience for your guests.
♦ Make your guests feel at home. Say "Hello" and ask them how their day is going if it is appropriate. Watch the table for signals suggesting they need attention; change ashtrays, and refill water glasses and coffee cups often. Let them know that you're happy that they're there, that they made your day!
♦ Smile, smile, smile.
♦ Sell, sell, sell. Suggest options to the guests, various appetizers, beverages, desserts.

❖ JOB DESCRIPTION: CAPTAIN

Job Summary

As leader of the service team, the captain is primarily responsible for ensuring that guests receive proper service, enjoy their meal, and want to return. The captain achieves this goal by providing guests with the highest possible standard in service.

A captain must be personable, be a people person, and be able to "read guests' minds"—being at the table before they wave their hands to get attention. The captain must be a proficient server capable of teaching the workings of a station, its organization, and its smooth operation; must possess excellent communication skills; coordinate team members; and ensure that everyone cooperates.

The captain must know the menu in detail—the ingredients, the preparation, the sauces, and the garnishes—so as to be able to answer guest questions and sell the food better. The captain must also know the wine list intimately—what wines complement what food items, and why.

The suggestive selling, or "upselling," of items such as specials, wine, liquors, desserts is a prime responsibility of the captain, increasing both check averages and tips. Showmanship in the dining room is the captain's responsibility—tableside cooking, flambéing, or the making of tableside dishes.

Another part of the captain's job is to ensure an orderly and staggered seating of the station so the team can properly serve all customers. If the team is overloaded, it is the captain's responsibility to alert management or the maitre d' so the seating of that station can be slowed, and the team given time to catch up.

Captains are held responsible for the servicing of all guests in their station, and therefore they must know where all team members are at all times, what they are supposed to be doing, and approximately how long each task should take. Captains provide leadership and organization for the team and are the primary sales representatives for the restaurant. The captain's role is crucial to the guests' enjoyment of their meal, the efficient functioning and professionalism of the service team, and the success of the restaurant.

Duties and Responsibilities

Prior to Opening of Dining Room

♦ Be on duty at least 30 minutes prior to the start of service, in uniform, well-groomed, and ready to work.

♦ Find station; learn names of servers and busser who will be on your team; and know station numbers, table numbers, and team members.

♦ Ensure that team members are ready to work; well-groomed; in full uniform; mentally alert; and knowledgeable regarding policies, procedures, menu items, and wines.

♦ Ensure that the station, including tables, chairs, carpeting or flooring, and sidestands, are clean, fully equipped, and neat. Correct placement, if necessary, of any tables and chairs. Dust or clean chair seats and banquette cushions if necessary.

♦ Check sidestand for proper setup (see Chapter One) of silverware, china, condiments, coffee- and teapots, water pitchers, pepper mill, linens, napery, clean menus for appropriate meal period, and wine lists.

♦ Check tables for proper setup (see Chapter One).

  · All pieces of silverware in a place setting parallel to each other and perpendicular to the edge of a square or rectangular table
  · Entree knife and entree fork 12 to 14 inches apart, to allow for the placement of entree plate between
  · Top of B&B plate even with the top edge of the tines of the entree fork, or B&B plate above the tines of the entree fork, per house policy.
  · Knife cutting edges pointing to the left
  · At tables with an even number of place settings, the settings opposite and parallel to each other (the entree fork and entree knife of opposite place settings being in a straight line across the table, all the way around the table)
  · Table linen being of appropriate design (if any) for that room; design centered; colors bright, not faded; linen in good condition, not soiled, stained, or torn.

♦ Review menu and check blackboard for specials of the day, soup, melon, sorbets of the day, and so on. Note all specials and "86" items, including wines.

♦ Sign out guest checks prior to opening. They are usually with the cashier or manager.

♦ Ensure that the service team has completed all assigned preservice responsibilities before the daily staff meeting, if the operation has one.

♦ Ensure that captain "house duties," if any, are completed prior to the service staff daily meeting (which most operations have 15 or 30 minutes prior to opening). These duties, which often rotate by station, may include the following:

· Checking of cake orders for the dining room for that meal period
· Ensuring that the blinds (or curtains) in the dining room are in the proper position, and that they are uniform—all up, or down, or where they should be
· Ensuring that sufficient napkins have been folded
· Noting and announcing to the staff at the staff meeting the "daily board," including all "86" items and wines, daily specials, melon, and sorbets

During Service

♦ Assist the maitre d' in seating guests.

♦ If a table setting is removed from a round table, remove the chair also, if feasible, to allow the guests to space themselves equidistantly around the table. This should be done prior to the guests' being seated.

♦ Pull out the tables and/or chairs when guests are arriving and leaving.

♦ Greet guests using their names if it is appropriate to do so. (If not known, obtain names from the seating card.)

♦ Present menu and wine list, and ask for beverage order and food order, if possible, within 2 minutes of guests' being seated. The captain should take as many orders as possible within the stations, and advise the front server when he or she should take an order.

♦ Sell cocktails, wines, and appetizers by suggesting possibilities. If alcoholic beverages are ordered, make sure the guests ordering such are of legal age for the purchase and consumption of alcoholic beverages.

♦ If a guest requests advice on wines, suggest a few wines in different price ranges, from different countries, describing each. Do *not* mention price—point to the wine suggestions with a pen, and allow the customer to note the price. Open and pour wines ordered (see the second guide in this series for details of wine service).

♦ Describe food items and specials, if asked to; suggest wines that complement the food items chosen.

◆ Sell vegetables, side dishes, tableside cooking, tableside preparation of items using the suggestion technique described in Chapter Two.

◆ Ensure busser fulfills initial tasks of serving hot bread and butter and water, if requested, and provides follow-up.

◆ Use seat designation system when taking an order, as described in Chapter Two. Usually the guest facing the kitchen is number 1. Circle the seat numbers of ladies as the order is taken. Proceed clockwise around the table.

◆ Ensure the servers do not ask who is having what, but use the seat designation numbers to serve the correct food to each guest.

◆ Ensure service team serves all courses in proper sequence, in a prompt manner, and in accordance with all service procedures.

· Placement of flatware and appropriate condiments (e.g., ketchup for french fries) *before* the food/soup arrives
· Drinks within 10 minutes of being ordered
· Appetizers within 10 minutes of being ordered
· Entrees within 30 minutes of being ordered
· Complete lunch service within 50 minutes of the guests' being seated, unless the guests request leisurely service.

See discussion of the timing of service at the end of Chapter Two.

◆ Take flatware from the sidestand upon a napkin-lined plate for use on a table during service. Flatware should never be removed from a set, empty table.

◆ Make sure soiled wares are cleaned properly, from the right side of the guest, using the right hand and stacking onto the left, promptly when the guests are finished.

◆ After the guests have finished their entrees, suggest desserts, sorbet, and/or coffee, espresso, cappuccino, dessert wines, and/or liqueurs. Offer cigars if in the smoking section. Crumb table (see Chapter Two) if another team member has not done so.

◆ Present guest checks upon request (or following house policy). The captain is responsible for correct check encoding and total, presentation of check, and collection of legal tender.

◆ Bid guests "Good morning," "Good afternoon," or "Good evening" as they leave, regardless of the tip.

◆ Ensure quick resetting of all tables in the station.

◆ Keep station clean and tidy at all times. Ensure that trays with dirty dishes are taken to the kitchen as soon as possible.

◆ Ensure that coffeepots, teapots are refilled with *hot* coffee/tea regularly. Refills of coffee should be offered to customers regularly, without their having to ask.

◆ Ask a busser or porter to sweep the station as often as necessary (floors should have been checked before service began).

- ◆ Ensure that the station is in proper order at the end of the shift: all tables reset; the station neat, clean, restocked.
- ◆ Make sure the service team has accounted for all unsettled checks before leaving the premises. At the close of the shift, any unused checks should be returned to the cashier to be accounted for.

❖   # GROUP SALES

Sales to groups of people, usually 15 or more in a party, are referred to as "group sales." To facilitate prompt service, a limited menu is offered. The seating is within public dining rooms (the a la carte dining rooms), and not in a private (banquet) room. The service is completed, start to finish within a specified time frame, often 2 hours. Captains coordinate the service of group sales, assisted by their regular team, or if it is a large group sale, by several servers and bussers.

Groups will have chosen their menu prior to arrival from several alternative group sales menus. See Figure 3.1 for examples. This enables the kitchen to prepare for expeditious service so the meal can be completed within the specified time frame. It also allows for faster turnover of tables.

Often timing is important to the group, as well as to the restaurant. For example, if the group is dining, and then going to a show, it is imperative that they are finished by 7:30 P.M. for an 8:00 P.M. show time. In any case, because of the competitive rates of group sales menus, the groups are not paying for the privilege of lingering! It is important to note that the group usually must vacate the seats reserved for them by the time specified on the contract as the finish time of the meal. Even if the group has arrived late, they must leave by the finish time. This allows the restaurant to rebook those seats to another group or to guests not in a group.

It is the captain's responsibility to ensure that the group leaves on time, whether they arrive on time or late! It is also the captain's responsibility to ensure that they enjoy the meal—word-of-mouth advertising is the best kind!

As the captain of a group sale, you need to do several things prior to the group's arrival and immediately upon their arrival to facilitate service. These tasks are outlined below, along with the order of service for a group sale using a four-member team. All members of the team work together to make everything happen quickly, and all work equally hard. For group sales, the term "server" is used for a person doing various tasks, even though it may be the captain or busser doing that task. Whoever is best able to do a particular task at a particular time does it, regardless of title.

GROUP SALES MENUS

LUNCH 1

Melon with Lime
Fresh Fruit Supreme

* * *

Assorted Breads

* * *

Fusilli with Seafood and Lobster Sauce
Cold Grilled Chicken Breast, with Radiatore Pasta Salad
Quiche Lorraine, with Seasonal Vegetables

* * *

Chocolate Cake
Praline Ice Cream

* * *

Coffee or Tea

$27.

LUNCH II

Chilled Melon, with Prosciutto
Home Smoked Norwegian Salmon
Tortellini with Sun-dried Tomatoes,
Basil and Cream Sauce

* * *

Assorted Breads

* * *

Tossed Salad with Vinaigrette dressing

* * *

Roast Sliced Filet of Beef, Bordelaise Sauce
Fillet of Sole Primavera, Lemon Butter Sauce
Roast Half Chicken, Tarragon Sauce
... All of the above served with Potatoes
or Rice and Seasonal Vegetables ...

* * *

Chocolate Mousse
Grand Marnier Charlotte with Raspberry Puree
Praline and Strawberry Ice Cream Cake with
Chocolate Sauce

* * *

Coffee or Tea
$33.

LUNCH III

Mozzarella, with Tomatoes and Pepper Salad
Home Smoked Norwegian Salmon
Seafood Terrine, Shrimp, Lobster and Sole
with Lobster Sauce
Pineapple Bowl with sliced Seasonal Fruits

* * *

Assorted Breads

* * *

Caesar Salad

* * *

Salmon Steak with Riesling Wine Sauce
Grilled Filet Mignon, Sauce Bearnaise
Roast Loin of Veal, Basil Sauce
... All of the above served with Potatoes
or Rice and Seasonal Vegetables ...

* * *

Chocolate Cake with Praline Ice Cream
Creamy Cheesecake with Sour Cream Topping
Fresh Strawberries (in season) with Schlag

* * *

Coffee or Tea

$42.

BRUNCH

Fresh Fruit Supreme
Chilled Melon with Prosciutto
Home Smoked Norwegian Salmon

* * *

Eggs Benedict, Hollandaise Sauce
(Maximum 25 guests)
Roast Sliced Filet of Beef, Bordelaise Sauce with
Seasonal Vegetables and Potatoes
Fusilli with Assorted Vegetables, Grilled Chicken, Sun-
dried Tomatoes, Red Onions and Cream Sauce
Quiche Lorraine and Seasonal Vegetables
Fillet of Sole Primavera, Lemon Butter Sauce with
Seasonal Vegetables and Potatoes or Rice

* * *

Croissant and Schnecken with Jams, Jellies
and Sweet Cream Butter

* * *

Chocolate Cake
Praline and Strawberry Ice Cream Cake
Cheesecake with Sour Cream Topping

* * *

Coffee or Tea
$35.

Please select one item for the group from each section separated by asterisk (*)

FIGURE 3.1   Examples of group sales menu.

The tasks that must be done before a group arrives include the following:

Prior to the Group's Arrival

1. Get a copy of the group's contract, containing the menu and terms, from the manager or group sales director.
2. Determine from the menu the flatware and glassware needed, as well as drink status (are the drinks included in the price? If so, what drinks—sodas, wine, beer, cocktails? How many? Or are cocktails to be available on a C.O.D. basis?).

If drinks are to be C.O.D., put drink tents (or other notice of drinks available and prices of each) on each table. Drink orders then will be taken upon the arrival of the group, and paid for by each member of the group when he or she is served.

3. Introduce yourself to the banquet chef, mentioning the name of the group being served. This allows the chef to place your team with a particular group, in the event that there are several group sales going on simultaneously. When it is time for the entrees, you want to pick up *your* group's food, not another group's!

4. The team must set tables, using the specified linens and flowers (if any were specified). Preset as much as possible, so the group can arrive, take off their coats, and begin eating. Preset all of these:

   · Flatware, including dessert
   · China, including cups and saucers
   · Glassware, including water and beverage glasses (wine glasses if having wine, soda glasses if having soda, and so forth)
   · Salt and pepper shakers
   · Bread and butter should be prepared and placed on each table 15 minutes prior to the arrival of the group (sometimes they arrive early and you want to be prepared for this).

5. The team must prepare the appetizers, or, if the kitchen is preparing them, transport them to the dining room.

   If the team must prepare them, go to the kitchen, usually the pantry area (all group sale appetizers are cold), and ask the chef the portion size and garnish, if any. Plate the appetizers. Wear plastic gloves—don't touch the food (e.g., melon slices) with your fingers!

6. Set the appetizers on the tables 10 minutes prior to the group's anticipated arrival.

7. Pour ice water into the preset water glasses 10 minutes prior to the group's anticipated arrival.

Upon arrival of the group, these are the tasks to be performed:

Upon the Group's Arrival

1. Get the final head count from the group's leader; tell the chef so the number of entrees can be adjusted (usually the final count must be within 10 percent of the guarantee figure).

2. Have the team serve beverages. If there are pitchers of soda or milk, pots of coffee, or carafes of wine, begin pouring.

   If C.O.D., then go to each table. Get the drink order of each guest. Open a check for the group and enter the beverage orders. If special drink prices have been prearranged, use those prices.

3. While one or two servers are taking care of beverages, and you are giving the final count to the chef, the remaining servers can be clearing appetizer plates of those who've finished.

4. When all appetizer plates have been removed, two servers go to the kitchen to get clean, empty plates, while two servers go to the kitchen to get platters of food.

5. Groups are served Russian, or platter, style. Therefore, begin by placing the empty entree plates from the right, with the right hand.

   Keep the stack of dishes on the left arm, and proceed *clockwise* around the table.

   If the entree will be hot, use hot dishes. If the entree will be cold, use cold dishes.

6. Serve the food Russian style (detailed in Chapter Two).

7. After the meal, while two servers are clearing entree plates, one server should fill coffeepots with regular coffee, decaffeinated coffee, and tea. Another server prepares the dessert in the kitchen—cutting and plating the cake, or placing prescooped scoops of ice cream into goblets and topping them with sauce, and so forth.

8. Serve dessert, coffee.

9. Check the menu/contract to see if the check is to be presented to the host of the group. Sometimes parties are billed directly to the tour organizer, and the tour group members should not see the bill.

   If drinks were C.O.D., money should have been collected as soon as they were served. Otherwise, at the end of the meal, everyone may be running for the bus or to catch the show, making it impossible to collect for beverages served earlier.

10. Present the check to the tour group leader, if it is to be presented.

11. Bid "Good day," "Good afternoon," or "Good evening" to guests as they leave.

The next few sections of this chapter—"Beverage Drama," "Special Dining Room Personnel," and "Advanced Techniques"—describe options available to restaurants to create opportunities for increased sales. If any of these ideas are implemented the captains and other staff members will have to learn how to use these merchandising tools effectively and how to do these procedures correctly.

These are ideas many restaurants might wish to implement to help increase tips and customer satisfaction by providing something different. These ideas have proved profitable at other operations. How-to details for the ideas mentioned in the next few sections are discussed after their presentation in the last section of this chapter.

❖ BEVERAGE DRAMA

In the service of spirits, wines, and other beverages, understatement is the ultimate in classic elegance: unetched, clear, thin lead crystal wineglasses; piperstem sherry glasses; a silver or burnished stainless steel coffee service. But although the classically elegant accessories and tabletop items may be affordable, they may also be overlooked by guests because of their simplicity.

Bold showmanship and apparent drama are much more noticeable to some customers. While in a classic restaurant it would be outlandish to decant wine in the dining room using a decanter and candle (it would be done at the side station), the show is appreciated by guests in less formal, although very expensive, establishments where it is part of the entertainment of dining out.

Management determines which aspects of beverage showmanship are incorporated into the operation. The show should fit the arena! In some cases, a house specialty, a unique concoction or a standard but rare cocktail, can be appealing to some guests. People frequent certain restaurants because those restaurants make the effort to produce exceptional daiquiris from fresh fruit or assemble genuine zombies, or margaritas, or whatever.

Specialized or distinguished glassware can also be used to draw attention to various drinks, especially those being highlighted and promoted by the restaurant. For example, an oversized all-purpose glass or an extra-heavy "cut crystal" highball glass or rocks glass, or long-stemmed or colored-stem wine goblets can stimulate customers' interest in drinks. Pewter or glass-bottomed pewter mugs help spotlight beers and ales, as do oversized pilsner glasses or the traditional German ceramic mugs.

Accessorization also includes the garnishes. Consider adding fresh flowers on the rim of the glass (rinsed in water first). Tropical drinks often have brightly colored umbrellas and cuts of various fresh fruits on a skewer. These and other items, such as plastic monkeys or other animals, can be used to add color, interest, and conversation pieces to drinks.

However, accessorization and specialized glassware can add to the level of beverage service only if you practice the basics: frosting glasses properly; coating the rims of glasses with sugar or salt evenly (frozen strawberry daiquiris, margaritas); and muddling sugar, bitters, an orange slice, and a cherry (an old fashioned).

Wine

Display

A wine display can be an important focal point—it can be very impressive and can sell wine. Some restaurants have built in a wall as a "wine cellar," being either open to the dining room air or enclosed with controlled temperature and humidity. Some restaurants have a selection of every wine on the wine list (or offered, if no wine list is prepared) on a shelf or in a window for guests to see.

If wine is displayed, a primary question should be answered: Is the wine being displayed also for consumption? If so, the wine should be stored on its side, to keep the cork in contact with the wine to prevent spoilage. Also, if the storage area is not temperature and humidity controlled, regular rotation of stock (first in, first out) must be ensured, as well as fast turnover. Wines deteriorate with exposure to heat, light, and vibration, so storage in a dining room is not ideal. If it's there, keep it on its side, and use it fast.

If the wine displayed is not for consumption, it must be evident to the guests that they are "show" bottles, without being too obvious. While it's not necessary to allow dust to accumulate on the bottles to indicate that they are display models only, a small placard near the storage case or shelf indicating that these are the selections available from the wine cellar suffices.

Accessorization

In a beautiful wine glass, even a rather mediocre wine seems to taste very good. A fine crystal tulip-shaped glass adds dignity to even the youngest commercial product. Again, this is part of showmanship, where guests want to have the elegance built into their meal.

There are some glasses, however, that, to a connoisseur, point out the faults as well as the strengths of the wine! A tasting glass that is truly well shaped will focus the bouquet of the wine so that it will linger near the mouth of the glass, showing off the wine's strengths and weaknesses. There are a very few restaurants that offer these true "tasting" glasses for wine. If they are available, "Les Impitoyables" as they are known, are usually presented to guests upon request only.

The wrong glass can also be wonderful! For example, for wine service some operations use large, oversized Burgundy wineglasses that resemble elongated tulip-shaped glasses with a smaller cylindrical mouth area. They may stand 12 to 18 inches high. These glasses are meant for special situations, but nobody can deny their theatrical effect.

If several wines are served at a banquet, the display of a half-dozen different glasses per person is dramatic, especially when they are arranged precisely, mirroring the opposite cover! Fragile glasses on excessively long stems, fishbowls, hollow-stemmed tulips, saucers, gallon snifters, and other unusual, odd, forgotten, or new glass shapes can amuse, enthrall, and entertain guests.

Wine Service

While wine service, and the how-tos, are detailed in the second guide in this series, the basics of wine service are detailed below. Some dramatic examples are given, but flourishes in wine service should be professional (if the atmosphere is informal, they might be a bit more daring), and stop short of overchilling, overheating, overshaking, or overhandling the wine—that is, stop short of damaging it.

Some General Rules for Wine Service

♦ Buckets and stands can be used for all wines. Ice is used only for wines that have to be chilled, generally white and rose wines and champagnes and sparkling wines.

♦ Decanting cradles can be used for all red wines when the wines are placed on the table or served from a sidestand, even if the wine has no sediment. However, if the establishment uses decanting cradles *only* for those wines with sediment, then other red wines should be stood on the table or sidestand.

♦ All wines can be decanted into crystal carafes in front of the customer, although few are. (Only wines with a sediment really have to be decanted; then it is done in the "wine cellar" or at the service bar.)

♦ The sommelier, wine steward, or server tastes a few drops of the wine from a silver taste-vin cup if that is the policy of the operation. Generally, unless there is an official sommelier, this practice is considered outdated, and the guest tastes his or her own wine. Unless it is refused by the guest, members of the service team do not generally taste guests' wines.

♦ An elaborate lever-action corkscrew can be used instead of the professional waiter's corkscrew if the operation has one.

♦ Champagne corks can be popped instead of slowly eased from the bottle at a gala celebration (e.g., New Year's Eve) when decorum and proper service are thrown to the wind. (The proper way to open a bottle of sparkling wine is to ease the cork from the bottle with a whisper, without a pop, resulting in more champagne to drink and less champagne to foam out of the bottle.)

Wine Service Techniques

Before a bottle of wine is poured, it is presented to the guest who ordered it. The presentation serves the following purposes:

1. Allowing the guest to see if the wrong bottle of wine may have inadvertently been brought
2. Allowing the guest to see if the vintage of the bottle agrees with the vintage printed on the wine list
3. Giving the guest the opportunity to see the wine he or she has ordered before it is opened

Technique: Presenting a Bottle of Wine

1. Approach the guest from his or her *right* side.
2. Hold the base of the bottle in the palm of your left hand, with a folded, clean napkin immediately beneath the bottle. Hold the neck of the bottle with your right hand.
3. Tilt the bottle so the guest can easily read the label.
4. Do *not shake* or make any sudden motions with the wine. There may be sediment in the bottle, especially if it's an old, red wine; you do not want to distribute the sediment throughout the wine.
5. Announce the name of the wine and the vintage (year) if there is one. For example, "Chateau d'Yquem, 1973, Madame."

Technique: Opening a Bottle of Still Wine

After presenting the wine, proceed to open it. Open red wines at the table, either on the tabletop, or in your hands, at the right side of the guest who ordered the wine. Open white wines, rose wines, and chilled Beaujolais wines in an ice bucket, which has been brought to the table, filled two-thirds to three-quarters full with ice water.

1. Using the knife portion of your waiter's corkscrew, cut the foil just below the second lip of the bottle, going all around the bottle with one motion. *Do not turn the bottle*—the label should be facing the customer at all times, if it is a red wine. And, if a white wine, you do not want to move the bottle unnecessarily. Twist your wrist, and turn your hand, not the bottle!
2. Remove the foil, and wipe the top of the bottle and the top of the cork with a clean napkin.
3. With the corkscrew, insert the point in the center of the cork, and twist, inserting the corkscrew until you reach the end of the cork, or until the corkscrew is fully inserted. *Do not turn the bottle—turn your hand!*
4. Pull the long handle end of the corkscrew down, so the lever rests on the lip of the bottle. With one smooth motion, pull the cork straight out of the bottle.

   If it is a long cork, the cork will not come out in one pull. Finish pulling the cork out with your hand. Unscrew the corkscrew.

5. Using a clean corner of the napkin, clean the bottle rim of any dirt or cork fragments. Wipe from the inside of the bottle to the outside, so you do not deposit any particles that were on the rim into the bottle!
6. Present the cork to the guest who ordered the wine.

Technique: Opening Sparkling Wines

Champagne and other sparkling wines are sealed with mushroom-shaped corks, which protrude from the bottle, and are, in turn, covered with twisted wire and a foil cap. This is to ensure that the cork stays in the bottle, as sparkling wines are under enormous pressure (about 6 atmospheres).

1. Be sure that it is *cold* (approximately 42°F). Use an ice bucket with salt, if necessary, to chill quickly.
2. Do *not shake* the wine while transporting it from the bar to the table, or while opening it.
3. Take the sparkling wine from the ice bucket. Use a clean napkin, and dry the bottle. Remove the foil.
4. Twist the wire hoop, and remove the wire, *keeping your thumb over the cork* so that it cannot pop.
5. Remember to keep the bottle slanted at 45 degrees. Keep your thumb on top of the cork at all times.
6. The pressure from the carbonated wine could force out the cork at any time once the wire has been removed. In addition, the motion from moving and handling the wine shakes it, and pressure is increased inside the bottle.
7. Holding the bottle at the 45-degree angle, and making sure the bottle is not pointing at anyone, *twist the bottle* to loosen the cork.
8. As you feel the cork start to loosen under your thumb, apply reverse pressure so *you* control the release of the cork from the bottle.
9. The cork should slide out of the bottle, without a pop!
10. Maintain the 45-degree angle for about 5 seconds to equalize the pressure. Then pour in two motions for each glass—The first pour will foam, then subside; the second will fill the glass.

Technique: Serving Wine

Wine is not necessarily poured once the bottle has been opened. For instance, quality red wines improve if they are allowed to stand at room temperature, opened, for about an hour. Only champagne and sparkling wines will lose quality (their bubbles), if allowed to stand, opened, for even a short period of time.

1. Approach the guest who ordered the wine from the guest's *right* side.
2. Pour about 1 ounce into the glass. Allow the wine to be tasted, and either accepted or rejected.
3. Proceed to serve the other guests at the table, serving ladies before gentlemen.
4. Pour from the *right* side of the guest, using your *right* hand, and traveling around the table in a *clockwise* direction, if possible.
5. Pour all the ladies first, then the gentlemen. Fill each glass with about 3 to 4 ounces of wine. The wineglass should be *no more than half full* at any time. If an oversized goblet, the 3- to 4-ounce pour may only barely fill the bottom. However, for champagne and sparkling wines, fill the glass to nearly the top, as detailed in step 10 below.
6. Replace the bottle in the ice bucket, if one is being used, or on the table, if not.
7. When pouring the wine, always hold the bottle *above the rim* of the glass. Never allow the bottle to touch the rim of any glass—it is the weakest part, and you do not want to chip it.
8. As you pour each guest's wine, make sure the label is visible to each guest. They want to know what is being served.
9. To pour, use your wrist. Tip the bottle slowly downward, until the wine begins to flow.

    When 3 to 4 ounces have been poured, or the glass is between one-third and one-half full, pivot the wrist, and twist the neck of the bottle upward, so the wine will not drip from the bottle.
10. Pour champagne or sparkling wines in two movements. First, pour about an ounce or two into the glass. It will foam and bubble. Allow the bubbles to subside, *then* fill the glass (about 3 to 4 ounces).
11. Touch the tip of the bottle with a clean, folded napkin to catch any drip from the bottle. This way, it will not drip onto a guest's clothing or food.
12. Refill glasses as they are emptied. Don't wait to be asked. However, if there is not enough for another round, ask the host if another bottle should be brought to the table *before* you finish the first bottle. That way, you know whether to skimp on the last portions or not.
13. If a second bottle is ordered, if it is the same wine, then the host gets a new glass. Everyone else can use the same glass for the same wine. The host needs a new glass to taste the new bottle, in the event that it is a "bad" bottle of wine. If it is a different wine, then *everyone* gets a new glass.

❖ SPECIAL DINING ROOM PERSONNEL

Special dining room personnel and special cooking techniques used in the dining room can enhance the guests' meals. While the captain might not be the person performing all of these techniques, he or she generally oversees the techniques, or sells the services of the specialists or various tableside preparations to customers at each table.

Therefore, a detailed description of some common dining room meal "enhancers" follows:

◆ Rolling cart servers (merchandising one course)
◆ Single-item passers (merchandising one item)
◆ Course specialists (preparing one course in the dining room)
◆ Employees, and guests, doing actual cooking in the dining room

These options can be important because your customer often identifies service with showmanship. While there may be culinary merit in some tableside preparations, the average customer is much more impressed by the show, the service team's attention, and the personalization of service, than by some real or fancied improvement in the quality of the dish.

Finding service personnel qualified for tableside preparation is difficult, but there is no reason why complex tableside preparations should be the only attention-getting device used in the dining room. It is possible to give customers personalized service with any course, using relatively inexperienced personnel and specialization—assigning one individual to one special task (e.g., flambéing coffees).

Classical servers are expensive and difficult to find, because they have many talents: They can serve graciously, carve fish and meats in the dining room, make salad dressings, serve wines, flambé, and so forth. However, if someone is taught to do only one of those tasks, with practice, that individual will be great at it! And that's the idea.

For example, from the customer's point of view, elegant platter service consists of being offered food items from a platter. The customer does not really care about all the other aspects of platter service, because if they are done properly, they will not be noticed.

The average part-time server might not make it through an evening of traditional platter service without getting burned, dropping a tray, pouring soup in somebody's lap, or panicking. However, with 15 minutes' training, a dramatic uniform, a gargantuan basket of popovers, and a pair of tongs, he or she can perform admirably in placing rolls of the customer's choice on B&B plates.

Customers appreciate the special service of popovers or rolls and the server who served them as much as they would a classical server serving three courses from a platter, because the quality of service customers enjoy—the attention to themselves—is present. In operations and in regions where classical service would not be appropriate because of the general informality of the ambience and the clientele, special service personnel can add new and exciting dimensions to service. Four types of special dining room personnel and/or techniques that can be used are discussed next.

Rolling Cart Servers

Dining room displays and dining room rolling carts can be attended by dedicated serving personnel. For example, dining room personnel dressed in chef's uniforms can attend carts of hors d'oeuvres. When guests require hors d'oeuvre service, the cart and "chef" are sent to the customer. (A more detailed discussion of the how-tos follows later in this chapter.)

Passers

In many operations it is possible to economically justify one or more nongratuity dining room workers on three bases: (1) they are potential trainees; (2) they can often replace a paid server, by allowing each server to handle more tables; and (3) they add an exciting dimension to service. For example, going out to dinner is often regarded as the evening's entertainment. Guests are pleased by the repeated attentions of specialized passers who have no other responsibilities than offering a single item (e.g., rolls, relishes, desserts). Passers give the customers something to talk about or something to do while waiting for their dinner. The passer also relieves the other servers of doing particular tasks.

Each operation has different opportunities for this treatment: Some might require several passers for a single item (e.g., bread), while others might require only one person presenting a succession of items (e.g., passing hot towels, offering complimentary cigars and/or flowers). Some make the item passed a signature item, as the corn pancakes served at Jimmy Kelly's in Nashville, Tenn. There they come, fresh and hot from the kitchen, a pile of 2-inch-across corn pancakes delivered to each table in lieu of bread. And, they're replenished with hot, fresh batches throughout the meal!

Another signature item that is passed to guests is the hot, fresh, home-baked French bread served at Bistro De Lion, also in Nashville. It melts in the mouth! What a first impression to make on guests as they walk in the door and are seated, what a great way to say that they are welcome and that you are glad they came.

Items lending themselves to this approach include the following:

- Lightly scented hot towels.
- Specialty breads, especially hot items such as corn muffins, popovers, garlic bread, oat bran muffins, pumpkin muffins, sour dough bread sticks, corn pancakes, and fresh baked breads.
- Complimentary hot and cold hors d'oeuvre items, such as canapes, puff paste products, dips, and crackers.
- Relishes and chutneys, including fresh crudities and dips for the health-conscious (e.g., dill-yogurt dip).
- Several kinds of butter (e.g., garlic butter, herb butter, horseradish butter).
- Steak sauces of every description in their original bottles. Most people will choose the better-known commercial products, but everyone is impressed by being offered a variety of regional specialties!
- Small portions of homemade sorbets—such as lemon, lime, grapefruit, raspberry, champagne, or liqueur—served in stemmed goblets and offered between courses as an "entremets" or "intermezzo."
- Bite-size portions of specials or new items—items the chef may be wanting to run as specials, but wants some customer feedback on first. Send bite-size portions to the guests (complimentary) and ask for feedback either at the table (to the captain, maitre d', or owner) or on the way out of the establishment (to the host/hostess, maitre d', or owner).
- Wine, if included in the price of the meal. A "keg" of wine can be carried and offered to guests of legal age by an employee, sort of a traveling sommelier, offering goodwill, good humor, and acting as a "traveling ambassador" of the restaurant.
- Meal closers: mints, cigars, flowers, chocolates from a large box, petit fours, homemade cookies.

Course Specialists

Unlike servers and passers, course specialists do more than carry, present, and sell the food items. Course specialists are taught the preparation (and some flourishes) for the dish they will be cooking. The specialists should be well merchandised with menu notes, table tents, and direct selling by servers. Also, the specialists sell just by being in the dining room, preferably in a uniform or outfit that is appropriate to the decor and ambience of the restaurant, but also flashy enough to be noticed by the diners (perhaps a different color bow tie or apron).

A good example of a food item for a specialist is coffee—plain or flaming coffee, or coffees, as there are many variations, or coffees and teas! The person could be equipped with a samovar of water, a dozen blends of coffee and tea, and a little chatter about each one. When the customer chooses a blend, the coffee specialist brews it on the spot and serves it. Or brews it, then blends in the flaming liquors!

In operations specializing in fresh seafood, a fresh oyster station can be implemented. The station, perhaps built like a seafood "bar" or a small rowboat filled with ice, seaweed, and a dozen or so varieties of oysters, can be wheeled to each table and guests can choose oysters that are opened before their eyes. The concept can be expanded to include more than fresh oysters—clams, oysters, mussels, and sea urchins can be included!

It might be effective to position the fresh clam and oyster station, with the person opening the fresh seafood in full fisherman's regalia, at the entrance to the restaurant, or perhaps in the bar or lounge area. That way customers there who are waiting for a meal or who have just stopped in for a drink or two can be tempted by the lure of fresh seafood to have "just a few"—dozen! The person in charge of the station can also prepare orders for tables in the dining room.

Other course specialists include

- ◆ The traditional sommelier or wine steward
- ◆ A salad maker for Caesar salad or the restaurant's own preparation
- ◆ A crepe maker, using Brittany-type crepe griddles
- ◆ An omelet maker
- ◆ A caviar specialist with a complete silver service
- ◆ A sushi and sushimi specialist
- ◆ A pasta Alfredo specialist, finishing off cooked pasta in a semi-hollowed-out wheel of Parmesan cheese, scraping fresh Parmesan cheese from the sides of the "bowl"

Cooking in the Dining Room

There are various ingenious, colorful, and healthy ways to actually cook in the dining room. One traditional method is on an open hearth where customers can watch their fish or meat steaks or hamburgers being prepared in front of them.

Having a broiler station or an auxiliary broiler station in the dining room as a showmanship device involves a significant initial capital investment—for a charbroiler, a ventilation system, and the sprinkler system it requires to meet fire codes. Also figure the lost sales from the space in the dining room the station occupies (generally one less table of four for every 20 square feet the station occupies). However, once the initial investment is made, the continuing cost of the broiler station is minimal.

A number of restaurants have an open hearth as their focal point, and even make it their theme. Guests feel involved as they see their food being seared; it is a healthy preparation method, with very little grease or fat being used. There is the crackle and the spitting of the fire when natural fat lands on the hot coals. Customers love the sight, the sounds, and the smells of an open hearth.

An open-hearth broiler station also is appealing to many operations because customers prefer broiled meats and fish ("fleshy" fish, such as salmon steaks and swordfish steaks, can be successfully broiled).

Another approach to the open-hearth idea is to open a wall to the kitchen and replace it with triple-pane glass. The large window allows guests to "participate" in the cooking, and to see the hearth, the grill, and the cooks while avoiding the smoke, the cooking odors, the kitchen sounds, and the kitchen heat. The American Bounty restaurant and the Escoffier Restaurant at The Culinary Institute of America in Hyde Park, N.Y., and Chef Sigi's in Nashville, Tenn., have used this approach, as have many other restaurants throughout the United States. It is effective, yet maintains the separation of the kitchen and the dining room.

Other low-fat methods of cooking in the dining room include "oriental" cooking stations: either Japanese griddles set into customers' tables or a separate dining room cooking area, or Chinese woks in a cooking area. These oriental cooking stations are not suitable for rolling carts because of the intense heat source required for the wok. But since the foods are generally prepared in the kitchen, and cut into small pieces, the finishing in the dining room can be done very effectively.

Guests' Cooking in the Dining Room

Offering the customer the opportunity to participate in the cooking is effective showmanship because it transforms a meal into an experience—the guests are doing something, they are busy, and they are often learning, as well.

Customers cooking their own meals is effective since service personnel are minimally involved; there is minimal accessorization (fondue pot, skewers, hot stones), and there are only minor production demands from the kitchen's viewpoint. It's relatively easy for everyone, and fun for the guests.

Customer cooking has three major variations:

- The hot pot or fondue pot
- Grills and/or hot stones
- The lobster pot

Hot Pots and Fondues

Cheese fondues have long been the most common example of customer "cooking." With these, guests dip bread chunks into a hot melted cheese mixture (usually Gruyere and Emmenthaler cheeses). The popularity of fondues and the availability of the accessorization from commercial suppliers have prompted operations to explore other fondues:

♦ Chocolate fondue utilizes the same fondue pot, forks, and accessories as cheese fondue. Instead of melted cheese, however, guests dip cake, fruit, or cookies into melted chocolate, sometimes flavored with liqueur.
♦ Fondue Chinoise offers the customer the opportunity to cook bits of vegetables and tender meat, such as filet, in a pot of well-flavored stock. When the raw ingredients have been consumed, the guests can enjoy the now very flavorful broth.
♦ Seafood fondue differs from fondue Chinoise only in the ingredients: shrimp, bits of white-fleshed fish, raw oysters, clams, and so on.
♦ Fondue bourguignonne represents an essential variation: The cooking medium is oil and butter, and it is not consumed. The customer "fries" tender meat and then dips it into prepared sauces.

Fondue Chinoise, seafood fondue, and fondue bourguignonne can be made in the traditional fondue pot or in a Mongolian hot pot, available from oriental supply stores. A traditional fondue pot is necessary for cheese and chocolate fondue sauces because of their thick consistency, which gets even thicker as they reduce over the flame.

Grills and Hot Stones

The popularity of backyard grills and hibachis on fire escapes of apartment buildings attests to our enjoyment of food cooked over an open fire and cooking it ourselves. It is possible to bring this same kind of enjoyment and flavor to the guests at restaurants. Some dining rooms incorporate grill tables under attractive hoods. For example, one has a 12-foot-wide circular table surrounded by chairs. In the center, there is a live charcoal fire under a copper hood. Guests are supplied with long metal skewers of meats, vegetables, and sausages.

Even without a permanent installation, customer grilling is possible. You can present individual-size, 500°F hot granite rocks (generally measuring 8 × 8 inches × $\frac{3}{4}$ inch thick) on a ceramic or wooden holder to each guest. On this holder surrounding the hot rock are the pieces of meat, fish, and/or vegetables to be cooked by the guest, with the sauces for dipping alongside the main items.

Guests place the food items on the hot rock, which retains its heat for about half an hour, and cook the foods to their desired degree of doneness. The food items should be small or julienned to ensure even cooking.

Foods appropriate for this type of cooking include

♦ Tender cuts of chicken, steak, veal, lamb, or pork
♦ Tiny sausages
♦ Mixed grills and mixed broilings
♦ Shrimp, lobster, scallops
♦ Riblets of pork, veal, or lamb
♦ Skewered items
♦ Marinated chunks of meat
♦ Vegetables, including red, green, yellow peppers; scallions

Lobster Pots

While lobster pots are not used in many restaurants, they are especially suited to those establishments along a seacoast featuring fresh lobster and can be an attraction for guests who like to do things for themselves.

Guests choose a lobster from a tank, and, instead of their turning the lobster over to the chef, a tank attendant places it in a net bag. The guest then signs his or her name to the tag on the bag and places the bag in the lobster pot (which can be anything from an old-fashioned black cauldron to a brick chimneylike steamer), cooking it for a recommended amount of time. The basic idea of lobster pots can be extended to other items: clambakes, spit-roasted chickens, even grills.

❖ ADVANCED TECHNIQUES

In many dining rooms, captains are in charge of doing the "show" or "entertaining" the guests. This can entail simply conversation, or it can mean rolling out the carts, first the appetizer cart, then the salad cart, then a gueridon, using French service to saute a main entree tableside; then rolling out the dessert cart and flambéing some coffees; and perhaps finishing with a liquor cart! While management decides whether they'll be implemented or not, it's up to the captain to make sure the execution of the tableside techniques is flawless.

The remainder of this chapter reviews special advanced techniques. Some of these techniques are useful in a great many restaurants, some are useful in only certain types of restaurants with leisurely service. These techniques include

- ◆ Rolling cart service
- ◆ Carving in the dining room
- ◆ Flambéing
- ◆ Tableside cooking
- ◆ Tableside preparation of cold items

❖ ROLLING CART SERVICE

Service from a rolling cart is dramatic. The silent progress of the cart across the dining room awakens all sorts of pleasant expectations in the diner. Whatever is served is ennobled by the regal presentation.

In addition to affording an opportunity for flourishes and grand gestures, rolling carts offer several practical benefits. For instance, if the rolling cart is used for a main course which needs no further kitchen preparation, it allows the dining room staff to aid the kitchen by selling the item from the cart. In a hectic dinner hour, 40 to 50 orders from the cart can mean the difference between quality preparation of the rest of the menu and rushed cooking. Or, it can prevent having to add a cook in the kitchen.

Or, if the rolling cart is used for appetizer service, antipasti selections, salads, or desserts, it has the effectiveness of a main course display with the added advantage of personalized service for the guests. To guests, it seems the ultimate in hospitality to be offered a few strawberries or an extra dollop of whipped cream, along with the piece of chocolate cake they have chosen. On the menu, suggestive selling words, such as, "Exotic treats and delicious confections from our rolling carts," evoke an interest that the same items listed on a dessert menu may not.

Bouillabaisse or any other soup or stew made of a variety of odd-shaped ingredients can be a house signature item, and also a main attraction. For example, if served from a giant copper cauldron, it can be a roving focal point in the room; served in a bowl from the kitchen, it loses that special appeal.

Rolling carts can make you seem proficient—you appear to be doing something difficult when preparing a customer's plate. The cart gives the air of mystery and professionalism that is associated with classically trained servers. In reality, all that you may be doing is saving a trip to the kitchen for dessert and saving the operation a pantry person to plate it.

Types of Rolling Carts

There are several types of rolling carts that are commercially available in a fairly wide price range. However, the restaurant should not ignore the possibility of having one or several carts built to specifications for special purposes. For example, there is no reason why a boat-shaped cart cannot be built from quality plastic and filled with ice to offer an assortment of opened shellfish worthy of Neptune. Or a cart to house a charcoal fire or a "witches' cauldron" cart that takes standard stainless steel inserts can be built. Whatever type of cart is used, be sure to spend time learning how to maneuver it quietly and seemingly effortlessly in the dining room. Make it look easy, even if it isn't!

Cold Rolling Carts

The basic cold cart is generally a rolling table with end flaps for resting plates while serving, a shelf for storing plates, and a tier for additional display. Generally there are structural differences between the expensive and the inexpensive models, even if they appear similar. The expensive ones are usually built of thicker and sturdier materials, and are reinforced in areas subject to stress, torsion, and wear and tear. If there are wheels, the more expensive ones usually have ball bearings. Once the use and the wear-and-tear factors have been determined, management (with your help) can decide on the model(s) appropriate for your restaurant.

Also consider the materials used. Those with higher-grade materials (e.g., stainless steel, copper, and/or brass) are more expensive than those built of fiberboard and contact paper or wood veneer; the price is directly proportional to the quality of the materials used.

Cold rolling carts are often used for the display and serving of desserts, cheeses, and hors d'oeuvres, or the making of salads. If used exclusively for cheese, they are often fitted with either butcher's block surfaces or (preferably) marble slabs.

Hors d'oeuvres in flat trays or in bowls can be placed on a rolling table, but their presentation is more effective if a dedicated hors d'oeuvre wagon is used. Usually it resembles a small ferris wheel which you rotate by turning large handles at each end. The hors d'oeuvre trays pivot in the frame. The only difficulty these carts present is that they must be restocked frequently since, as favorite items are emptied, the wheel becomes unbalanced.

Liqueur carts and wine carts are specially fitted to hold bottles and glasses. They can be very dramatic if the cart allows a large display of bottles and glassware. Some of the newer models also have casks with spigots for carafe wines.

Hot Rolling Carts

The traditional rolling cart for hot food service is the voiture, sometimes called a roast beef wagon. It consists of a dome-shaped hood, either a sphere or a rounded cylinder, that slides into itself when it is opened. The hood covers a compartmentalized metal base that accommodates inserts filled with sauces or vegetables, while a central compartment houses a large joint of meat. There is a compartment with water beneath the base and a place for Sterno (canned heat) under that. Usually the wagon has plate holders, shelves, and flaps for service. They are often very ornate and beautiful, and act as a natural centerpiece for the room.

Better models cost several thousand dollars. The difference between the inexpensive and the expensive models is the metals, materials, and workmanship. The best are sterling silverplate and mahogany wood; the less expensive models are stainless steel and wood veneer. There are also attractive units in copper.

Someone skilled in dining room carving is a necessity if one of these carts is used. It defeats the purpose of having a fantastic cart if there is no one who can carve well! (Detailed carving instructions are included later in the chapter.)

Food from Rolling Carts

Hors d'oeuvres, soups, salads, main dishes, desserts, wines, and liqueurs all lend themselves to service from rolling carts. The number of courses which can be served from carts is determined by the amount of space available in and adjacent to the dining room for holding carts when they are not in use. Cart service should stop short of turning the dining room into a bus station where servers jockey among the tables for position or line up to "take their turns at the wheel." Except for the very large facility that uses a number of carts for each course almost as a booster station for the servers, three carts seem to be the workable maximum. Any more and the essence of showmanship—novelty—is lost.

Hors d'Oeuvres

For the operation, the principal advantage of hors d'oeuvre service from a rolling cart is that it allows the restaurant to use preprepared, cost-controlled products along with a few easy-to-prepare salads. For example, a 16-tray wagon can be filled with some of the following:

- Homemade mozzarella with fresh plum tomatoes and fresh basil in an olive oil marinade
- Shrimp and bean salad
- Anchovies and roasted red peppers
- Pickled figs
- Alaskan king crab salad
- Snails and wild mushrooms with herbs
- Ripe olives

- Dilled brussels sprouts
- Cucumber, dill, and yogurt salad
- Stuffed baby eggplants
- Virginia baked ham and Jarlsberg cheese rolls with Dijon mustard sauce
- Marinated herring or sardines from Sicily
- Marinated artichoke hearts
- Smoked oysters in pâte à chou puffs
- Smoked salmon on seven-grain bread
- Assorted spicy sliced sausages
- Fresh fruits

Soup

Soup sales can be increased by effectively merchandising from a wagon. The image of a copper cauldron seems to make the prospect of soup more inviting: "Homemade soup du jour from our copper kettle" sounds better than simply "Soup du jour."

Salads

Salads from a rolling cart offer several opportunities for a sale to a customer. A special salad wagon, with a sunken bowl holding a bushel of mixed exotic greens (dandelion, chicory, baby endive leaves, Bibb lettuce) and satellite bowls holding toppings and dressing, can make a salad hard to refuse. Or the salad setup can be an empty large wooden bowl where you prepare the salad of the customers' choice (usually made for two) before their eyes. Usually it is a Caesar salad or a house specialty salad, where it is not the ingredients, but the show that is the main attraction. See "Tableside Preparation of Cold Items (pages 190–195)."

Main Dishes

You usually won't serve main dishes from a cart except as part of a buffet or private party where they might be wheeled from table to table, with you offering the guests a bit of this or a bit of that and adding to the festive atmosphere. Otherwise, guests generally prefer their food prepared fresh in the kitchen.

If main dishes are to be served from a cart, those that are hard to serve or less spectacular when divided into portions—such as large joints of meat, whole birds, and fish—are suited for rolling cart service or buffet service. Some examples are steamship rounds (roast beef), legs of lamb, legs of veal, haunches of venison, fresh hams, baby lambs, turkeys, geese, pullet-sized chickens (poulade), whole poached salmon, and whole braised bass. Other dishes that lend themselves to this type of service are sauce dishes that can be dramatically assembled (such as curry with all the condiments, or chicken or veal marengo), and dishes that are hashed when they are served (such as game pies, beef en daube, moussaka, lasagna).

Desserts

Whereas people often find that a single portion of any one dessert is too much to eat, a dessert cart gives customers the opportunity to enjoy a variety of desserts, eating only a small portion or bite of each. The cart also gives the operation an opportunity to feature the pastry chef's specialties and suggestively sell many more desserts than might be sold otherwise, especially with many people being health-conscious. When guests see healthy, fruit-based desserts and low-calorie desserts next to the rich chocolate and cream desserts, they truly do have a choice, and can afford (calorie-wise and cholesterol-wise) a sampling.

Desserts on a cart might include

◆ Fresh fruit salad
◆ Poached pears with sauce anglaise or raspberry puree
◆ Fresh fruit tart of the day (apple, blueberry, raspberry, kiwi—whatever is in season)
◆ Chocolate mousse
◆ Double chocolate cake
◆ Creme caramel or a custard or pudding
◆ Fresh grapefruit and orange compote
◆ Fresh fruit cobbler, plain or with whipped cream or homemade ice cream or gelato
◆ Cheesecake
◆ Rum cake or baba au rum
◆ Angel food cake, plain or with fresh fruit salad or grapefruit-orange compote topping

Liqueurs and Wines

Liqueurs and wines finish off a meal elegantly, and also increase sales. Customers can be watching a rolling cart, with elegantly displayed liqueurs and wines, being shuttled from table to table throughout their meal, or they may notice it subliminally. Either way, selling to them is easier at the end of their meal because they have already seen and tasted the drinks in their imagination several times.

Liqueurs and wines on a cart allow you to suggest particular bottles, especially the out-of-the ordinary ones, the ones people would love to try, but don't want to buy a whole bottle of. Few people can resist when a bottle of an old port or sherry or aged cognac that they've been wanting to sample is held before them. Wheeling the cart over to the table before asking if the customer would like an after-dinner drink is essential—let them see what's available, and sell the "new" ones on the cart, or the unusual ones!

 # CARVING IN THE DINING ROOM

Basic Carving Techniques

Guests are impressed with carving stations and with tableside carving. Not only are they assured that their portion is freshly cut, but they receive personalized attention and a show as well. Often items are served that are most attractive when whole—a whole sea bass, salmon, or Dover sole—or a joint of meat.

Carving stations and tableside carving require more skill and training than display courses or rolling carts, because the carver must be proficient in carving techniques. Usually the carver at a carving station is a chef or cook; the person performing tableside carving is a captain or senior person who is competent in carving and presentation techniques, French service (finishing the meal in the presence of the guests), and techniques for plating in the dining room.

The carver must be a good conversationalist, able to entertain the guests while the cooking, carving, and plating of the dishes is occurring. And, of course, this person must be immaculately dressed and groomed, since he or she represents the establishment to the guests, and spends a great deal of time at an individual table with those guests. It is imperative that the carver leave a good impression. The fundamentals of carving are equally applicable to carving stations and tableside carving, and are detailed below.

Carving Stations in the Dining Room

A carving station creates excitement in the dining room, allowing for the merchandising of cuts and items which because of their size are not generally served whole, and once cut, often are not as spectacular. Carving station displays can use these meats effectively, whether or not the food is actually cooked in the dining room.

Carving stations in the dining room must be impressive, immaculately clean and inviting, and cost-effective—in terms of food cost, labor cost, profit per serving, and merchandising or advertising effect. Especially effective are less expensive cuts or large cuts, if they can be merchandised. A steamship roast is more impressive and less expensive than a prime rib if the volume of sales can justify the cost of a carver and a piece of meat as large as a steamship round. Although a carving station needs only a means of keeping the meat hot and a place to cut, most operations attempt to make better use of the presence of a carver in the dining room.

Carving From a Rolling Cart

When food is served from a gueridon or rolling cart, the server coordinates efforts with those of the captain (or carver, if the captain is not doing the carving) using the rolling cart at tableside. The captain cuts the meat and places it on the plate, and the server completes the garnishing and service. This type of coordinated effort provides faster service to the guests—while one is carving, another is garnishing, and so on. Specialized carts can be purchased for roast beef and for steamship roasts.

Buffet Carving

If a regular buffet is offered to guests, a carving station can be made part of the dining room buffet. When several items are offered, this system has the advantage of allowing a permanent facility with adequate heating and holding units. Even infrared lights can be made permanent, with a decorative casing enclosing them, suspended from the ceiling. A steamship roast holder stand can be installed. Additional meats can be kept hot in a cabinet. Plates can be heated.

Either the servers or the guests can approach the carver. If guests serve themselves, pricing can be adjusted to allow for unlimited servings.

Cooking and Carving Displays

The most impressive displays include cooking as well as carving stations. Special units are available which allow a large steamship round to be hung in chains over a bed of coals or between heating units. The roast rotates slowly and self-bastes.

Other cooking stations use spits over charcoal or gas fires. The stations may be oriented horizontally so that the unit resembles a giant fireplace, or several spits and grills may lean together, in a tepee shape, over a bed of coals in the "floor."

Foods that are suited for cooking and carving stations are listed below. Many of these items can also be used for tableside carving stations; however, those that are quite large (e.g., steamship rounds) are suitable only for carving stations.

◆ Spit-roasted chicken
◆ Spit-roasted turkey
◆ Steamship rounds

♦ Haunch of venison
♦ Whole baby lamb
♦ Whole suckling pig
♦ Whole side of beef
♦ Baron of beef
♦ Whole roast veal
♦ Whole sheep
♦ Slabs of spareribs
♦ Mixed broilings
♦ Saddle of veal
♦ Whole ham
♦ Sirloin of beef

Carving at Dining Room Stations

Carving in a dining room is relatively easy if the carver understands the anatomy of the animal or fish being cut and if the items have been adequately prepared by the kitchen. The best training is several days in the butcher shop and several days in the kitchen, learning the natural "seams" of whole roasts and primal cuts, the location of bones, and the qualities of different parts of the same piece of meat.

Problems in the dining room usually involve lack of preparation for service or for being on display. Carvers have been known to scurry around fetching forgotten items or, forgetting that they are on display, touch their hair with their hands. Problems can also arise if carvers are sloppy in dishing out sliced meats—guests might not feel that they are getting their money's worth. If it looks elegant, it looks expensive; if it's sloppy, it appears to be of lesser quality.

Carving Station Guidelines

♦ Carving stations and equipment must be clean at the start of service, and kept clean throughout service.
♦ Only the highest standards of personal grooming are acceptable. Beards, sideburns, and mustaches, if present, must be well-trimmed. Hands and fingernails must be scrupulously clean, with no nail polish. No heavy after-shave lotion or perfume.
♦ Uniform must be clean and starched, without rips, holes, or stains.
♦ Carver must be extremely careful of personal behavior: no smoking, leaning, sitting, gum chewing, scratching, sneezing, coughing, and so forth.
♦ Guests who approach the station must be greeted and thanked as they are served.
♦ Food cannot be touched by fingers.
♦ Plates must be hot.
♦ Setup for the service must be complete at the start of the service.

◆ Knives must be sharp, but should not be sharpened in the dining room. Sharpening should be done before or after service.
◆ Knives must be handled carefully: not flipped, thrown, or abused.

Equipment and Preparations for Carving

Equipment

The carver generally uses a large (12-inch), broad-bladed knife for roasts and a shorter (7-inch), narrower, less flexible knife for poultry, as well as a two- or three-pronged fork with a safety guard on the shaft. For salmon a long, flexible, thin blade is used. The tools may be of modest, functional, professional quality, or they may be a good steel set with elaborate handles. For deboning fish tableside (e.g., Dover sole), a serving fork and spoon are all that are required.

The knives must be sharp to ensure good yields and clean cuts. Many restaurants use a professional service that supplies sharpened knives on a regular basis; otherwise, the carvers are usually issued knives and are then responsible for maintaining their own equipment. Sharpening stones and a butcher's steel can be used to keep the edge on the knife. These should not be used in the dining room itself, however. Poultry shears, if used at all, also remain in the kitchen. A "fish slice" of silver or stainless steel is needed for broiled or braised fish.

Kitchen Preparation

The kitchen has several responsibilities to the captain when an item is to be carved in the dining room.

Fish, especially salmon, may or may not have been smoked first. Salmon usually has the skin on the outside of the fillet, and has had the small bones along the fillet removed with a tweezers.

Before any meats are cooked, or after they are removed from the oven, any bones which are likely to give the carver difficulty should be removed—for example, the chine in ribs, and the ilium (hip) in ham and lamb legs.

The meat or fish must be cooked properly, to the desired degree of doneness. After cooking, all meats except steak should be allowed to sit for 20 minutes so the juices can be redistributed evenly within the roast or piece of meat and they can be carved easily. If the roast or meat is cut immediately after removal from the oven, the juices will run out, and the meat will taste dry. "Carry over" cooking will keep the meat hot for at least 30 minutes, and finish the cooking process.

All possible bones, skewers, string, and excess fat should be removed in the kitchen after cooking for aesthetic carving in the dining room. When an item is presented to be carved tableside, it must be suitably and attractively garnished, yet the platter on which it is served must have sufficient space to maneuver the item and work with the knife and other utensils needed.

It is also necessary to assemble the complete course, including garnishes and sauces, so the captain can serve the guests immediately after carving. There must be bowls, sauceboats, and platters filled with vegetables, potatoes, sauces, parsley, and whatever else is needed for the meal.

General Rules for Carving

In general, meats are cut across the grain. Steaks are the most notable exception; they are tender enough to be cut with the grain. In meats that present several grains, like center-cut leg roasts, the meat is divided at the natural seams and then placed so it can be cut across the grain. In all carving, the first rule is to conserve the natural juices so the meat will be tender.

Slices of hot meat should be six to the inch; slices of cold, eight to the inch. Lamb may be cut thinner (ten) and mutton, if it should be encountered, thicker (four).

Beef

Prime Rib   Position a rib roast on its heavy side. Plant the fork between the second and third ribs from the top. Make the first cut by pulling the knife toward yourself, parallel to the table. The required slices can be cut, then loosened at one time, or the carver may come up around the bone with each slice.

Rolled Rib   Cut a rolled rib like a prime rib. Position it vertically, and slice. There is no bone, so a full stroke can be used (cut all the way through the roast).

Steak   Remove any bone with the point of the carving knife. Then push the meat together into one pile on the cutting surface (retaining the heat) and cut into thin slices of 2 or 2½ inches across (not long strips). Cut the steak on an angle and not exactly vertically (at right angles to the table) if it is at all possible to avoid it. If cut on an angle, each piece will appear larger.

Fowl

Before carving, remove the legs and wings by cutting between the limb and the body until the bone is exposed, then gently and quickly forcing back the limb until the joint is laid bare. As these are ball-and-socket joints, they don't need to be cut through, but can be taken apart with the point of the knife.

There are two basic methods for carving the breast meat. The carver can insert a knife under the breast meat, loosen the meat from the breast bone, and remove the breasts. Then the breasts are cut in sections 1 inch wide. This method conserves the juices. In the second method, the breast is sliced in one of three ways.

◆ The slices can be taken longitudinally, following the general V shape of the bird.
◆ The slices can be slices parallel to the breast bone.
◆ The meat can be cut across the breast in a series of slices the full width of the breast.

With chicken or turkey, ask guests if they desire white meat, dark meat, or a combination of both. If white meat is desired, place sliced breast meat on the plate, following the chef's plating instructions, and garnishing accordingly. If a guest desires dark meat, separate the thigh from the leg at the joint. If it is a large fowl, slice the thigh meat off the bone. Place slices of thigh meat on the plate. If it is a small fowl (e.g., chicken), place the thigh, thigh meat, and one leg on the plate. If a combination of white and dark meat is desired, add some breast meat slices to the dark meat.

Any fowl can be sliced in any of these ways, but small birds lend themselves to the first method, duck and goose to the second, turkey and other birds to the third.

Small Birds   Duckling and small game birds can simply be split, divided as chicken, or if they are very small (e.g., quail or cornish hens), deboned and stuffed, which would be done in the kitchen. Duckling can also be cut into four pieces, in exact quarters. Partridge and pheasant can be cut into three pieces by dividing them in thirds lengthwise, making two legs with breast sections and the center breast portion served with the backbone.

Lamb and Mutton

Rack of Lamb   A rack of lamb, or for that matter any rack, can be carved in flat slices parallel to the line of the ribs. This can be accomplished by cutting away from the ribs, or by making a series of successively larger wedge cuts toward the line of the ribs.

Saddle of Lamb   The saddle of lamb and also the saddle of any other meat are best carved by first mentally dividing the whole saddle into fourths. Then half of one slice is cut at right angles to the backbone.

Afterward a wedge-shaped slice is made in this fourth by cutting toward the backbone in a parallel line, perhaps a half-inch away. Successive wedges are then cut toward the backbone, until that quarter is finished and another is started.

Forequarter of Lamb   The forequarter of lamb is first cut from the back with a slanting slash beneath the shoulder blade. Then the rack is carved as usual. The front leg is removed from the shoulder section and served as one portion. The shoulder is sliced across the blade bone.

Hindquarter of Lamb   The hindquarter is divided into the rack and the leg, and then these parts are carved separately.

Legs of Lamb and Mutton   Legs of lamb or mutton are cut in two ways: in slices at right angles to the bone, or in slices parallel to the bone. In either case, the thick, meaty section is placed on the far side of the platter or pan on which the lamb is being held for carving.

Cut a slice or two from the bottom to make a base, turn the roast, and starting at the shank end, cut either full slices or a series of parallel cuts to the bone, and then insert the knife under the slices, running it along the bone, to free them.

Veal

Most veal is carved like comparable cuts of lamb and beef.

Pork

Loin of Pork   When the chine bones have been removed by the kitchen, the loin can be cut into ribs. Otherwise, it is carved like rack of lamb.

Suckling Pig   Start a suckling pig by inserting the fork between the shoulders, straddling the backbone. Cut down the backbone toward the tail. Reinsert the fork in one of the split ends and rip toward the head, dividing the pig into long halves. Divide each half into a forequarter, a rack, and a ham. Slice the forequarter. Cut the rack into chops. Carve the ham.

Ham   Ham is cut in slices toward the bone through the fleshy section on both sides or, for a less attractive but more economical service, in slices parallel to the bone, starting at the shank. Hams like prosciutto or Westphalian are dry-cured and should be carved with the grain in thin parallel slices, starting at the shank end. The procedure is facilitated by using a ham stand.

Salmon

Salmon is often sliced as part of a buffet. In the kitchen the salmon is dressed and the small bones are removed from the fillets. Starting at the tail end, very thin slices are cut on the diagonal, at about a 38-degree angle to the cutting surface, not parallel to the cutting surface, but not at a 45-degree angle either. Each slice should be paper-thin and about 4 inches long, cutting across the width of the salmon fillet. With a large fillet, two "rows" can be cut, alternating first from the right side then from the left side, working up toward the head end of the fillet. Any dark flesh (as opposed to the salmon-colored flesh), usually found right against the skin, should be cut off before serving to the guests.

Tableside Carving

Tableside carving requires skill, dexterity, and a good eye for placement of the food on the plates, in addition to the usual server skills. As an initial venture, it is usually best to offer a few dishes that can be carved by captains or carvers after minimal instruction from the chef and some practice. After a few months of experience with those items, their success in terms of sales, customer acceptance, the skill of the service personnel, and the enthusiasm of the service teams for tableside carving can be evaluated. If cost-effective, tableside carving can be expanded to include additional items.

Foods Suited to Tableside Carving

There are five categories of items that are usually considered for tableside carving:

1. Items which are portion-cut from primal cuts: lamb chops, pork chops, sirloin steaks, filet steaks
2. Items which are really for two, but are cut in the kitchen: duck, chicken, whole fish
3. Items which are best presented by tableside carving, because they are much more attractive whole than cut: braised dishes, pot roasts, meats in a crust
4. Items which cannot be served effectively except by tableside carving: family steaks, turkeys, suckling pigs
5. Quality items which, once cut, cannot be readily distinguished from less expensive but similar items (e.g., Dover sole), and so should be shown whole to guests, then prepared tableside

Table 3.1 offers some suggestions for items suited to tableside carving in each category.

TABLE 3.1   Items Suited to Tableside Carving

Items From Primal Cuts, Carved for Two or More	
Sirloin steak	Mixed grill
Chateaubriand	Filet
Rib of beef	Porterhouse steak
Marinated steak	Lamb chops (rack)
	Pork chops (loin)

Items for Two	
Pullet chickens	Whole bass
Grouse	Duckling
Whole sole	Rabbit

Items Best Presented by Tableside Carving	
Beef tongue	Fish mousse
Braised beef	Veal Orloff
Beef Wellington	Lamb breast
Salmon Koulibiac	Shoulder of lamb
Game pies	Braised liver

Items That Should Be Presented by Tableside Carving	
Suckling pig	Poached salmon
Fresh ham	Haunch of venison
	Veal loin
Goose	Rump roast
Turkey	Roast sirloin

Quality Items That Should Be Presented at the Tableside	
Dover sole	

Equipment for Tableside Carving

Captains need all the standard carving tools—knives and a two- or three-pronged fork—and, if they are working with Dover sole, a serving spoon or fork. They need as well a place to work near the guests' table, a place to keep vegetables hot, a place to heat plates, the utensils and tools for that dish or item, and the gueridon or trolley.

There are several approaches to tableside carving. Rectangular tables can be fitted with a flap on one narrow side, with the customers seated only on the broad sides. The captain then pulls up the flap and uses it as a carving station. In certain dining rooms, sideboards can be used. The captain presents the dish and then carves it at a sideboard a few feet away.

The most popular and the easiest in terms of positioning the carving station and cleaning up is the low rolling cart or gueridon. Station one next to the table where the carving is to be done, proceed to do the carving, then wheel it away when finished. Some operations use more elaborate, higher carts, topped with butcher block wood fitted with racks and with a trough for meat juice.

Heat sources are necessary to keep the foods warm. Common sources of heat include the small heavy-wire food warmers that use either alcohol or canned heat, canned heat alone, or electric warming or carving trays. When sideboard carving is possible, each unit can be equipped with an electrically heated flat tray as well as a carving board.

Technique: Carving Tableside

Although the carving of specific items may differ, the overall service does not, except in a few minor details:

1. After placing the order, prepare for carving: Gather tools, plates, wagon, and cutting board, and position them so that the food can be served promptly.
2. Pick up the order, vegetables, and garnishes from the kitchen.
3. Light the heat source on the sideboard or gueridon, unless using canned heat, in which case it should have been lit. Place the vegetables, starch, garnishes where they will keep warm. Warm the plates.
4. Present the dish to the customers (if possible, to the host first, from the host's left side).
5. Make any relevant inquiries: "Would the lady like white or dark meat?" or "Would you like dark meat, ma'am?"
6. Carve, cut, debone, or divide the item completely on the serving platter.
7. If necessary (if the carving has taken more than a few moments) heat the platter.
8. Prepare the ladies' plates first (starting with the lady on the host's right), then the gentlemen's plates. If there are more than four guests, plates should be prepared in sets that will fit conveniently on the service station, or ask another server to assist with a second gueridon station, ensuring all guests will be served at approximately the same time with hot food.
9. Make the plate attractive. If the plate were marked with numerals, like a clock, the meat should be placed across numerals 4 through

7, any garnish or a separate sauce at 3, the potatoes/starch at 1 and 2, and the vegetable at 8, 9, and 10. The 6 is placed directly in front of the guest.

10. Don't touch the food with your fingers, or allow your fingers to touch the area of the plates with which food has contact.

Here is a finishing flourish to use with meats: When steaks, for example, chateaubriand or double sirloin, are cut, leave the trimmings and bits of fat on the platter after the dishes have been portioned. Take a plate, place it over the trimmings on the platter, and decorously squeeze the juices from the trimmings. Then spoon it over the prepared plates.

Training for Tableside Procedures

Every item that is prepared tableside should have extensive step-by-step documentation to follow, especially while learning to execute the tableside procedure. In addition to documentation, training is necessary by a carver proficient in the tasks and able to teach. This involves watching the carver demonstrate each procedure and talk about every step in the operation as it is performed. The carver must be able to break down complicated maneuvers into simple steps, and must have a good eye for noticing when a new captain misses a step or performs it improperly. And the carver must be able to instruct new captains, if they are performing a maneuver improperly, how to perform it properly—by showing and by talking.

Finally, practice is needed. New captains must practice, usually with each other while a captain adept in the procedure supervises. While this results in a high food cost while they're practicing, it is more than justified with the increase in sales of those items as soon as they are with customers, since those newly trained in each procedure will want to show off in the dining room, and will merchandise those items expertly as they perform the tableside procedure expertly!

An example of step-by-step documentation for a tableside preparation follows, the deboning of Dover sole, which is a popular dish, and usually deboned in front of the customer. Knowledgeable customers like to see the whole fish, as the shape of the Dover sole is the primary means of differentiating it from other members of the sole family. Dover sole being the most expensive, and most tasty to many, if it is ordered, customers want it delivered.

Similar documentation should be developed for every tableside item.

SAMPLE DOCUMENTATION: *Tableside Dover Sole*

DOVER SOLE PRESENTATION

Utensils Needed: Serving spoon and fork
Procedure
Once the Dover sole has been received from the kitchen, immediately take it to the dining room. Present it to the guest, in the bimetal (lined copper pan) in which it was sautéed.

Ask if the customer would like you to fillet (debone) it.

If the response is NO, return to the sidestand with the sole in the bimetal, and place it on a flat surface.

Remove the sole by gently loosening the skin from the pan with the serving spoon. Once completely free from the pan, lift the sole by placing the spoon under, and the fork above the sole.

Place the sole in the dinner plate, whole, and garnish. Serve to the customer.

If the customer's response is YES, return to the sidestand with the sole in the bimetal, and place the pan on a flat surface.

Remove the fin sections, top and bottom, of the sole by placing the fork gently into the fish meat at the edge of the bones, and pulling the fin bones away from the fish with the edge of the serving spoon.

Work on one small section at a time, holding the fish meat with the fork and separating the bones with the spoon.

Start at the HEAD area, and work gradually toward the TAIL, checking all areas for any fin bones you may have missed.

Place the sole on the dinner plate by gently loosening the skin from the pan with the serving spoon. Once completely free from the pan, lift the sole by placing the spoon under, and the fork above.

Place in dinner plate.

With the edge of the spoon, penetrate the meat at the center until the spinal column can be felt.

Gently separate the meat from the bone by moving the spoon downward, following the spinal column, working from HEAD to TAIL.

Remove the two halves of the exposed fillet by placing the serving spoon edge in between the bones and top fillet.

In a scraping-type motion, separate the fillet from the bones, working from the HEAD to the TAIL.

Gently slide each fillet half to either side of the plate.

At this point, the spinal column and bones (the skeleton) should be visible.

Place the fork under the spinal column at the head. Use the spoon to keep the dish in place. Lift the spinal column and bones up, and bend toward the tail. Snap off the spinal column at the vertebrae closest to the tail. Remove the skeleton to bimetal.

Arrange fillet halves on the plate.

Wipe the rim of the plate with a napkin. Garnish. Spoon any pan juices over the fillets.

Serve.

❖ FLAMBÉING

Flambéing is a variation of tableside cooking, although technically there is no cooking to be done! Much of the equipment and supplies are the same, and the effect—customers enraptured with the show— wonderful.

Flambéing is simply setting food alight in the dining room, largely for the entertainment of the guests, perhaps with some minor flavor enhancement. When done perfectly, customers enjoy it, willingly pay for it, and return for more!

Flambéing basically differs from tableside cooking in three ways:

1. The food is cooked in the kitchen by the chef, so the captain does not need to judge doneness.
2. It's easy—any captain who can light a match can flambé a dish.
3. Flambéing takes a fraction of the time needed for a tableside preparation—it is, therefore, practical to perform in busy restaurants without charging an outlandish price.

There is always the danger that upon discovering how easy this supposedly arcane act is, a captain's zeal for the procedure may border on pyromania (it truly can be dangerous). Flambéing, like other showmanship, is more dramatic and more effective in moderation.

Equipment

Most flambéing requires three pieces of equipment:

1. A cart on which to work
2. A lamp, stove, or heat source (e.g., rechaud)
3. Pans or vessels that can be easily handled in the dining room

Additional equipment—skewers, flaming swords, and chafing dishes—expands the flambé possibilities of the operation and embellish conventional tableside flambéing.

Carts

The most common cart for flambéing and other tableside preparation is simply a rectangular table 18 by 30 inches on four small casters called a gueridon (other carts may also be called gueridons), as described earlier under "Cold Rolling Carts." It is easily wheeled through the dining room and nestles nicely against the customer's table. Some versions have only two large wheels and are maneuvered like wheelbarrows. Others have shelves and hinged extensions. More complex versions incorporate a propane-fired stove.

Wheeled tables can be used if more space is needed. In most instances, these tables are purchased for tableside preparations like pressed duck, which can require two tables, and are only incidentally used for flambéing.

Lamps, Rechauds

The lamp or heat source for flambéing does not have to be as powerful as one that actually cooks foods. The food is already hot, and the spirits used in flambéing need only slight heating. If the operation plans to flambé only, then the least expensive system consistent with the general quality of the restaurant's equipment should be purchased. However, if tableside cooking is intended, then powerful units should be purchased.

Some who flambé prefer "flare" lamps, which are actually alcohol-burning stoves consisting of a reservoir for fuel, a wick with an adjustment screw (not unlike a kerosene lantern), a ventilated chimney, and a grid. In silver or copper, these lamps may be somewhat expensive. A less expensive alcohol device, of considerable versatility for heating, flambéing, and light cooking, consists of a wire cage with a small alcohol lamp in a universal joint that allows the captain to turn the stove without spilling the alcohol.

Most restaurants favor rechauds, two-tier metal devices that use Sterno, a solid jellylike fuel on the lower tier, with a snuffer regulator, and have a flat upper tier as the work surface. Other units using canned heat are even simpler, with little more than a place for a can of fuel and a rack to hold a pan.

Butane-fired units of various types are also available. While they are excellent, they are expensive, and local safety regulations may prohibit their use. Propane gas cylinders can be used, especially for stoves built into rolling carts.

Pans

Cooking in the dining room can require a number of specialized pans, or a few basic ones. Many restaurants have adopted a "crepes suzette pan" or "blazer," really a fancy copper frying pan lined with a corrosion-resistant nonreactive metal (e.g., tin, stainless steel, or nickel) as their all-purpose pan.

Some find it easier to flambé in variously shaped bimetals (or pans of two metals, usually copper on the outside for appearance and a corrosion-resistant nonreactive metal on the inside). These can be any shape, from round to oval to square, and any size. A crepes suzette pan can be a bimetal, although all bimetals are not crepes suzette pans. Plain stainless steel vessels or silverplate can also be used.

Sizzler plates have also been used. As long as the vessel can be placed over an open flame and does not react with alcohol to produce undesirable flavors, as cast iron does, it can be used for flambéing.

Flaming Swords

Specialty swords are made for flambé service. They resemble narrow military swords, except that the "cup" near the handle is inverted so that drippings are caught when the sword is held aloft.

Skewers and Skewer Sets

Meat, fish, and vegetables can also be flambéed on metal skewers or brochettes about 1 foot long. They can be plain metal or quite elaborate with decorated handles.

Chafing Dishes

A chafing dish consists of a small compartment for solid fuel or a can of solid fuel, a lower pan for water, and an upper pan for holding a sauce dish or a liquid. The flambéing is done in the upper pan.

Brandy Snifter Warmer

A specially fitted small heater, usually fueled by alcohol, for warming oversized brandy snifters.

Supplies

A restaurant with a bar has the supplies for flambé showmanship in its stocks of spirits, brandies, and cordials. No special products need be purchased, although some operations do use extremely high-proof specialty products made expressly for flambéing. On the one hand, these products are foolproof, since they can be ignited quite easily. On the other, due to their ease of igniting, one can start fires quite easily, spreading to jackets or hair or the tablecloth.

In addition, there is an argument for using a drinkable product in food that will be eaten. Quality liqueurs, cordials, and brandies leave their flavor in the food that is flambéed, as do the "flaming products," their flavor being somewhat bitter and distasteful. Also, guests enjoy seeing quality products being used in their foods and beverages.

Table 3.2 lists some flavors for flambé preparation, which products

TABLE 3.2   Flavors for Flambéing Food: Cordials, Liqueurs, and Spirits

Flavor	Product	Food
Almond	Creme de Almond	Any food . . . discreetly
Anise	Anisette Ouzo Pernod Ricard	Fish Lamb Vegetables
Apple	Applejack Apple brandy Calvados	Fruits Fruit pies Ice creams Pork
Apricot	Abricotine Apricot brandy Apricot liqueurs Apry	Fruits Lamb Fish Desserts
Blackberry	Blackberry brandy Blackberry liqueurs	Fruit Fruit soups Desserts
Cherry	Cherry brandy Cherry liqueur Maraschino Kirsch Kirschwasser	Vegetables Desserts Soups Sweet sauces Lamb Fish
Grapefruit	Forbidden Fruit	Fish Dessert

TABLE 3.2   (*Continued*)

Flavor	Product	Food
Orange	Cointreau	Fish
	Curaçao (in several colors)	Lamb
	Triple sec	Pork
	Grand Marnier	Desserts
		Crepes (suzette)
Herbs and spices	Benedictine	Any dish . . . with great discretion
	Chartreuse (yellow and green)	
	Izarra	
	Strega	
Peach	Peach brandy	Fruits
	Peach liqueur	Lamb
		Pork
Caraway	Kummel	Pork
	Aquavit	Vegetables
Cocoa	Creme de cacao (white or brown)	Desserts
	Chocolate liqueurs	Fowl . . . discreetly
Coffee	Creme de cafe	Desserts
	Kahlua	Fowl . . . discreetly
	Tia Maria	
Plum	Mirabelle	Fowl
	Quetsch	Fish
	Slivovitz	Red meats . . . discreetly
Tangerine	Aurum	Dessert
		Game
		Duck
		Fish
Mint	Creme de menthe	Dessert
	Peppermint schnapps	Lamb . . . discreetly
Raspberry	Framboise	Desserts
		Fowl
		Lamb
		Pork
		Red meats . . . discreetly
Strawberry	Fraises	Fowl
		Lamb
		Pork
		Red meats . . . discreetly
		Desserts

offer them, and some of the dishes to which they are suited. Beverages can be flambéed with any whiskey or liqueur of high enough proof.

Flambéing Basics

Flambéing, reduced to its basics, is setting alcohol on fire. Being that basic, the decision whether or not to flambé is based on other factors than the practicality of flambéing: It is practical under many circumstances.

Flambéing does not require elaborate uniforms or ingredients to make it work. The paraphernalia and pretensions with which most restaurants accompany flambéing is showmanship at its "best." The dress and show may be entirely merited and successful in those circumstances, but they are also entirely divisible from the actual procedure of flambéing.

It is possible to consider flambéing as a series of techniques ordered on the basis of their difficulty, the time they take, the equipment they require, the dishes they suit, or even the showmanship they offer. A technique should be chosen that suits the circumstances.

For example, at a cocktail party, a live cooking station with an almost continuous display of flambéing is attractive, but it presents several problems that would not occur if you were flambéing for four people in an a la carte restaurant.

Four or five hundred orders of anything, even cocktail size, are quite a challenge to a single flambéer, and most of the standard flambé items are too expensive as cocktail party fare. You could choose, however, to "flambé" a standard cocktail hors d'oeuvre item such as spiced meat balls or cocktail franks. The actual food could be in a chafing dish, hot and in its sauce. The continuous flambéing would be in a standard suzette pan on a small burner. The captain would ignite a quantity of brandy and pour it, still burning, into the chafing dish from as high as he or she could reach. Or some of the sauce might be added to the suzette pan and then poured over the mixture into the chafing dish. In either case, the showmanship is there without the captain attempting to cook 500 orders of meatballs in a 10-inch pan.

Better yet would be a station of flaming coffees, made to order. While it would take longer, the preparation of each is spectacular and adds more to the festive atmosphere than flambéing meatballs or cocktail franks. Consider the event, then find the right blend of showmanship and ingredients for that event. Don't flambé just to flambé.

Kitchen Preparation

The food for flambé service in the dining room must leave the kitchen cooked. The only exception might be steaks which are going to be flambéed in a pan and should be slightly underdone. Some further cooking will take place in the dining room, as it is necessary to heat the pan in which the steak will be flambéed.

The kitchen must also make sure that the food is hot, or else the food itself will cool the flambéing pan. For example, sautéed sliced mushrooms added to a steak can easily be flambéed if they are hot. If they are taken from the refrigerator, however, it is necessary to preheat them so that they are warm and easy to flambé in the pan, without cooling the rest of the dish.

If the food is presented and flambéed on the same platter, the kitchen must heat that platter as well as the flambéing liquid. When swords are used, the food must be hot and the flambéing liquid poured over the food must be hot, as the liquid will be lit with a match, not heated on a burner and ignited from the burner's flame.

Dining Room Preparation

Flambéing becomes ineffective and unglamorous if captains must look for equipment during the meal service. Flambé service, if offered, must be supported by sufficient equipment for captains to prepare setups before the service.

Captains then have an obligation to make sure there are sufficient measured portions of cognac in sauce boats, if this is the system, or they have prepared enough burners, or even completely assembled a number of gueridons and parked them in the pantry—whatever the preparation is for the flambé service.

When the item for flambéing is ready, the captain must be ready to take the item, grab the flambé equipment and utensils and proceed to the customer's table. It is even better if the equipment is positioned at the table before the captain goes into the kitchen to pick up the order, so there is no delay and no scrambling.

Flambéing Methods

Five methods of flambéing, or flambé techniques, follow:

1. Two-pan flambéing, which requires two burners and is almost cooking
2. One-pan flambéing, which is especially suited to a dish which can be "finished" in the dining room on a single burner
3. No-pan flambéing, which is especially suited to the dishes which have no sauce, can be taken from the kitchen in a combination presentation/flambé/service vessel and do not require a burner

4. Sword-presentation flambéing, which does not require either a pan or a burner
5. Foodless flambéing, which is flambéing for effect only

Two-Pan Flambéing

Liquids, from soup to beverages, require two burners for flambé presentation because they themselves cannot be flambéed. An ounce of cognac cannot be poured into 2 cups of hot soup and ignited, as the strength of the alcohol in the mixture would be entirely diluted. The liquid (soup, stew, coffee) must be kept warm on one burner while the sautéed item or garnish or brandy is flambéed in a pan on the other burner. For the soup, a few bits of vegetable garnish might be sautéed then flambéed; for the coffee some sugar might be caramelized. The garnish or brandy is warmed, then ignited; then the liquid is poured into the flames or the flames into the liquid.

One-Pan Flambéing

When an item has little or no sauce, it can be flambéed in a single pan. The flambéing is done right on top of the item. For example, suppose the item is duckling a l'orange, or something similar, duckling with pineapple. The captain presents the dish to the guests, presumably attractively arranged on a serving platter. The captain places a pat or two of butter in the suzette pan and heats it until it begins to sizzle. Sugar is then put into the pan and caramelized; then the pineapple is glazed. The meat and garnishes, everything except for parsley, can be transferred from the platter into the pan. An ounce of warmed or room-temperature liqueur, cognac, or a mixture of them is poured into the side of the pan, and the instant it "steams" (almost immediately), that part of the pan is tilted into the flame of the burner, and it ignites. The almost nonexistent liquid is then spooned over the duck. As the flames die out, the food is portioned onto the customers' plates.

Before the food is flambéed, any dry ingredient or a wet ingredient in modest quantity can be added. In other words, the dish can be "finished" with the addition of any garnish or flavoring. After the dish has been flambéed, any liquid or wet garnish can be added. In the instance of the duckling, the server might add orange peel, chopped parsley, chopped candied fruit, or a drop of two of red pepper sauce before flambéing, and orange juice, orange sauce, brown sauce, or fresh orange segments after flambéing.

If the item were a steak or chop, a sauce could be concocted by adding drops of bottled steak sauce of many varieties, shallots, parsley, mushrooms, or tomatoes, as long as nothing creates so much liquid that the liquor is diluted, making the dish impossible to flambé.

If there is a lot of liquid in the pan, one way to handle it is to create a hot spot. Suppose the item or the creation is so moist that when the pan is level, the liquid entirely covers the bottom. Unless a great deal of liquor is added, which is both expensive and potentially disrupting to the flavor of the item, the dish will not flambé. If the pan is moved and tilted slightly so that the liquid runs into the part of the pan that is off the flame, a dry spot is created directly over the flame. When this has dried and the little residue of the sauce on it begins to color, the liquor can be poured directly on the spot, and the pan dipped into the flame without allowing the sauce to wash back over the spot, igniting it. By this method, it is possible to fill a pan with crepes suzette for four people (three apiece), pour a quantity of prepared sauce over the crepes, and flambé the pan.

No-Pan Flambéing

No-pan flambéing requires something on the order of a sizzler platter set: a heavy metal broiler-proof pan and an insulating wooden or plastic holder platter in which it sits. No-pan flambéing is simple. The cook heats the sizzler insert in the kitchen under the broiler or over a direct flame. If the item being flambéd will not be harmed by the heat, it can be put on the "red hot" platter as it leaves the kitchen. If it will be harmed, it should be presented on a separate platter.

The captain has ready a glass or sauceboat containing an ounce or two of liquor, depending on the size of the platter. The red hot sizzler is taken on its holder to the dining room. The item is presented. A match or, more elegantly, a thin wood or paper taper from a candle, is lit. The liquor is poured on the sizzler (not on the item), it "steams" instantly, and is then ignited for a flambé effect. With a very hot, very thick sizzler and a solid insulating holder, the liquor can be ignited as much as 6 or 7 minutes after the platter leaves the kitchen, because the sizzler remains hot enough to quickly vaporize the alcohol in the liquor.

Even an item with sauce can be prepared this way. Once the flames on the sizzler platter have died, the captain can add some of the sauce to the item, in effect "deglazing" the sizzler, and then serve it.

Flaming Swords

Flaming-sword presentation is usually reserved for broiled or grilled meats, but anything that is solid enough to stay on the sword may be strung on it and flambéed, from jumbo shrimp to pineapples, dates, and prunes.

There is no difficulty in flambéing the sword, either at the table or as the server enters the dining room, if the food is hot and the liquor used is heated. (The food item alone is not hot enough to heat the liquor so that it vaporizes quickly enough to flame.) Lacking the ability to actually heat a small quantity of liquor, you can keep a capped bottle of liquor in the steam table.

It is also possible to heat and ignite the liquor and pour it over the item still flaming. Either of these two methods can be used on items which do not flame well, even ice cream. The heated liquor is poured onto a sugar cube or piece of sponge cake on top of or between the scoops of frozen ice cream and flambéed, or flaming sauce is poured over it.

Foodless Flambéing

There are items which will not flame readily. It is possible in these instances to flambé something that is not eaten. For example, a suckling pig spouting flames from his mouth is very dramatic in a darkened dining room. Unless the pig's head is soaked (very unpractical), however, the flames will not last. The alternative is to stuff the pig's mouth with cotton, soak it in cheap high-proof alcohol, and ignite it. The cotton should be sufficiently soaked with alcohol to maintain the flame until the pig is returned to the kitchen after the presentation or else the cotton could smoulder in the dining room.

Flambéing Sauces

Flambéed Sauce Items

Flambéed sauce items are simply flambés of items, usually main courses, that have sauces. Knowing how to flambé the sauce leaves you with a repertoire of thousands of items to flambé. Just flambé the sauce and vary the main ingredient, or vary the sauce and use the same main ingredient.

When flambéing sauces, the captain can perform the final step in the cooking and plating of the food in front of the guests, imparting even more the "made-to-order" feeling. Sauce items which can be acceptably flambéed range from appetizers such as shrimp scampi or some variation of sauteed shrimp to vegetable side dishes such as mushrooms with red wine sauce (champignons Bordelaise) to sauces to be napped over meats. Once the basic procedures have been learned, any dish of this sort can be flambéed. Some of the many sauce dishes that can be flambéed are listed below, followed by a sample dish which outlines the steps for flambéing the sauce. (Please note that the same basic procedure can be followed for any number of meats and sauces—the procedure and the sequence of steps are the important points to remember, rather than whether the meat is chicken or steak, or the sauce is tarragon- or dill-based.)

Repertory of Flambéed Sauce Dishes

Seafood

- ♦ Shrimp scampi with tomato sauce or garlic butter
- ♦ Soft-shell crab with brown butter, flambéed with cognac
- ♦ Frog's legs with garlic butter and tomatoes, flambéed with cognac
- ♦ Snails sans shell with garlic butter, flambéed with cognac
- ♦ Fish fillets with brown butter, flambéed with orange or fruit liqueur
- ♦ Shad roe with bacon and cream sauce, flambéed with cognac
- ♦ Trout with brown butter, flambéed with cognac
- ♦ Salmon steaks with brown butter, flambéed with orange liqueur

Meats

- ♦ Beef tournedos with all standard sauces and garnishes
- ♦ Sirloin (New-York-cut steaks), especially minute-size and butterflied, with mushrooms, sauce, and so on
- ♦ Brains with brown or black butter, flambéed with apple brandy
- ♦ Liver with brown butter and bacon, flambéed with cognac
- ♦ Kidneys with cream sauce and tarragon, flambéed with cognac
- ♦ Lamb chops with Colbert sauce, flambéed with cognac
- ♦ Pork chops with piquant sauce, flambéed with fruit liqueur
- ♦ Venison steaks with pepper sauce, flambéed with gin
- ♦ Lamb steaks with Madeira sauce, flambéed with cognac
- ♦ Veal escalope with cream sauce, flambéed with fruit liqueur
- ♦ Veal steaks with brown sauce, flambéed with fruit liqueur

Poultry

- ♦ Whole small birds with brown sauce or lightly thickened stock, flambéed with cognac or fruit liqueur
- ♦ Duckling with sweet orange sauce, flambéed with cognac or fruit liqueur
- ♦ Turkey steak with brown butter, flambéed with banana liqueur
- ♦ Chicken supreme with all standard sauces and garnishes

Vegetables

- ♦ Mushrooms with red wine sauce, flambéed with cognac
- ♦ Fruit garnishes flambéed with similar fruit liqueur (for example, apple for pork, flambéed with applejack)

Technique: Flambéing Sauce: Chicken Supreme with Tarragon Creme Sauce

Note: If only one flaming technique is learned, it should be this one. It is the most versatile and often-used technique. The same sequence can be used with hundreds of foods, and with as many sauces. The steps, sequences, and procedures are the important points to note.

Kitchen Preparation

The kitchen supplies the dish, garnishes, and sauces:

♦ One chicken or capon supreme per person, fully prepared and cooked in the kitchen. (The supreme is the breast with only the upper joint of the wing left on.) Chicken pieces are placed on a flameproof tray.
♦ Heavy cream
♦ Chopped fresh parsley and chopped fresh tarragon
♦ Butter
♦ Shallots, "sweated" (shallots sauteed until they are transparent, not brown)
♦ Light cream sauce
♦ Parsley sprigs and any vegetable garnishes

Captain's Preparation

Auxiliary ingredients, burners, and plates for the completed chicken supreme.

♦ Two burners or a lamp and a chafing dish
♦ A gueridon or trolley
♦ Peppermill
♦ Bottle of red pepper sauce
♦ Dinner plates (hot, if possible)
♦ Bottle of cognac
♦ Bottle of white wine
♦ Jar of Dijon-style mustard
♦ Bottle of Worcestershire sauce
♦ Lemon half wrapped in cheesecloth
♦ Serving forks and spoons

Procedure

1. Set up the gueridon at tableside.
2. Bring the chicken on a serving platter from the kitchen.
3. Light the lamps or burners.
4. Place the pats of butter in the pan and allow them to sizzle on one lamp (the more powerful of the two, if they differ).
5. Place the cream sauce in the chafing dish on the other lamp, or place the plates on the other lamp if they are not hot, or place the vegetables on the other lamp if the procedure will be so protracted that they will get cold.
6. Add the shallots to the sizzling butter and stir them around with a fork.
7. Place the chicken breasts in the pan with the shallots. Since they are already cooked and hot, this is for show; the length of time in the pan alone depends on the time available, the guests' demeanor, and so on.
8. Add the cognac and flame it. As the flames die, spoon a little over each piece of chicken, then remove the chicken pieces to the flame-proof platter.
9. If the process is protracted, place the platter on the other lamp over low heat to keep warm.
10. Add white wine to the pan and allow it to cook away. The flame should be as hot as possible.
11. Add cream and let it cook until almost gone.
12. While the cream is cooking, any or all of the optional ingredients, or none of them, can be added, depending upon how elaborate the dish is to be.

    Note: Steps 10 to 12 can be eliminated (as well as the ingredients required, if the light cream sauce is well flavored and it's necessary to speed up the flambé procedure).
13. Add the light cream sauce, a drop or two of pepper sauce, and a grinding or two of pepper from the mill. Allow the preparation to cook 1 minute.
14. Sprinkle the chopped fresh herbs into the sauce.
15. Spoon the sauce over the chicken breasts, either on the service platter (for Russian service) or on the dinner plates. Garnish with the parsley springs and vegetables.

Grill Flambé

A rarer technique is a combination of charbroiling and flambéing. A plain broiled item can be prepared using the above technique if there is a sauce, or by flambéing the garnish items, if there is no sauce.

But to impart additional flavors to a broiled item without adding any fats or oils, the grill flambé technique can be used. With this technique, the broiled item is flambéed on a grill over a few hickory or maple chips or, lacking them, some dried herbs or even dried onions. The object is to burn something that can flavor the meat without making too much smoke.

Few broiled items are hurt by being splashed with a little cognac; some are actually enhanced, with showmanship added as well. Unique flavors can be imparted to the grilled items by using exotic woods such as mesquite, apple, or pear for grilling. Otherwise standard smoking woods, combined with dehydrated vegetables, or dried fruits can be used to provide complementary flavors. Some items suitable to the grill flambé technique are listed below, followed by a step-by-step example of the technique.

Repertory of Grill Flambés

- ◆ Pork chops over dried bananas, flambéed fruit liqueur
- ◆ Trout over wood chips and onions, flambéed with cognac
- ◆ Half chicken over dried figs, flambéed with fruit liqueur
- ◆ Lamb chops over wood chips and a little dried mint, flambéed with cognac
- ◆ Game over juniper twigs or wood chips and juniper berries, flambéed with gin
- ◆ Steak over wood chips and peppercorns, flambéed with cognac

Technique: Flambéing Grilled Items: Hickory Onion Steak

Kitchen Preparation

1. The kitchen prepares sirloin steaks, preferably double cut if the server carves, to almost the desired doneness on a portable grill or on a small cake rack.
2. Leaving the steak on the grill or on the rack, the kitchen gives the portable grill to the captain on a flameproof serving tray or bimetal pan, with garnishes and vegetables in a separate pan.

Captain's Preparation

- ◆ One burner or lamp or a chafing dish and lamp
- ◆ A gueridon or trolley
- ◆ Cognac

- ◆ Dinner plates
- ◆ Peppermill
- ◆ Hickory chips, dried onions

Procedure

1. Set up the gueridon at tableside.
2. Light the lamp or chafing dish.
3. Heat the cognac. The cognac should be warm when the steak is brought from the kitchen, but should not boil.
4. Bring the steak into the dining room on the grill or rack from the kitchen.
5. Present it to the customer.
6. Sprinkle the chips and dried onions on the pan under the steak, lifting the rack or grill carefully.
7. Light a match or, more elegantly, a taper.
8. Pour the warmed cognac over the steak and the chips beneath.
9. Ignite it immediately. It may be necessary to light the chips separately.
10. The steak may be turned over and flambéed again, depending on the show desired.
11. When the flames have died, the steak can be served, or carved and served.

Flambéing Desserts

Flambéed desserts offer the opportunity of creating a distinguished dessert menu from relatively undistinguished ingredients. The perennial flambé favorites, crepes suzette and cherries jubilee, illustrate this. Crepes suzette are thin, delicate pancakes in a sweet, slightly caramelized Grand Marnier sauce, and cherries jubilee is vanilla ice cream with hot cherries and cherry liqueur sauce.

But the combination of something sweet after a dinner and flames and showmanship is seemingly irresistible, as these and other flambéed desserts sell well year after year. There are two basic flambé desserts:

1. The crepe dessert, whether it is suzette or any other
2. Flambéed fruit, whether it is served alone or spooned over ice cream

Crepes

Crepes are often made ahead and even frozen, which greatly increases their versatility on a menu. They can be made plain or with herbs and featured as entrees (filled with meat, vegetable, and/or cheese mixtures) or luncheon entrees (filled with spinach and cheese or even fresh fruits). For dessert usually a bit of sugar is added to the crepe batter, for a sweeter crepe. There are three ways of varying the basic crepe recipes:

1. Adding something to the batter
2. Changing the liqueur
3. Adding something to the sauce in the pan

The combinations and permutations of these variations are infinite. Try adding coffee to the batter, then flambé with coffee liqueur, and add chopped hazelnuts; or add hazelnuts to the batter, flambé with pear liqueur, and add diced apples to the sauce.

A repertory of additional examples of flambéed crepes is listed below, followed by a step-by-step example for that perennial favorite, crepes suzette.

Repertory of Flambéed Crepes

Basic crepe, with

- ◆ Flambéed peach liqueur, with or without stewed peaches
- ◆ Grated chocolate, and suzette treatment
- ◆ Coffee flavor, flambéed with coffee liqueur
- ◆ Flambéed rum, with bananas glazed in sauce
- ◆ Diced pineapple, flambéed with cognac
- ◆ Flambéed applejack, with stewed diced apples
- ◆ Flambéed cherry liqueur, with stewed or canned pitted cherries
- ◆ Flambéed scotch whiskey
- ◆ Flambéed cognac, with stewed or fresh strawberries

Technique: Flambéing Crepes: Crepes Suzette

Kitchen Preparation

The kitchen supplies two or three light, thin pancakes (crepes) for each order, usually four crepes for two people.

Captain's Preparation

Assemble everything beforehand so there is a minimum of preparation in the dining room:

◆ Lamp or burner with suzette pan
◆ 2 ounces granulated sugar (superfine preferred)
◆ 3 ounces sweet butter
◆ Grated orange zest (from about one-quarter of an orange)
◆ 3 ounces orange juice and 1 ounce lemon juice in a sauce boat
◆ 1 ounce orange liqueur, or half liqueur and half cognac, or Grand Marnier liqueur, in bottle or sauce boat
◆ 1 ounce cognac in bottle or sauce boat
◆ Dessert plates, preferably hot
◆ Serving fork and spoon; small spoons for zest, butter, and sugar
◆ Gueridon or trolley

Procedure

1.   Set up the gueridon at tableside.
2.   Bring the crepes from the kitchen, unfolded, on a plate.
3.   Light the lamp and heat the pan over high heat. Add the sugar by sprinkling it over the pan.
4.   When the sugar just begins to color slightly, add the butter and stir the mixture thoroughly with a fork.
5.   Gradually add the lemon and orange juice.
6.   Add either a sugar lump impregnated with oils from an orange, or orange zest.
7.   Add the orange liqueur and lower the flame.
8.   Stir the mixture with a fork.
9.   Using a spoon and fork, pick up a pancake and swish it through the sauce in the pan so that it is coated. Then fold it first in half and then in half again, to form a triangle. Push the completed triangle to the side of the pan.
10.   Repeat step 9 with the remaining pancakes.
11.   When all four pancakes have been folded, move them to the center of the pan. Turn up the flame.
12.   Create a "hot spot" by tilting the pan and moving it off center. Pour the cognac into the hot spot and dip the pan into the flame to flambé.
13.   While the flames are still present, turn each pancake over.
14.   Dish them out still flaming. Spoon the sauce over the pancakes.

Service Variations

The captain has several preparation alternatives, depending on how much of a show is desired and how many crepes must be flambéed. The fastest way to produce bulk flambéed crepes, for example, for a party of 100, is to prepare the sauce ahead of time (as indicated above, but in the kitchen in a large pot) and keep it hot, while flambéing cognac in the pan on prefolded crepes.

For a la carte service, the captain should prepare a panade, a paste of butter, sugar, orange liqueur, orange juice, and grated orange rind (zest). The panade is heated in the pan, the crepes are moved in the panade a bit, and then the preparation is flambéed.

The full three-act presentation has several additional steps performed before the guests, which were outlined above, but even these can be elaborated. Instead of supplying orange juice and orange peel as indicated, the captain may tightly wrap an orange in a napkin as though strangling it, so that some of the peel is exposed. A sugar cube in tongs is rubbed against the exposed portion of the orange so that it absorbs the orange oil. The cube is added to the granulated sugar normally used. To extract the juice, the orange is pierced with a fork, the insides mashed and squeezed. The procedure can be repeated with a lemon for more elaboration.

Fruit

Fruit flambés are usually one of two types:

1. Flambéing an already cooked or poached fruit, actually flambéing only some of its syrup
2. Slightly cooking and flambéing a raw or partially cooked fruit in the dining room

The first method is the easiest. It is not even necessary to use a pan; many captains flambé the spirit in a ladle and then pour it over the fruit in serving dishes (with or without ice cream underneath). The second method is usually used when more show is desired: The captain appears to be actually preparing a dessert, especially if able to peel the fruit elegantly.

For example, an orange can be peeled by cutting off one end and forcing the fork through this end to the base of the tines. Spear the whole orange, cut side up, with the fork, and remove the peel with a knife in one continuous ribbon, while turning it with the fork. Then, either slice the orange or remove each segment by cutting it away from the membrane which holds it, still without touching the fruit by hand. Or a banana can be peeled by halving it lengthwise and lifting the fruit from the peel by sliding a spoon under it.

Whether the captain peels the fruit or it is sent from the kitchen peeled or partially cooked, the flambéing procedure in the dining room is the same.

Any fruit that can be heated without falling apart can be treated as a flambé. Perhaps the only further consideration, if the fruit is to be slightly sautéed before flambéing, is the fruit's compatibility with butter: pears, apples, and peaches seem to go well with butter, while cherries, melon, and grapes do not.

The choice of liqueur and moistening liquid offers the major variations. Since many fruit liqueurs or fruit juices are compatible with many other fruits, the combinations are numerous. A further dimension can be added by using different ice creams or various jams and jellies instead of sugar, adding them with the moistening liquid.

Combinations can be conventional or highly exotic, as illustrated in the following list:

Repertory of Flambéed Fruits

- ◆ Bananas flambéed with rum
- ◆ Pears flambéed with pear liqueur or cognac
- ◆ Apples flambéed with applejack
- ◆ Peaches flambéed with raspberry liqueur
- ◆ Pears flambéed with chocolate liqueur
- ◆ Pineapple flambéed with coconut liqueur
- ◆ Oranges flambéed with ginger brandy
- ◆ Cherries flambéed with gin

Technique: Flambéing Fruit: Peaches

Kitchen Preparation

The kitchen's role usually consists of preparing the fruit. Peaches should be peeled by blanching in boiling water, have the pits removed, and be halved or sliced attractively.

Captain's Preparation

- ◆ Lamp or burner with suzette pan
- ◆ 2 ounces granulated or superfine sugar
- ◆ 3 ounces of sweet butter
- ◆ 3 ounces of liquid—for example, orange juice, peach juice, apricot nectar, or the liquid from maraschino cherries
- ◆ 1 ounce of liqueur—for example, peach liqueur
- ◆ 1 ounce of cognac or peach brandy
- ◆ Toasted coconut
- ◆ Dessert plates, preferably hot, or ice cream in cold plates or perhaps in glasses

- ◆ Serving fork and spoon
- ◆ Gueridon or trolley

Procedure

1. Set up the geuridon at tableside.
2. Bring the fruit from the kitchen.
3. Light the lamp and heat the pan over high heat. Add the sugar by sprinkling it over the pan.
4. When the sugar begins to slightly color, add the butter and stir the mixture thoroughly with a fork.
5. Gradually add the juice or liquid, and then the liqueur.
6. Add the fruit, and turn it in the sauce.
7. When the fruit is hot, create a hot spot by tilting the pan and moving it off center. Pour the cognac into the hot spot, dip the pan into the flame to flambé.
8. While the flames are still present, turn the peaches around.
9. Dish them out while still flaming and sprinkle them with coconut.

Flambéing Beverages

Flambéed beverages are easy and dramatic. Most often two chafing dishes are used, one for the coffee (or tea, hot chocolate, or hot punch), and the other for the spirit, sugar, and seasonings.

If necessary the process can be made much simpler: A high-proof spirit can be flambéed on a lump of sugar in a warm teaspoon and poured into a single cup of beverage. Or it can be made more complex. For example, hot beverages, especially flavored coffees, are often served in a glass. The liqueur can be heated over the flame in the glass, then the liqueur is flambéed by igniting it, then the coffee and additional ingredients (e.g., whipped cream) are added to the glass. A variation on this, if two portions are being made, is to pour the flaming liqueur from one glass to the other, holding one glass much higher than the other. Especially at night, this is quite spectacular. After pouring from glass to glass a few times, set them on the work surface, add the coffee, and finish the drinks.

Another variation (eye appeal) is to frost the rim of the glass with sugar by dipping it into the liqueur, then in confectioner's or superfine sugar. The sugar can even be slightly caramelized.

Most guests are relaxed and well fed when they order coffee service, so coffee showmanship is usually greeted with pleasure and can be an elaborate procedure without the guests' becoming impatient.

Any liqueur can be used to create a unique house drink. For example, an Italian restaurant might use Grappa or Strega, while a Spanish restaurant could use Fundador brandy, or a Greek restaurant Metaxa brandy liqueur. Irish coffee is the most common example of an ethnic treatment of a flambéed coffee beverage. Lightly whipped cream can be floated on any of these preparations, as it is on Irish coffee, by pouring it over the back of a service spoon.

Scotch, rum, bourbon, whiskey, chartreuse, and fruit liqueurs should not be neglected, and beverages other than coffee offer a novel variation. Tea is excellent with most liqueurs and brandies, while cocoa or hot chocolate is excellent with orange, coffee, cocoa, and mint liqueurs, as well as rums and brandies.

The whole area of hot toddies is virtually unexplored as flambé creations. The major difference between a toddy and the coffee drinks is the use of hot water instead of coffee, and perhaps the floating of a slice of lime, lemon, or orange in the customer's glass.

The step-by-step procedure for a flambéed beverage is detailed next, using coffee diable (or café diable) for the example of the technique.

Technique: Flambéing Beverages: Café Diable

Captain's Preparation

There is not a great deal of preparation needed for the average, straightforward café diable or other flambéed beverage. To add to the show, and given the time and the equipment, you can make it quite unusual. For example, you can roast green coffee beans in a suzette pan, grind them at the table, and make the coffee by the filter method. While the coffee is brewing, heat and then flambé the liqueurs. Or, you can roast a few token crushed beans, just to lend the aroma of roasting coffee to the preparation.

Equipment

◆ Two chafing dishes (small double boilers of metal with burners or lamps underneath)
◆ Dramatic glassware: four tempered wine goblets, glass mugs, or demitasse cups, preferably hot or to be heated by the captain
◆ 4 teaspoons brown sugar and one lump white sugar
◆ Peel of one-half a lemon and one-half an orange

- ♦ Two cloves
- ♦ Stick of cinnamon
- ♦ 4 ounces cognac
- ♦ One ladle
- ♦ Enough coffee to fill cups of glassware three-fourths full
- ♦ Gueridon

Procedure

1. Set up the gueridon at tableside.
2. Bring the coffee to the table, and light both chafing dishes.
3. Pour the coffee into one of the chafing dishes to keep hot or, if in a decorative (e.g., silverplate) coffeepot, position the coffeepot directly above a heat source to keep it hot.
4. Slowly heat all the other ingredients, except the lump of sugar, in the other chafing dish.
5. When the brandy is warm, dip in the ladle and remove about $\frac{1}{2}$ ounce (1 tablespoon).
6. Put the sugar cube in the ladle and ignite it with the open flame of the burner.
7. Lower the flaming ladle into the brandy, which will ignite.
8. While it is still burning, pour in the coffee.
9. Or instead, pour the flaming brandy into the chafing dish of coffee from a height, carefully, so as not to splash the customers or the furnishings.

Café Diable: A More Flamboyant Technique

Proceed as above except:

1. Have two stemmed wine goblets of tempered glass available.
2. Bring the coffee to the gueridon in a decorative coffeepot that will keep the coffee hot during the preparation stages.
3. Heat 3 ounces of cognac in the chafing dish with the orange peel, lemon peel, brown sugar, and so on, as above.
4. Heat 2 ounces of cognac in the goblets, 1 ounce in each.
5. Hold the goblets by the stem and turn slowly above the heat to prevent the glassware from overheating in one spot and breaking.
6. When the cognac in the goblets is sufficiently warm, ignite it.
7. Pour the cognac from one goblet to the other, holding one high above the other for effect. Transfer the flaming cognac back and forth, between goblets, a few times, then pour the contents of both into the chafing dish with the remainder of the warm cognac, igniting it.
8. Continue with step 8 or 9 of the original method.

❖ TABLESIDE PREPARATION OF COLD ITEMS

Tableside preparations require captains with skill and confidence. All procedures must meet professional standards, including crisp, efficient, rapid hand motions and a purposeful style. Captains cannot fidget with the food or fumble with the accessories. While many table preparations do not require any more culinary technique than does flambéing, the need for a professional air in their preparation makes it difficult to offer them successfully with an inexperienced or inadequately trained captain.

Tableside preparation can be arranged on a scale of difficulty, from easiest to hardest, as follows:

- ◆ Cold preparations tend to be simplest, requiring little more than the assembly of ingredients.
- ◆ Hot, cooked-to-order preparations are more difficult.
- ◆ Classical specialty dishes are most difficult, because the captain is actually creating a dish almost entirely from raw ingredients. For example, pressed duck is extremely difficult, requiring carving, sauce making, using the duck press, and so on.

The most apparent advantage of preparing cold foods at tableside is that they do not require very much equipment. Generally vessels for the ingredients, a gueridon or trolley, and a large mixing bowl suffice. Accessories include a large peppermill, condiments, and mixing and serving utensils.

As a class of preparations, cold items offer a further advantage: Many appetizers, salads, and main courses need only a cold dressing or sauce, often a mayonnaise or olive oil type, mixed into or with the major ingredients. The dressing or sauce ingredients are placed in the bowl, mixed, and then the main ingredients are added: cooked shrimp, raw meat for steak tartare, or romaine lettuce and croutons for Caesar salad.

There are also many salads that can be made as cold preparations —literally any "composed" salad from the classical repertory or a simple salad made of greens tossed with oil and vinegar, with a few grindings from a giant peppermill and perhaps topped with some fresh, edible flowers, such as zucchini blossoms if they are in season.

Basic Sauces and Dressings

Since many cold dishes are similar in preparation, a large repertory of items can be mastered quickly. Three basic sauce and dressing variations are usually encountered:

1. A mixture of already prepared ingredients
2. Emulsion-based (mayonnaise-based) sauce or dressing using raw or slightly cooked egg yolk
3. Emulsion-based (mayonnaise-based) sauce or dressing using hard-cooked egg yolk

Mixtures of Already Prepared Ingredients

This procedure involves placing many dishes of already prepared ingredients around a mixing bowl, arranged attractively and taking the color of each ingredient into consideration. Each ingredient has its own serving utensil, whether a spoon or fork or a pour spout, if it is olive oil or another liquid. Extra serving utensils should be available on a shelf below the main ingredients so that no utensil is ever taken from one item and used in another item's bowl, causing contamination of the food item.

If parsley, chopped egg white, chopped egg yolk, anchovies, garlic cloves, a cruet of olive oil, ketchup, chili sauce, or Worcestershire sauce are on a gueridon, the colors should be considered: The green of the parsley might be next to the chopped egg white, next to the red ketchup, and so on. Grated parmesan cheese would not be placed next to the egg whites or egg yolks—there's not enough color contrast!

The captain approaches the table with the prepared gueridon. The main ingredient (e.g., romaine lettuce for a Caesar salad, or chopped raw meat for steak tartare) is in a large bowl, often on a shelf under the "fixins" area, or to the side of it.

The ingredients for the sauce are taken, a bit at a time, from the small bowls or cruets and mixed in the large mixing bowl. You could be making cocktail sauce for shrimp, Thousand Island dressing for salad, or any one of the hundreds of preparations of this sort that are usually put together in the pantry.

For instance, for shrimp cocktail sauce, a bit of tomato ketchup is placed in the main bowl, then a dollop of chili sauce is added, then horseradish, followed by a squeeze of lemon juice from a cheesecloth-wrapped lemon, a splash of Worcestershire, and a grinding or two of pepper. Voila—the sauce has been made!

The trick is to leave something in each bowl, and to add at least one or two ingredients in two passes instead of one. In this way, you appear to be an artist perfecting a creation, not a chemist. The more bottles and jars used, the more creative it seems. Some even put chopped parsley in three different bowls!

Emulsion-Based Sauce with Egg Yolk

A number of dishes use this procedure, among them steak tartare and Caesar salad. The gueridon has the ingredients for making mayonnaise, the base sauce:

- a raw egg yolk
- some vegetable or olive oil
- an acid ingredient (usually vinegar or lemon juice)
- the ingredients for garnishing or seasoning

The basic procedure is to combine the egg yolk with the dry or pasty ingredients. Alternately add drops of oil to thicken the mixture and drops of acid product to thin it. When the sauce has been made, add the garnish and seasonings, then the main ingredients. As long as too much oil is not added or added too quickly, the preparation will be a success.

If you are making steak tartare, mash the anchovies first, then add some of the acid (lemon juice), which will dissolve any of the small bones present in the anchovies. Then proceed with the egg yolk, mustards, Worcestershire, Tabasco, and fresh ground pepper and mix. Gradually add in the olive oil and finally the garnishes—chopped cornichons, capers, chopped raw onion—and the sauce is done.

Emulsion-Based Sauce with a Hard-Cooked Yolk

Some salad dressings start with a hard-cooked egg yolk. The preparation parallels making a sauce with a raw egg yolk, except that the hard yolk will not absorb as much oil. In the dining room this is seldom a problem, since the amount of oil added, even to a raw yolk, is nowhere near the limit of its absorbent powers (one raw yolk usually absorbs 2 to 3 ounces of oil).

A repertory of cold preparations that might be offered for tableside preparation follows.

Repertory of Cold Preparations

Appetizers

- Avocado chunks with sauce of ketchup, Worcestershire sauce, chili sauce, lemon juice, yogurt or heavy cream
- Lobster cocktail with mayonnaise-based sauce with capers, pickle relish, tomato ketchup, crushed anchovies
- Herring chunks with sour cream, chopped onion, lemon juice, chives, chopped dill, black pepper
- Oyster cocktail with horseradish, chili sauce, lemon juice, red pepper sauce
- Shrimp cocktail with sauce of ketchup, Worcestershire sauce, chili sauce, horseradish, lemon juice, with countless variations
- Melon balls with bar sugar, port wine, and powdered ginger or creme de menthe (alone)
- Poached mussel cocktail with Dijon-style mustard, horseradish, mayonnaise

Main Courses

- Chicken salad with yogurt or mayonnaise, chopped olives, chopped parsley, Worcestershire sauce, pickle relish, black pepper, grated onion
- Steak tartare (ground or chopped raw beef) with capers, onions, chopped hard-cooked egg white and yolk, raw egg yolk, mustard, oil and vinegar, Worcestershire sauce, red pepper sauce, black pepper, anchovies
- Tuna salad, turkey salad, salmon salad, shrimp salad, and the like
- Crabmeat and melon chunks, in the scooped-out melon shell, with mayonnaise-based sauce plus curry powder and concentrated orange juice

Salads and Salad Main Courses or Appetizers

- Thin strips of chicken with diced celery, celery root, diced apples, asparagus tips, and a mayonnaise dressing with chopped chives, parsley, and ground pepper on top
- Cooked stringbeans, navy beans, kidney beans, wax beans, diced onions, diced tomatoes, chopped celery, and chopped egg, with hard-cooked egg-yolk mayonnaise
- Diced tongue, ham, salami, strips of cheese, pimiento, green peppers, mixed greens, and mayonnaise-based Russian dressing
- Avocado chunks, melon balls, diced seeded cucumbers, chopped hazelnuts, grapefruit segments, and oil and vinegar dressing
- Diced, peeled, and boiled potatoes, carrots, turnips, chopped celery, cooked red kidney beans, cooked elbow macaroni, diced salami, chopped olives, anchovies, and capers, with mayonnaise

Technique: Preparing Steak Tartare

This is a preparation of an emulsion-based sauce using a raw egg yolk. It is based on the preparation of the primary sauce, mayonnaise, with the steak and other seasonings added. This is just one presentation; yours may vary.

Kitchen Preparation

In most cold preparations the kitchen has the primary responsibility for the assembly of the ingredients: 6 ounces (one portion) of lean, freshly ground or chopped tender beefsteak on a silver platter or wooden board, shaped in a flat smooth oval, surrounded by two large bibb lettuce leaves; six slices of cocktail-size pumpernickel bread (or other bread).

On the side of the platter, in tiny 2-tablespoon bowls or glass ramekins there should be

minced raw onion or shallots
whole nonpareil-size capers
minced cornichons
chopped parsley
two lemon halves, wrapped in cheesecloth covers

Atop the ground sirloin there should be

egg yolk in an eggshell half, making a slight hollow in the top center of
the meat (made with the eggshell)
crossed anchovy fillets on either side of the egg, or wrapped around the
eggshell

Captain's Preparation

♦ Gueridon
♦ Large mixing bowl
♦ Oil and vinegar cruets
♦ Peppermill
♦ Salt
♦ Dijon mustard in a jar
♦ Red pepper sauce
♦ Worcestershire sauce
♦ Iced plate
♦ Two serving forks and spoons for mustard, tastings

Procedure

1. Set up the gueridon at tableside with all accessories.
2. Bring the steak tartare setup from the kitchen.
3. Present the steak to the customer; ask how he or she would like it prepared (with cornichons? capers? anchovies?).
4. Remove the anchovies from the top of the steak and puree them well in the bottom of the mixing bowl using two forks.
5. Squeeze the juice of one lemon half and mix well to dissolve any small anchovy bones. The sauce will turn creamy. Add about ½ teaspoon of Dijon mustard, and the raw egg yolk to the anchovy mixture.
6. Mix them well. Add Worcestershire sauce, Tabasco sauce, freshly ground pepper.
7. Slowly drip a few drops of oil into the mixture, beating constantly with a fork to incorporate the oil into the sauce.

8. As the sauce begins to thicken, squeeze a few drops of lemon juice (or vinegar) to thin it, then add more oil. Continue adding oil until sauce is thick and creamy. Add lemon juice to thin, add oil to thicken . Make about ¼ cup of sauce for a pound of ground sirloin; about two tablespoons of sauce for one portion.

9. When the sauce has been made, add the extras:

   Minced cornichons
   Capers (mix in without crushing, unless the house policy is to crush the capers)
   Minced raw onion or shallots

10. Mix in the meat. Combine well, but do not mash. Using a clean teaspoon and B&B plate, offer a "taste" to the guest. Adjust for seasonings.

    If not "hot" enough, add ground pepper, Worcestershire, and/or Tabasco. If too spicy, add more oil. Mix again. Ask customer to taste again.

11. When seasoned to the guest's taste, transfer the bibb lettuce leaves onto the serving plate. Using the mixing bowl, roll the steak tartare into a ball until it is smooth and without seams. Roll it out onto the lettuce leaves. It should be a smooth oval. If it is not, push it together into a rough oval with the serving fork.

12. Finish with a grinding or two of fresh black pepper; garnish with the chopped parsley. Place toast triangles or pumpernickel bread around the sides of the plate. Serve.

Once you've practiced this, you'll be able to perform the whole procedure, including the offering of the "taste bite" to the customer and adjusting to taste, in 5 to 10 minutes. It is a popular dish, and once customers learn that you'll prepare it the way they like it, they'll be back for it again and again.

❖ TABLESIDE COOKING

Since tableside cooking is really cooking, not assembling or flambéing, it takes time. The captain must be at the tableside from the start of the dish to its service—usually at least 20 minutes. Tableside cooking entertains only the customers for whom the item is being cooked. Guests eating other dishes may be disturbed by the sputtering pan, the heat, or the fumes. Finally, tableside cooking requires a captain with presence, confidence, and skill. Tableside dishes can be excellent—as good as, but usually no better than, the same dishes prepared in the kitchen. They can also be easily ruined by a captain who misjudges the doneness of meat, who is hurried and does not bother to let the sauce "come together," or who is unable to control the cooking flame on a lamp or burner.

Before an operation attempts tableside cooking, the following factors should be weighed:

◆ The place of tableside items on the menu—will they be a house specialty? Merchandised effectively? Do the customers want such items? Will they pay for them?

◆ The reduced productivity of the service staff—can the decrease in staff productivity be covered by the increased price for the "show items"?

◆ The skill of the personnel—it will be necessary to have training sessions, someone to write the procedures, practice sessions, and perhaps additional service staff to cover for those engaged in tableside cooking.

The attractions of tableside cooking are apparent; its problems may not be. It is a limited process, with only two types of dishes being made with any frequency: sautés and cream reductions. Both of these techniques are discussed next. Some dishes for tableside preparation—vegetables, starches, eggs, omelets—are then discussed, followed by a brief discussion of the classical specialties steak au poivre, steak Diane, zabaglione.

Tableside Sautés

Sautéed preparations—dishes that are cooked in a small amount of fat with a sauce developed in the pan—lend themselves well to tableside preparation. They are quickly prepared and are attractive, though sometimes expensive.

The cuts of meats and fish that are tender enough to lend themselves to this type of preparation include tenderloin and sirloin steaks, lamb chops and noisettes, veal loin cutlets, veal escalopes, chicken breasts and tenderloins, pork tenderloin cutlets, shrimp, fish steaks and fillets from solid fish, kidneys, sweetbreads, and brains. They can be flambéed as a legitimate part of the process.

The kitchen has three tasks in preparing for dining room sauté cooking:

1. Preparing the meat by trimming it, removing excess fat and gristle, and portioning it
2. Preparing the sauce or sauce base
3. Preparing the garnish elements

An alternative is to have the chef do the actual cooking in the kitchen, then place the meat on a serving dish, cover it with the sauce, and surround it with the garnish. In the dining room, the captain can flambé it again for effect and then dish it out onto the customer's plate.

Sauté Procedure

Whatever the dish, the sauté process consists of 10 steps:

1. Heating a small quantity of fat (butter, or butter and oil) in the pan until it begins to brown
2. Searing the item so that it develops color
3. Cooking the item
4. Removing the item but keeping it warm
5. Deglazing the pan by swishing it with a liqueur, usually but not necessarily cognac
6. Flaming the pan
7. Adding a liquid (e.g., wine) and an already prepared sauce
8. Allowing the liquid in the pan to reduce and "come together"
9. Seasoning and garnishing the sauce
10. Returning the item for finishing in the sauce

For true tableside cooking, this whole process takes place at the customers' tableside. It is readily apparent why the captain needs to be skilled in this procedure—the timing of each step is crucial and the ingredients expensive.

Technique: Sautéing Tableside: Escalope of Veal with Fresh Peppers

Kitchen Preparation

- 2-ounce veal escalopes on flameproof platter
- Sauceboat of tomato sauce and brown sauce together
- Dish of sweated shallots
- Julienne of skinned, lightly sautéed red, yellow, and green peppers
- Garnish of blanched, skinned, lightly sautéed cherry tomatoes or sautéed mushrooms
- Sweet potato croquettes

Captain's Preparation

- Gueridon
- At least one lamp or burner and pan, preferably two (one to keep the veal warm while the sauce is being made)
- Dish of butter

♦ Appropriate seasonings: red pepper sauce, salt, peppermill
♦ Chopped parsley
♦ Hot dinner plates
♦ Serving fork and spoon
♦ Bottle of liqueur for flaming (e.g., cognac)

Procedure

1. Set up the gueridon at tableside.
2. Bring the items from the kitchen and arrange them in order of use on the gueridon.
3. Light the lamp. Melt the butter in the pan, heating it until it sizzles.
4. Sear and slightly brown each veal escalope.
5. Remove them from the pan and place them on the flameproof platter with the sweet potato croquettes to keep warm.
6. Add shallots and peppers to the pan and sauté them, stirring with a fork.
7. Deglaze the pan by adding about 1 ounce of cognac, swishing it in the pan to pick up the material adhering to the pan's bottom.
8. Flame the cognac by dipping the pan into the burner flame.
9. Pour in the tomato sauce and brown sauce from the sauce boat.
10. Allow them to cook together for a few moments so that the flavor develops.
11. Add garnish of cherry tomatoes or mushrooms and warm 30 seconds.
12. Return the veal to the pan from the platter. Since the escalopes are thin and tender, almost no further cooking is required; simply heat them through.
13. Season the dish with salt (optional) and a grinding or two of the peppermill.
14. Heat some cognac in a ladle and flambé for effect.
15. When the flames have died, sprinkle with parsley.
16. Dish it out onto the customer's plate, and garnish the plate with sweet potato croquettes.

Tableside Cream Dishes

Tableside cream preparations are similar to sauté preparations, but they have another dimension. Heavy cream thickens as it is reduced; that is, as the water in the cream evaporates. Any item that can tolerate being simmered in liquid will yield very attractive results—a rich dish with a made-to-order sauce (e.g., chicken breasts, veal escalope, beef tenderloin tips, lobster tail medallions). These dishes can be made more quickly and with less expense if some already thickened white sauce (or a sauce based on white sauce, such as Mornay sauce) is used in place of some or all of the cream.

Cream Dish Procedure

1. Heat a small quantity of butter in a suzette pan or a chafing dish over a burner or lamp.
2. Add the item—for example, lobster meat—and toss it in the butter without browning it.
3. Flambé the pan with a liquor (e.g., cognac).
4. Add the heavy cream.
5. Slowly simmer the item until the cream thickens. In actuality it goes through three stages: It simmers like water, it foams once, and then it begins to bubble slowly and thicken. This will take a few minutes, depending upon the amount of cream used and the amount of liquor added.
6. Add seasonings and garnishes and let the sauce blend.

The procedure for a sample cream preparation, seafood curry, follows.

◆ *Technique:* Preparing Seafood Curry

Kitchen Preparation

◆ 8 ounces of assorted seafood (two portions) attractively arranged on a platter: shrimp, crabmeat chunks, raw shelled oysters, raw lobster or langouste tail meat, and the like
◆ Steamed white rice
◆ Curry powder, or preferably curry powder ingredients for assembly in the chafing dish: turmeric, coriander, cumin, pepper, cloves, cardamom, white ginger, cayenne pepper, mace, cinnamon, fennel
◆ Chutney, toasted coconut, chopped green onions, and diced tomatoes as garnish for the final dish
◆ 8 ounces heavy cream in a pitcher
◆ One ripe banana
◆ 4 ounces partially sautéed onions

Captain's Preparation

◆ Gueridon
◆ Lamp or burner and pan or chafing dish
◆ Dinner plates, preferably hot
◆ Serving spoon and fork
◆ Individual spoons for condiments

♦ Butter in dish
♦ Orange liqueur for flambéing

Procedure

1. Set up the gueridon at tableside.
2. Bring the food from the kitchen and arrange it in order of use.
3. Melt butter over medium heat.
4. Add the seafood and onion and toss it in the butter without browning.
5. Flambé with orange liqueur.
6. Add heavy cream, then curry powder or curry powder ingredients.
7. Reduce the heat.
8. While the cream is thickening, mash the banana.
9. When the cream has thickened, slowly stir in about one-third of the banana.
10. Let the dish heat through.
11. Mound white rice in the center of the dinner plates. Make a hollow in the center of the rice and divide the seafood among the plates, placing it in the hollows.
12. Surround each mound of rice with a little of the garnish ingredients.
13. Spoon the sauce over the seafood.

Other Dishes for Tableside Preparation

Vegetables and Starches

Generally restaurants using tableside cooking will not use the procedure on items which cannot be sold at a high menu price. It is possible, of course, to sauté any vegetable in the dining room that can be sautéed in the kitchen, or to make various starches and vegetables as cream preparations. Usually the captain starts with a partially cooked item. For example, quality noodles or macaroni can be finished as a cream dish with herbs and parmesan cheese in the dining room (e.g., fettuccini Alfredo or carbonara, or linguini with four cheeses).

Eggs

Eggs can also be prepared in the dining room with excellent results. Omelets and scrambled eggs are probably the only dishes which actually do taste better prepared in the dining room than in the kitchen, because there is no time lost in serving them. Only a few operations, however, can justifiably offer them as dining room preparations, since they require the inflated prices of a brunch or supper menu for the effort. The asking price can often be justified by adding other food items, for example, lobster chunks to the seafood omelette or seafood sauce, or as a garnish to create a special dish.

The steps in making an omelet in the dining room follow.

Technique: Preparing Rolled Omelet Tableside

Captain's Preparation

- ♦ Gueridon
- ♦ Lamp or burner with a suzette pan or ideally, a heavy 9-inch omelet pan
- ♦ Three eggs per omelet
- ♦ 2 tablespoons of butter for each omelet
- ♦ Garnishes and/or fillings for each omelet
- ♦ Beating bowl
- ♦ Warm plates
- ♦ Serving fork and spoon

Procedure

1. Set up the gueridon at tableside.
2. Beat the three eggs together.
3. Heat the pan over the lamp, using medium heat.
4. Add 2 tablespoons of butter.
5. When the butter has just begun to brown, pour in the egg mixture.
6. Holding the pan in the left hand, move it vigorously back and forth, while at the same time briskly stirring the eggs with a fork held in the right hand.
7. When the eggs have begun to set on the bottom, stop agitating the pan. Lower the heat. Add desired fillings.
8. Lift the far side of the omelet with a fork and proceed to roll it tightly toward the handle of the pan.
9. When the omelet is completely rolled, slide it toward the front of the pan and over onto a warm plate.

Technique: Preparing Scrambled Eggs Tableside

Scrambled eggs can be made with the same equipment as an omelet, but a genuine silver chafing dish is preferred, as this gives the captain complete control over the doneness of the eggs, just as though they were being prepared in a double boiler.

1. Set up the gueridon at tableside.
2. Light the lamp and heat the chafing dish water to near boiling or heat the pan to medium hot.
3. Beat three eggs together with 1 tablespoon of milk or cream.
4. Add the eggs to the pan and continue to stir until the eggs are cooked the way the customer has ordered them—soft, medium, or hard. If additional items are to be added (e.g., chopped chives, parmesan cheese, diced ham, diced peppers), add these items while the eggs are "setting."
5. Spoon the cooked eggs onto a warm plate.

Some Classical Specialties

If there are some captains who are trained in culinary skills as well as dining room service, then "classics" that are somewhat more complex than the basic sautés and creams might be attempted. Two of the more popular are described below.

Steak au Poivre

This is a combination of a sauté and a cream reduction, cooking filet mignon steaks or sirloin steaks with peppercorns. A filet steak is lightly pressed into coarsely ground or crushed white peppercorns. The captain can crush the pepper at the table in the bowl of one heavy service spoon with the bowl of another. The steak is started as a sauté, half cooked, and removed. The captain then deglazes the pan with cognac and makes a cream reduction, enhances it with brown sauce, Dijon mustard, and sauce Robert. The steak is then returned to the pan to finish. The captain's main concern is controlling the doneness of the steak.

Steak Diane

Steak Diane is a classic presentation of tender filet mignon steaks, usually for two or more. Sauté the shallots in butter. Then sear flattened (in the kitchen) filet steaks, deglaze the pan, and finish with brown sauce, mushroom garnish, fresh seasonings, and chopped parsley. The captain's concerns are controlling the doneness of the steak, searing it so that it appears appetizing, and making large orders in small pans (e.g., making steak Diane for four in a standard suzette pan that comfortably accommodates only a single steak at a time).

Zabaglione

Zabaglione is an impressive Italian dessert sauce, a light, foamy frothy combination of egg yolks and Marsala wine. It is often served alone or over fresh fruit. It is easiest to make with a double boiler chafing dish, although it can be prepared over an open flame, but the difficulty is at least doubled because the eggs will "scramble" much faster.

Beat four raw egg yolks, 4 ounces of granulated sugar (superfine preferred), and 3 ounces of Marsala wine with a silver or plastic whip (an ordinary whip may turn the mixture green). When it has doubled in bulk and become a semistable semifoam, remove the inner pan and beat it a little more off the heat to improve its aeration without overcooking it. The captain's concern is control of the mixture. If the heat is too low, it will take too long to thicken. If the flame is too high or it is beaten too long, the mixture loses its air because the eggs have completely cooked and can no longer form elastic bubbles. The result is a sort of scrambled egg dish.

If done correctly, the result will be a light, airy "foam" that can be ladled over fruit or ice cream, or eaten alone!

ELECTRONICALLY TRANSMITTING AN ORDER

As an example of opening a guest check (using the NCR system and a keyboard similar to that in Illustration 2.4), you would follow this procedure:

Steps in Opening a Check, Using the NCR 2160 System

1. Hit the numeric #s for server number
   Hit "Server #" key
2. Hit numeric #s for the number of guests at the table
   Hit "New Check/# Covers" key
3. Hit numeric #s for the table number
   Hit "Table #/ Data Enter" key

Then the check is "opened" and ready for the items being ordered. Once opened, a check can be continued from any terminal connected to the controller. You need not return to the same terminal over and over again. Whichever one is available is the one used.

Consider these general rules when you are entering an order:

◆ If there is a word button, the word button should be used.
◆ If there is a PLU number, the PLU number should be used.

♦ If neither, use Misc buttons—Misc Food, Misc Liquor, Misc Wines, and so on.

Continuing to enter the order, for instance for two glasses of wine, you would first open the check using the method described above. Then you'd hit the number "2" key, followed by the word button "Glass Wine":

```
┌──────────┐              ┌──────────┐
│          │              │  GLASS   │
│    2     │              │  WINE    │
│          │              │          │
└──────────┘              └──────────┘
```

If there is no word button, for instance to order a hamburger from the brunch menu (PLU 331, found on the order dupe, Figure 2.1), the numbers 3-3-1 would be pressed, followed by the PLU key:

```
┌────────┐    ┌────────┐    ┌────────┐    ┌────────┐
│        │    │        │    │        │    │        │
│   3    │    │   3    │    │   1    │    │  PLU   │
│        │    │        │    │        │    │        │
└────────┘    └────────┘    └────────┘    └────────┘
```

If the guest wanted the hamburger medium rare, the word buttons "Medium" then "Rare" would be hit after the PLU key:

```
┌──────────┐              ┌──────────┐
│          │              │          │
│  MEDIUM  │              │  RARE    │
│          │              │          │
└──────────┘              └──────────┘
```

If two hamburgers were desired by different guests, one wishing it cooked to medium and one rare, they would be entered as follows, using the above-described system:

```
┌────────┐    ┌────────┐    ┌────────┐    ┌────────┐
│        │    │        │    │        │    │        │
│   2    │    │  QTY   │    │   3    │    │   3    │
│        │    │        │    │        │    │        │
└────────┘    └────────┘    └────────┘    └────────┘

┌────────┐    ┌────────┐    ┌────────┐    ┌────────┐
│        │    │        │    │        │    │        │
│   1    │    │  PLU   │    │  ONE   │    │  MED   │
│        │    │        │    │        │    │        │
└────────┘    └────────┘    └────────┘    └────────┘

              ┌────────┐    ┌────────┐
              │        │    │        │
              │  ONE   │    │  RARE  │
              │        │    │        │
              └────────┘    └────────┘
```

CREDIT CARD PROCEDURES

When a credit card is offered as payment for the guest check, proceed as follows:

1. Request the guest who offered the credit card to sign the check.
2. Compare the signature on the credit card with the signature on the guest check. Make sure they match.
3. If there is any doubt in your mind, call a manager.
4. Check the credit card for both starting date and expiration date. Today's date should be somewhere in between.
5. If it is an Amex, Visa, MC, Diner's, or Carte Blanche card, run it through the credit card approval machine—magnetic stripe on the bottom, on the right-hand side, for most machines.
6. At the "amount" prompt (some are simply "A"), enter the amount to be charged to the credit card. Go a bit high to allow for a tip.
7. Wait for the approval code. Amex has a two-digit code; Master Card and Visa have a six-digit code. If you get an "07" or other nonapproval code, call. Numbers should be posted near the credit card approval machine.
8. While you are waiting, copy the credit card number onto the check. You now have the credit card number and the guest's signature on the check.
9. Choose the appropriate credit card slip for the credit card. Transfer the check number to the upper right-hand corner of the voucher slip.

10. Run the voucher through the credit card machine, with the credit card underneath the voucher, if your restaurant is using that type of voucher machine. Run it through in both directions! If using the automatic imprint machine, place the card in the back and the voucher in front; close the machine.

11. Check all copies of the voucher to ensure the imprint was made. Check for clarity of the numbers and letters from the credit card on all copies of the voucher.

12. Fill in the subtotal amount. Do not fill in the tax amount if it was figured automatically by an electronic system, rather draw a line through the tax block.

13. When the approval code is received, enter it on the voucher. Make sure your first name initial and last name are on the top, right-hand corner of the voucher.

14. Copy the check number onto the top, right-hand corner of the voucher. Now the credit card number, the check number, the approval code, and who obtained the approval code for this transaction are on the voucher.

15. If the approval code does not appear, you will have to call for verbal approval. Step-by-step directions, including all phone numbers, merchant numbers, and bank numbers for each credit card are posted by each credit card approval machine.

16. If the guest has a tax-exempt number, see the cashier.

17. Allow the guest to complete the voucher, adding a tip, if he or she so desires. The completed voucher is returned to the guest, on a plate (if that is the house policy), with a pen.

18. Ask the guest to sign the voucher. Do not allow a guest to leave without signing the voucher. Restaurants cannot collect payment without an authorized signature on the voucher.

19. Check the signatures again!! If the signatures match, return the credit card to the guest, with the customer copy of the voucher receipt. *Note:* If the credit card is not signed, ask the guest to sign it in your presence. Then, holding the card, ask for other forms of identification with signatures. Compare. If there is any discrepancy, call a manager.

GLOSSARY OF TABLESERVICE TERMS AND PHRASES

a la carte   Literally, from the menu, but meaning a menu on which individual items are individually priced.

abboyeur   The individual in the classical kitchen who shouts or "barks" the servers' orders to the cooks. The expediter or announcer.

American plan   Daily room rate includes three meals.

American service   The most widely used method of service in use in America. Basic rules include: serving guests' food plates from their left side using one's left hand; clearing plates and beverages from the guests' right sides using one's right hand; serving beverages from the guest's right side, using one's right hand.

announcer   The individual who shouts the servers' orders to the cooks in large American kitchens.

arm service   Service of foods and beverages on plates without the use of trays or wagons.

bar   A room or an area in a restaurant operation devoted to serving drinks, generally at a counter. (Compare lounge.)

bin number   The number of the shelf or case in which wines are stored; a means of identifying and ordering wines.

blue plate special   The specialty of the day in low- or medium-check-average restaurants, sometimes served on a plate (blue or otherwise) divided into three compartments.

booster   Or booster station. A serving stand or cabinet in the middle of a dining room floor; may be equipped with a hot plate, refrigerator, or even cold running water.

bottle bonus   Server's commission on wine sales.

bread boats   Bread baskets.

buffet   A display of food from which patrons serve themselves.

burnishing machine   A mechanical device filled with cleaning solution and ball bearings; for polishing silver and stainless steel flatware.

bus   To remove serviceware from a table after guests have finished with it.

bus box   A plastic or metal container about 2 feet square for carrying or storing dishes.

bus stand   A small table or a folding metal rack for holding trays or bus boxes.

butter chip   A small plate of permanentware or single-service ware for butter. Or, individual butter chips, or three-quarter-inch squares, unwrapped, usually served on a small plate.

carafe   A glass container without a handle for serving wine or water; 4 to 64 ounces.

carbonated water   Water charged with carbon dioxide gas, for sodas in fountain service and for drinks.

carrier   A closed cabinet that accommodates covered plates and accessories being transported from the kitchen to a guest's room; may be heated or chilled.

casserole   A heavy oven-proof dish of metal or earthenware; and by extension, a dish cooked in it—for example, tuna casserole.

cellar   The place where wine is stored; may or may not be below ground.

chafing dish   A two-part container and serving vessel for food, with a heat source beneath it; the upper compartment contains the food, the lower boiling water.

chef   The person in charge of the kitchen or major department in the kitchen (for example, the sauce chef); other individuals are cooks.

chef de rang   The head station server in a classical restaurant team.

china   Plates and cups of opaque material.

clear   To remove serviceware from tables when guests have finished.

coaster   A small flat dish of either permanentware or single-service ware on which bottles and glasses are placed.

coffee whitener   A nondairy product for coffee.

commis   An assistant server in a classical restaurant team.

continental breakfast   Coffee, bread and butter, and sometimes jam; often complimentary.

convenience foods   Processed or partially manufactured foods.

cooler   A bucket, fitted into a stand, to contain ice for cooling white and sparkling wines.

cover The table place and table appointments of an individual guest; by extension, the guest himself or herself.

cradle A metal or wicker basket used for holding wine during decanting (see decanting) and sometimes for serving wine. Usually used for red wines.

creamer A container for cream, milk, or nondairy coffee whitener.

crockery Refers to all opaque dishes and cups.

crumbing a table Removing debris from a table during a meal, often using a special device. Table crumbers or "silent butlers" or a clean napkin are often used.

cutlery Table knives, forks, spoons.

decanter A bottlelike vessel for liquids, with a stopper; meant to be used more than once. Usually used for old wines. (See decanting.)

decanting Pouring an old wine from its original bottle into a serving vessel, so that the sediment is left in the bottle and is not poured into the customer's glass.

draught beer Beer dispensed from kegs through piping and a faucet, as opposed to beer in bottles and cans.

du jour Literally, of the day, meaning a daily special. Often soup du jour, or soup of the day, will be featured on menus.

dumbwaiter A small elevator between two or more floors of a restaurant to transport trays and bus boxes, not staff.

dummy waiter See sideboard.

dupe Short for "duplicate check."

duplicate check A copy of the customer's original check, used by servers to obtain food from the kitchen.

European plan Signifies that no food is included in the room rate (compare with American plan).

expediter An individual who calls servers' orders to cooks in a kitchen and facilitates the gathering of orders for servers.

family style A service concept in which platters of food are placed on the table and the guests help themselves to their own portions.

fast food A restaurant operation which relies on many transactions at low-check averages to make a profit.

finger bowl A bowl of warm water, with either perfume, lemon slice, or rose petals, served after finger-dirtying foods in some restaurants, or routinely at the end of the meal.

flatware All table utensils.

food checker An individual in the kitchen who makes sure that the food on a server's tray matches the customer's check.

fountain A piece of counter equipment containing ice cream freezers and carbonated water faucets; by extension, any restaurant featuring ice cream specialties.

French service Serving food from gueridons or wagons to guest plates in the dining room using a serving spoon and serving fork. Often using rechauds to finish the food in the presence of the guests.

freshen   To heat baked goods; to remove staleness.

garnish   A supplemental food item added to a dish or a platter for visual appeal.

goblet   A footed water glass of at least 8 ounces.

granulated sugar   Sugar in small particles.

gratuities   Monies left by a guest for a server's services. Also called "tips."

griddleman   The cook who prepares food on a heated flat metal plate called a griddle: usually items like eggs, hamburgers, pancakes.

gueridon   A serving cart or wagon, generally with a small built-in stove or a standing stove unit.

half and half   A mixture of cream and milk for coffee; contains less cream than coffee cream.

highball   A drink of spirits and either ginger ale, lemon soda, tonic, or plain soda over ice in a tall glass. Also refers to a tall glass used for such drinks.

inhaler   A bell-shaped glass with a foot and stem, used for the service of brandies.

kitchen stub   The part of a check used to transmit an order to the kitchen (compare duplicate check).

lay plate   An elaborate plate placed in the center of each place setting to add interest to the table; removed after the soup course. Also called a show plate.

lead item   The food item on a menu (for example, soup) which is expected to sell best.

linen   Refers to all table accessories made from cloth, whether they are actually linen (from flax) or some other material.

linen box   A standing container, not unlike a mail box, for receiving dirty linen from the dining room. Often in the kitchen.

liqueurs   Preparations of alcohol, sugar, and some flavoring, used in drink preparation and as after-dinner drinks.

liquors   Alcoholic beverages containing at least two-fifths pure alcohol.

liter   A measure in the metric system equal to slightly more than a quart; by extension, a carafe with a flared mouth and narrow neck which contains a liter, more or less.

live stock   Refers to salads, relishes, and the like set as a matter of course on tables.

lounge   A separate room in a restaurant operation that contains a bar and small tables, is devoted to selling alcoholic beverages, and may offer entertainment and/or light foods.

lump sugar   Or cube sugar. Sugar which has been pressed into square or rectangular blocks for individual servings.

microwave oven   An electronic oven based on heating via microwaves, usually about the size of a 21-inch television set, used for heating, defrosting, or reconstituting food and freshening baked goods.

mise en place Literally, put in place; to get one's station ready. The French term for preparation or sidework; widely used.

mixed drink An alcoholic beverage prepared by combining a liquor with wine, fruit juice, fruit, sugar, syrup, or the like; a cocktail.

mixer Ginger ale, lemon soda, cola, tonic, or plain soda used with alcoholic beverages.

modified American plan Indicates that breakfast and dinner are included in the room rate.

monkey dish A bowl-like dish, about 3 inches across, used for single orders of vegetables.

napery Refers to all table linen.

nappy dish See monkey dish.

neat Refers to a beverage. Served in a glass without ice or other accompaniment.

nondairy creamer A white vegetable product used in coffee in place of milk or cream.

on the rocks An alcoholic drink served over ice.

overchip A plate chipped on the upper surface, visible to the customer.

pantry An area between the kitchen and the dining room in which servers can keep supplies, make coffee, open wine, and prepare trays. Or, the area of the kitchen devoted to cold items.

par stock The number of items thought to be suitable inventory for normal business.

passing Transmitting a customer's order to the kitchen or preparation area or bar.

perishables Items which need refrigeration but are often left unrefrigerated for limited periods, for example, milk and butter.

pilsner glass A conical glass on a foot, usually used for beer.

plate service A service concept in which food items are portioned by the cooks in the kitchen directly onto the customer's plate (compare wagon service, French service, and Russian service).

platter service See Russian service,

pony A small glass, on a stem and a foot, vaguely cylindrical, used for serving straight liquors, liqueurs, and brandies.

pooling Dividing all gratuities earned in a dining room among all floor personnel.

portion control The standardization of individual customer orders to a definite size or weight.

portion pack Individually packaged servings of salt, pepper, condiments, salad dressings, and the like.

reading the plates Checking all the plates that will be used during a meal service for dirt and damage.

rechaud A small stove used in the dining room for heating food or finishing the cooking of food tableside, in front of the guests; generally stands on a table or a cart.

reconstitute   To restore a frozen product to eating temperature; to add water to a dry product.

rocks   Ice cubes.

runner   A member of a dining room staff who shuttles between the kitchen and the floor or the kitchen and a buffet carrying food items.

Russian service   A service concept which includes serving individual portions from large service platters using a serving fork and spoon; also carving of large roasts in the dining room, and serving individual portions from large service vessels kept in the dining room.

salver   A round silver tray about 1 foot in diameter used for glasses, wine, drinks, and sometimes coffee; by extension, any small round tray of any material.

seltzer   See carbonated water.

service cloth   A cloth used by a server to handle hot serviceware, to use in opening and pouring wines.

serviceware   All the articles used in the dining room for holding, serving, or eating food or drink: china, glassware, flatware, and all disposable single-service items.

short order   An item that can be cooked quickly, and by extension, the person on the flattop who usually cooks those items, and/or the type of restaurant that features those items.

show plate   See lay plate.

sideboard   A fitted wall cabinet which contains supplies needed during the meal service.

side dish   An accompaniment to a main dish; for example, potato salad or onion rings; seldom ordered as a separate course.

side towel   Service cloth.

sidework   All duties assigned service personnel in addition to table-service.

silence pad   A heavy cloth of felt or foam rubber placed under a table-cloth.

single service   Serviceware of paper, plastic, or metal meant to be used once.

smorgasbord   A buffet featuring "Scandinavian" items, generally including canned and pickled fish. Also, a buffet restaurant that urges customers to eat as much as they want.

snifter   See inhaler.

sommelier   A person specializing in wines—types, storage, service, and sale of wine.

specials   Items introduced to a permanent a la carte menu on a daily or cyclical basis.

splits   Small bottles, usually 6 to 8 ounces, of wine or nonalcoholic beverages.

station The tables assigned to a single server or team of servers, bussers, captains.

steward A wine steward or sommelier; also the individual in charge of the operations' inventory of foodstuffs and serviceware.

stillroom A continental term for an area similar to the servers' pantry (see pantry).

straight In referring to drinks, means undiluted.

straight up In referring to mixed drinks, means served without ice, although usually made with ice and strained into the serving glass so as to chill the drink.

strip a table Remove everything from a table, including tablecloth and silence pad. (Compare bus and clear.)

supper club A restaurant specializing in service after 10 o'clock.

supreme cup A glass or metal dish of two parts. The lower part allows for the placement of shaved ice for chilling foods; the upper part is where the food to be chilled is placed; for example, a seafood cocktail.

sweet The continental term for dessert.

sweetener A chemical substance other than sugar used by some guests in beverages to sweeten the beverage.

tally sheet A record of a server's services.

tips Monies left for a server's services. (See gratuities.)

tonic Carbonated water flavored with quinine; a mixer often used with gin and vodka.

trolley A continental term for wagon or gueridon, often left in the dining room with cakes or hors d'oeuvres.

tulip A glass vaguely shaped like a tulip flower, with a long stem and small foot. Usually used for wines.

tumbler A cylindrical glass without a foot or stem often used for highballs, milk, sodas.

turnover The "turning over" of a table, meaning to have one party leave and "turn over" the table to the next party. To serve two or more parties of customers during a meal period at a single table.

twist A small piece of lemon peel, usually about one and one-half inches by one-quarter inch; twisted to release lemon oil into mixed drinks.

underchip A plate chipped on the lower surface; the chip is invisible to the customer.

underliner A plate used under another plate or glass for ease of handling, or to make the service more attractive.

vintage A wine produced from the grapes of only one year; by extension, that year.

wagon A rolling cart for the service of food (wagon service); generally elaborate and left in the dining room with serving vessels full of food.

wardrobe items   Heavy, large pieces of serviceware which belong to the dining room rather than to individual stations: for example, duck presses and wine coolers.

wine steward   See sommelier.

INDEX